HAPHAZARD FAMILIES

FORMATIONS: ADOPTION, KINSHIP, AND CULTURE
Emily Hipchen and John McLeod, Series Editors

HAPHAZARD FAMILIES

Romanticism, Nation, and the Prehistory of Modern Adoption

Eric C. Walker

THE OHIO STATE UNIVERSITY PRESS
COLUMBUS

Copyright © 2024 by The Ohio State University.
All rights reserved.

Library of Congress Cataloging-in-Publication Data
Names: Walker, Eric C., author.
Title: Haphazard families : romanticism, nation, and the prehistory of modern adoption / Eric C. Walker.
Other titles: Formations: adoption, kinship, and culture.
Description: Columbus : The Ohio State University Press, [2024] | Series: Formations: adoption, kinship, and culture | Includes bibliographical references and index. | Summary: "Examines literary and historical adoptions associated with Queen Caroline, Jane Austen, the Wordsworths, Mary Shelley, the Lambs, Letitia Landon, and others to demonstrate how Romantic constructions of childhood supply foundational structures of modern adoptee subjectivity"—Provided by publisher.
Identifiers: LCCN 2023057251 | ISBN 9780814215661 (hardback) | ISBN 0814215661 (hardback) | ISBN 9780814283455 (ebook) | ISBN 0814283454 (ebook)
Subjects: LCSH: Levasseur, Marie-Thérèse, 1721–1801—Family. | Austen, Jane, 1775–1817. | Shelley, Mary Wollstonecraft, 1797–1851. | Rousseau, Jean-Jacques, 1712–1778. | L.E.L. (Letitia Elizabeth Landon), 1802–1838. | Moxon, Emma Isola, 1809–1891. | Lamb, Charles, 1775–1834. | Lamb, Mary, 1764–1847. | Adoption—Great Britain—History—19th century. | Adoption in literature. | Adopted children—Great Britain—History. | Abandoned children—Great Britain—History. | English literature—19th century—History and criticism. | Romanticism—Great Britain.
Classification: LCC HV875.58.G7 W35 2024 | DDC 362.7340941—dc23/eng/20240226
LC record available at https://lccn.loc.gov/2023057251

Other identifiers: ISBN 9780814259085 (paperback) | ISBN 0814259081 (paperback)

Cover design by Nathan Putens
Text design by Juliet Williams
Type set in Adobe Minion Pro

♾ The paper used in this publication meets the minimum requirements of the American National Standard for Information Sciences—Permanence of Paper for Printed Library Materials. ANSI Z39.48-1992.

CONTENTS

List of Illustrations — vi

Preface — vii

Acknowledgments — xi

INTRODUCTION   Thérèse Levasseur's Lost Children — 1

CHAPTER 1   The Burden of Romantic Childhood — 11

CHAPTER 2   National Children: The Madness of William Austin — 37

CHAPTER 3   Natural Children: Jane Austen and Adoption — 69

CHAPTER 4   Abandoned Children: Mary Shelley, Rousseau, and *Frankenstein* — 105

CHAPTER 5   Unexplained Children: Basil Caroline Montagu and the Wordsworth Circle — 128

CHAPTER 6   Found Children: Emma Isola and Charles and Mary Lamb — 163

CONCLUSION   Untimely Adoption — 194

Appendix   Austen Family Accounts of the Edward Austen Adoption — *203*

Bibliography — *211*

Index — *223*

ILLUSTRATIONS

FIGURE 1	William Austin satirical cartoon, 1813	48
FIGURE 2	Edward Austen adoption silhouette, 1783	73
FIGURE 3	London Foundling Hospital, 1816	109
FIGURE 4	Basil Montagu adoption memoir manuscript, ca. 1817	134
FIGURE 5	Emma Isola Moxon, 1858	193

PREFACE

Marginal or remarkable, neglected or remembered, if not
still—and once again—intolerably contemporary, these
nonpersons, in every case, demand our attention.

—Daniel Heller-Roazen, *Absentees*

This book addresses two sets of readers, students and scholars of adoption and students and scholars of Romanticism. Because the bookshelves and bookmarks of these two groups do not overlap seamlessly, when I introduce new topics I err on the side of what may appear obvious to one audience or the other. For example, when I turn to the history of Romantic childhood, the legacy of which I argue burdens modern adoption, I register that early poems shaping Romantic childhood appeared in a book titled *Lyrical Ballads* in 1798, a set of facts that Romanticists carry around like an overworn passport. When I turn to the topic of the adoptee Fanny Price's abrupt return to her birth family in Jane Austen's *Mansfield Park,* I locate this episode within a set of headings long familiar to adoption specialists, such as reunion, repatriation, and rehoming.

The assumption of the book is that Romanticists and adoption scholars have much to learn from one another—that adoption opens a new window into Romantic subjectivity and that Romanticism supplies foundational structures of modern adoptee subjectivity. Although the book offers new approaches to well-traveled material such as Austen's novels and *Frankenstein,* there is also much that is unfamiliar: an adopted London waif, William Austin, disruptive on the royal national stage; a laboratory sample of the Romantic child, Basil Caroline Montagu, whose broken adopted life measures the cost of that figure; and the adopted life of a Cambridge orphan of an immigrant family, Emma

Isola, whose de facto care in a culture where adoption did not legally exist speaks to ways in which modern de jure adoption might recover benefits of open-ended and contingent adoptive care, glimpsed in practice.

Writing as a social historian, a latter-day Tolstoy might put it this way: all families are haphazard, but adoptive families are haphazard in their own particular ways. To which I would add: adoptive families across history are haphazard in time-bound and place-bound ways. This book focuses on adoptive families in Great Britain in what literary and cultural historians designate the "Romantic century," the late-Enlightenment and pre-Victorian span from 1750 to 1850 that produces revolutionary France and the new United States of America. In 1851 the state of Massachusetts passed the first de jure adoption law in the English-speaking world, legislation that would not be adopted in England until 1926, in Scotland until 1930, and in Ireland until 1953.[1] A primary goal of this study is to spotlight the immediately antecedent forms of de facto adoption, both historical and literary, that usher in modern adoption in Anglophone culture.[2]

When I refer to "the Romantic century" or, more often, "the Romantic period," I signify basic chronology: events and people from the middle of the eighteenth century to the middle of the nineteenth century.[3] Within that span dwell many Romanticisms, of course. The chapters that follow about Romantic-period adoption testify to forms of Romanticism that behave in what Jerome Christensen terms "untimely" ways, in forms oppositional, disruptive, and nonnormative, a Romanticism that "challenges the present state of things" in "a conspiracy against the given."[4] These histories of Romantic-period adoption forge alliances with rich bodies of theory and scholarship about subjectivity, identity, and personhood on the margins, in the figures of subalterns, migrants, exiles, strangers, and the various "diminished individuals" understood as nonpersons by Daniel Heller-Roazen, figures at the center of some of the most pressing ethical and political challenges of moder-

---

1. During the period of this study, the name of the nation shifted in 1801 from Great Britain to the United Kingdom, encompassing England, Wales, Scotland, and Ireland. Because separate legal systems among that set are at issue in these materials, when I refer to "England," it signifies that distinct legal and cultural subset of the larger nation. Instead of "the UK" (the boundaries of which shifted a century later, and may yet again after Brexit), with abundant others I use "Britain" often anachronistically as a shorthand signifier for the nation.

2. For a helpful discussion of the methodological challenges in writing about adoption in earlier historical periods, see the introduction to Nelson, *Little Strangers*.

3. I do not employ an alternative term from British studies, "the Georgian era," which takes its name from a series of monarchs from 1714 to 1830.

4. Christensen, *End of History,* 12–13, 2.

PREFACE

ix

nity, such as immigration.[5] In adoption, strangers and familiars pass as one another. In H. J. Todd's 1818 revision of Samuel Johnson's 1755 *Dictionary of the English Language,* Todd added this definition to Johnson's entry for "adoptive" ("He that is adopted"): "He that is not native."[6] The many adoptees in the following chapters—Charles Aikin, Sabrina Bicknell, William Austin, Emma Watson, Fanny Price, Dido Elizabeth Belle, Elizabeth Murray, Frank Churchill, Jane Fairfax, Edward Austen Knight, Elizabeth Lavenza, Bessie Florence Gibson Shelley, Basil Caroline Montagu, Emma Isola, Emma Stuart Gregson, Fred Stuart, Laura Stuart—are all untimely, diminished strangers in their native land.

In the "Theatre" column in the London *Universal Magazine* in October 1796, there appeared this notice: "On Saturday, October 19, a new comedy, entitled FORTUNE'S FOOL, was performed for the first time, at Coventgarden theatre."[7] The new play, by Frederick Reynolds, hangs upon a central character, Haphazard, whose comic misfortunes hang upon adoption.[8] A rich disgruntled uncle disinherits his nephew and bestows his fortune on his new adopted heir, Haphazard, an opportunistic Welchman on the make in London ("Life's a lottery!") who is racialized as the disruptive outsider. In London in the middle of the Romantic century, adoption circulated in popular culture under the unruly banner of the random and the contingent, played to an aleatory tune.

---

5. Heller-Roazen, *Absentees,* 75–143; the epigraph is found on p. 82.

6. Todd, *Johnson's Dictionary.*

7. *The Universal Magazine,* 1796, 377.

8. Reynolds, *Fortune's Fool.*

ACKNOWLEDGMENTS

I first floated ideas and material for this book at a 2003 conference in New York on "Romanticism and Parenting," concurrent with a meeting of NASSR (the North American Society for the Study of Romanticism), and I am grateful to Elizabeth Fay for organizing that meeting and for the responses of those around the table, including Alan Richardson, Chris Rovee, Kim Wheatley, Michael Macovski, Cheryl Nixon, Jonathan Gross, and Carolyn Weber. Panels at subsequent NASSR meetings in Boulder, Montreal, Toronto, Durham, and Vancouver provided welcome opportunities to continue to explore this work. My gratitude to Talia Vestri Croan for organizing a session on "Romantic Genealogies of Kinship" at the 2016 Modern Language Association meeting in Austin and for Charles Rzepka's always good questions.

My work on Austen and adoption received a timely boost from the 12th British Women Writers Conference at the University of Georgia in 2004 and especially from the 2009 New Directions in Austen Studies Conference at Chawton House, Hampshire, in conversations there with Gillian Dow, Laurie Kaplan, Susan Allen Ford, Eric Lindstrom, Mary Ann O'Farrell, Linda Bree, Christine Kenyon-Jones, Clara Tuite, Angela Esterhammer, Marilyn Francus, Michelle Levy, John Wiltshire, and Deborah Weiss. My work on the Lambs and adoption took penultimate form in the Lamb panel at the Friends of Coleridge Biennial Summer Conference at Jesus College, Cambridge, in 2018, helped by conversations there with Felicity James, Michael Gamer, Emily Stanback, Jared Richman, Justin Shepherd, Ed Weech, and Tim Fulford. While the Coleridgeans were punting on the Cam, I was off locating Kenmare House, the Trumpington Street home where Emma Isola met the Lambs in the summer of 1820.

But my greatest organizational debt is to ASAC, the Alliance for the Study of Adoption and Culture. Starting in 2005, ASAC conferences have been a steady anchor of this work, and I'm especially grateful to meeting organizers in Tampa, Pittsburgh, Cambridge Mass., Claremont, Tallahassee, Minneapolis, and Oakland. Primary thanks are due to the ASAC founding members and other officers and hosts: Marianne Novy, Emily Hipchen, Carol Singley, Claudia Nelson, Karen Balcom, Margaret Homans, Cynthia Callahan, Kim Park Nelson, Marina Fedosik, John McLeod, and Sally Haslanger. Special thanks to Emily Hipchen for her sustained and sustaining work on the house journal, *Adoption & Culture*. At ASAC conferences, I have profited enormously from many panels, speakers, and conversations, a roster that includes Lori Askeland, Laura Briggs, E. Wayne Carp, Alice Diver, Jennifer Kwon Dobbs, Daniel ElAwar, Janet Ellerby, Shannon Gibney, Jena Heath, Tobias Hübinette, Susan Ito, Jackie Kay, Eleana Kim, Frances Latchford, Kimberly Leighton, Deann Borshay Liem, Kimberly McKee, Carolyn McLeod, Kit Myers, Ellen Peel, Bruno Perreau, Sayres Rudy, Martha Satz, Kay Trimberger, and Barbara Yngvesson.

Archivists, librarians, and curators have provided essential help at key points. My thanks to Jeff Cowton at the Jerwood Centre in Grasmere for his great care of the Wordsworth Trust archive; Mike Rogers and Jan Dann at the Lincolnshire Archives; Pam Clark at the Royal Archives, Windsor; Elizabeth Denlinger at the Pforzheimer Collection, New York Public Library; and Emma Yandle at the Chawton House Museum. Most generous with family archives has been John Moxon, the great-great-grandson of Emma Isola and her publisher husband Edward Moxon. I remain indebted to research collections at Strozier Library, Florida State University; Davis Library, University of North Carolina at Chapel Hill; and Joyner Library, East Carolina University. I am very grateful to Kristen Elias Rowley at The Ohio State University Press for exemplary editorial care.

An earlier version of chapter 2, "Adoption, Narrative, and Nation, 1800–1850: The Case of William Austin," appeared in *JBS: The Journal of British Studies* in 2014. I am grateful to Cambridge University Press for permission to adapt that material here.

Earlier versions of Austen material in chapter 3 appeared in 2010 in *Persuasions On-Line*, edited by Susan Allen Ford ("'In the Place of a Parent': Austen and Adoption") and in 2014 in an online volume edited by Eric Lindstrom on *Stanley Cavell and the Event of Romanticism* ("Cavell and Austen") in the Praxis series at the Romantic Circles website, and I am grateful to the editors of these publications for permission to adapt that material here.

An earlier version of Lamb material in chapter 6 appeared in the *Coleridge Bulletin* in 2019 ("Charles Lamb, Emma Isola, and the Politics of Adoption, 1820"), and I am grateful to the editors, Graham Davidson and Jeffery Barbeau, for permission to adapt that material here.

Now into a third decade, I have learned far and away the most about adoption from Meg Walker and Sarah Walker. This book, then, is dedicated to both Meg and Sarah, beyond measure.

Montreat, North Carolina
September 2023

INTRODUCTION

Thérèse Levasseur's Lost Children

In Paris in any one midcentury year around 1750, thousands of babies were abandoned at a charitable institution, the Hôpital des Enfants-Trouvés, founded in 1670. Relinquished to the care of nuns and wet nurses, four of every five of these infants perished before six months. Protestant London meanwhile lagged nearly a century behind Catholic Paris on this desperate social services front. In 1739 a retired naval officer, Thomas Coram, spearheaded the establishment of a foundling hospital in the northeast corner of what is now Bloomsbury. Sometime late in 1746 or early in 1747—the exact date is unknown—one particular infant was left at the Paris Hôpital. The father later insisted that this child—whose gender is also unknown—was "deposited" (*déposé*) rather than, euphemistically, "found" (*trouvé*), a distinction surely lost on the baby, who was handed off to the nuns by a midwife. The mother, Thérèse Levasseur, a native of Orleans, was a young laundress at a nearby boarding house. An unemployed boarder, the older father later claimed that he attempted at least one gesture at childcare: he passed along to the mother or the midwife two cards with an identifying cipher, one to go in the baby's blankets, the other to keep, perhaps later to claim kinship. In spite of such desultory paperwork, this unregistered child entirely disappeared from the historical record, lost and erased.

But at least one other fact survives about this abandoned baby. Thérèse Levasseur's first baby was soon followed by four full siblings, all of whom were

· 1 ·

born over the next half decade—and all of whom were also abandoned, one by one, at the Paris Hôpital. We know even less about these latter four abandoned siblings than the bleak mystery of the oldest. In their father's later account, their lives appear and disappear without any other detail, not even a tale of cards and ciphers. And of the mother? Across the channel, a verse survives in a poem by a despairing mother compelled to leave her infant at the London foundling hospital in 1759: "And death almost to me to part."[1] No trace of a shared grief survives from Thérèse Levasseur, a mother who witnessed five babies disappear, never to be known or recovered. Perhaps it played out this way: after the first death, there is no other.[2]

On the part of the boarding-house father, those deaths at least disrupted his repose, and he much later rehearsed a published explanation, in these terms. Abandonment was the best way to protect the honor of the unmarried mother. Abandonment was also the best way to give the offspring of a feckless father a chance at real survival with real people. And if those arguments might not fly, blame Plato: in the ideal republic, children belong not to individuals but to the state. In fairness, the father's case in his own words:

> I fashioned my way of thinking according to what I saw prevail among these very amiable and fundamentally very decent men, and I said to myself: "Since it is the custom of the country, one may, if one lives there, follow it. Here is the way out that I have been looking for." I made up my mind to take it, blithely and without the least scruple; indeed, the only one with which I had to contend came from Therese, whom I had the greatest difficulty in the world in persuading her to adopt the only course of action that would preserve her honor. But when her mother, who feared, in addition, the burden of another unwanted child, came to my aid, she let herself be overruled. . . . I will only say that this error was such that in handing over my children to be raised at public expense, since I had not the means to bring them up myself, in ensuring that they became labourers and peasants rather than adventurers and fortune-seekers, I believed that I was acting as a true citizen and father, and I looked upon myself as a member of Plato's republic.[3]

Thus reasons the biological father of those five babies, Jean-Jacques Rousseau, in the first volume of his *Confessions* in 1782, published four years after his

---

1. Pinsky, *Foundling Hospital,* 20.

2. Historical details in these paragraphs are based on the narratives and extensive sources in Cranston, *Early Life*; Damrosch, *Restless Genius*; McClure, *Coram's Children*; and Blum, *Republic of Virtue.*

3. Rousseau, *Confessions,* 335, 347–48.

death and more than thirty years after the births and disappearance of these five lost children.

Whatever grim actuarial fates befell the bodily selves of the five abandoned children of Thérèse Levasseur, their anonymous afterlives were remarkably lively—and prominently literary. Before prerevolutionary France and Britain digested the two volumes of posthumous *Confessions* in the 1780s, Europe had already heard abundantly from Jean-Jacques Rousseau about childhood and children. In *Julie, ou La Nouvelle Héloïse* in 1761, Rousseau gallantly assigned sacrificial parenthood to the eponymous mother, who dies while rescuing a child from drowning. In *Emile* a year later, a proper father took center stage, mapping proper care for the eponymous child: "I have already said what must be done when a child cries to have this or that. I shall only add that as soon as he can ask by saying what he desires, and, to get it more quickly or overcome a refusal, he supports his request with tears, it ought to be irrevocably refused him."[4] An old set of irrevocable refusals haunts the book.

Rousseau confessed his shaky credentials as a parent in a throwaway passage early in *Emile*: "He who cannot fulfill the duties of a father has no right to become one. Neither poverty nor labors nor concern for public opinion exempts him from feeding his children and from raising them himself. Readers, you can believe me. I predict to whoever has vitals and neglects such holy duties that he will long shed bitter tears for his offense and will never find consolation for it."[5] After his posthumous broadcast of his serial offenses, Rousseau suffered the scorn of antirevolutionary polemic in Britain. Edmund Burke in 1791 twisted a tight tether between bad politics and bad parenting. Celebrated by revolutionary France, Rousseau smugly proclaims "universal benevolence," glared Burke, but "his heart was incapable of harbouring one spark of common parental affection." In his "mad Confession of his mad faults," the champion of sentiment "melts with tenderness for those only who touch him by the remotest relation, and then, without one natural pang, casts away, as a sort of offal and excrement, the spawn of his disgustful amours, and sends his children to the hospital of foundlings. The bear loves, licks, and forms her young; but bears are not philosophers."[6]

Literary London teemed with radical philosophers in the early 1790s, who sometimes behaved parentally as bears, and sometimes not. Sharing occasional paths with Burke, Mary Wollstonecraft also scorched Rousseau's "wild chimeras" in *Vindication of the Rights of Woman* in 1792, her target his empty

---

4. Rousseau, *Emile*, 86.
5. Rousseau, *Emile*, 49.
6. Burke, *Letter*, 34–35.

afterthoughts ("what nonsense!") about the education of women in *Emile*.[7] A year later, however, William Godwin, soon to be the father of Wollstonecraft's most famous daughter, celebrated *Emile* and Rousseauvian childhood as a primary inspiration in the most radical work of philosophy in British Romanticism, *An Enquiry Concerning Political Justice*—the first section of which, written by an unmarried man without children, is all about how to raise them.

Godwin's busy London circle in the 1790s is the epicenter of the literary afterlives in Romantic-period Britain of Thérèse Levasseur's lost children. The chapters in this book track manifold cross-channel aftershocks in the wake of seismic Rousseauvian childhood, which supplies background noise throughout. Instead of pan-European Romanticism, this book foregrounds adoption in late eighteenth- and early nineteenth-century British culture. Modern Anglo-American de jure adoption emerges from distinctly English jurisprudence, sharply different from French tradition. Adoption does not exist in English common law, whereas adoption in France navigates a civil code heritage of Roman jurisprudence, where adoption was a tool of dynastic and state power. Adoption, in short, marks a sharp cultural divide between British and French practice, and this book tracks for modern Anglophone adoption the vexed and formative British side of that fault line, exemplified in a set of untimely de facto adoptions that help focus the prehistory of modern adoption.[8]

Chapter 1, "The Burden of Romantic Childhood," introduces the culturally constructed figure of the Romantic child. Instead of relitigating long-running debates about the origins of western childhood, this chapter assumes the persuasive claims that Romanticism in the wake of Rousseau turbocharged the stakes of childhood identity. As Adam Phillips maps the new plateau, "in that familiar cliché of Romanticism, and of the Romanticism that is Freudianism, we are always really the children we once were," the flip side of which is the paired cliché that understands Romanticism as defined by loss: we are always separated from the lost children we once were.[9] My arguments about Romantic childhood do not pursue such outworn clichés but explore the fraught legacy of that history for adoption. In the vexed history of liberal universalism, children in the eighteenth and early nineteenth century became a new human subset separated out as different and *not* equal in multiple senses: set apart, strange, exceptions to normative rule, a political differentiation that amplified the new exceptionalism of Romantic childhood taking root more generally in

---

7. Wollstonecraft, *Vindication*, 177.

8. Foregrounding adoptive parents instead of adoptees, Rachel Bowlby assembles "a hinterland of antecedent stories and situations for many of the forms of contemporary parenthood" (*Child*, x).

9. Phillips, "Left Out," 13.

the culture. Because this period marks the regnant tasking of differentiated children as primary engines of affective value—what the sociologist Viviana Zelizer terms the "sacralization of children" and the historian Hugh Cunningham the "sanctification of children"—adoptees in the wake of Romantic childhood shoulder a doubled weight of difference, born naturally into exceptionality but then displaced elsewhere, culturally.[10] This latter removal shapes what Daniel Heller-Roazen terms "lessening" as he tracks historical forms of "diminished individuals" who belong, variously, to a set of nonpersons.[11] Adoptees in the wake of Romantic childhood inherit identitarian knots that entangle the elevation of childhood exceptionalism with the diminishing abjection of familial remove.

Especially in the narratives of marginal historical adoptees such as William Austin, Basil Caroline Montagu, and Emma Isola, this book works to disentangle the vexed cultural figure of the Romantic child from what it would erase, the children of history. These case histories exhibit de facto adoptions behaving disruptively and oppositionally, for better and for worse, in untimely forms. These chapters do not pose unruly British adoptions as discrete invasions of cross-channel revolutionary principles, which still circulate in popular definitions of the term "Romantic." The radical contingency of French family formation in the revolutionary decades rendered the British biological family even more emphatically a counterrevolutionary redoubt, refortified like the Martello towers ringing the southern coast in fear of attack. Instead of French landing parties from without, the scenes of British adoption in these chapters exhibit oppositional disruptions staged more complexly from within the closed structures of familial and national biocentric power. These British histories of haphazard adoptive families thus measure distance between the haste of revolution and the untimely pace of justice. In Jerome Christensen's account, these adoptive histories belong to a Romanticism that is "inescapably anachronistic because it is the politics of the future and always will be until something better comes along."[12]

Chapter 2, "National Children: The Madness of William Austin," navigates the tabloid waters of royal scandal. In the history of William Austin, a London waif adopted in 1802 by Princess Caroline, the estranged spouse of the Prince of Wales, I read the figure of the "national child" in Britain as a displaced echo of Rousseauvian France, where, in the words of Ala Alryyes, "Rousseau created the national child who does not naturally belong to the family."[13] The

---

10. Zelizer, *Priceless Child*, 10; and Cunningham, *Children and Childhood*, 59.
11. Heller-Roazen, *Absentees*, 8–9.
12. Christensen, *End of History*, 31.
13. Alryyes, *Original Subjects*, 76.

preposterous life of William Austin displays how the figure of the adopted child separated from consanguineous origins and planted disturbingly on the royal stage spotlights the fictiveness of the nation—a liberating spectacle in France but an unruly prospect for the British nation, whose power remained deeply rooted in the bloodline guarantees of biological genealogy. Sufficiently alarmed, a secret government tribunal in 1806 investigated the disputed identity of "THE CHILD," as Austin was styled in clandestine documents. Rendered exceptional as a child in near-fantasy form, Austin simultaneously suffered the diminishment of both separation from and connection to a birth family whom he knew, who were throughout his life stigmatized as irredeemably ill-bred. The cost to this adoptee of such doubled differentiation—its bundled elevation and abjection—played out after the uproar of the divorce trial of Queen Caroline in 1820 in a subsequent history of madness. The untimely effect of adoption in Britain brandished threat rather than promise.

Chapter 3, "Natural Children: Jane Austen and Adoption," opens by tracking Austen's interest in the family battle between the Princess of Wales and the prince regent. As Austen pondered "what to do about" this royal scandal and its contested history of parenthood both biological and adoptive, she was at work full speed on *Mansfield Park,* quickly followed by *Emma,* two novels that offer a superabundance of adoption tales and form the focus of this chapter. Prefaced by an account of the historical adoption Austen knew best in her own family—the kinship adoption of her older brother Edward Austen—my reading of Austen's fiction inventories an extensive range of human motives and consequences bound up in the manifold historical practices of de facto adoption. Her abandoned fragment of a novel from 1804–5, *The Watsons,* foregrounds a repatriation adoption narrative, a form that she then deploys in both *Mansfield Park* and *Emma.* Doubly differentiated, the adoptees in these fictions—Emma Watson, Fanny Price, Harriet Smith, Jane Fairfax, Frank Churchill—suffer diminishment as their lives chafe against the bionormatively bounded spaces of familial and tribal power that constrain them: "the town of D. in Surry" in *The Watsons* fragment, the Mansfield estate in *Mansfield Park,* and Highbury in *Emma.* The redundancy of surrogate identity in *Emma* supplies a generalizing force which suggests that all its family narratives threaten to look like untimely adoption tales. At the level of form, surrogacy operates in the novel as a figure for the novel's own fiction-making procedures, doubled up by the busy narrative machines of both Emma Woodhouse and the narrator. In the crucial Box Hill episode late in the novel, in loaded banter about marriage and adoption between Emma Woodhouse and the adoptee Frank Churchill, Rousseau casts an anachronistic and unsettling shadow.

Chapter 4, "Abandoned Children: Mary Shelley, Rousseau, and *Franken-stein*," turns to the most famous Romantic-period representation of abandoned parenthood, a book long adapted in forms faithful and fantastic in drama, film, and fiction. Prompted by critiques voiced in disability studies, I resist the temptation to exploit *Frankenstein* to exhibit the Creature as a prototypical cyborgian adoptee, which risks swerving into a contest to stake premium outsider status or a privileged site of the uncanny. I thus detour from eye-popping post-Romantic ways of remediating the novel to circle back and spotlight, historically, the culture of Romantic-period adoption in the Romantic-period book. All the other chapters of this book foreground the lives of adoptees; in this one chapter, I spotlight the life of a mother who navigates the perilous pressure to abandon or relinquish children. As in the life history of William Austin on the national stage, what is at stake in this chapter is the contested figure of a child, to be cared for by either a biological parent or surrogate strangers. The first section foregrounds the widowed Mary Shelley's fraught return to England in 1823, fearful that she might lose the custody of her one surviving child while she settled a few streets away from the Foundling Hospital, the signature London location where mothers and infants were cast apart institutionally. In Shelley's fierce maternal ledger, to surrender her son Percy to surrogate care coldly arranged by her late husband's coldly powerful father was to yield to certain diminishment. In the wake of her contest with the bionormative fortress that was Sir Timothy Shelley, the second section shifts to the most extensive alterations Shelley then made to the 1818 text of *Frankenstein* for the 1831 edition, when she revisits her earlier representations of adoption. The first is a long passage early in the book about Elizabeth Lavenza, who in 1818 is Victor Frankenstein's blood relative (a cousin) in a kinship adoption but in 1831 is a twice-abandoned and twice-adopted stranger. In Shelley's new 1831 introduction to the novel, references to her own childhood experiences of abandonment prepare untimely and disorderly ground for a later Shelley text that is not well-known, her fierce attack on Rousseau and his abandonment of his children in her 1838 biography of Rousseau for Dionysius Lardner's *Cabinet Cyclopedia*.

Chapter 5, "Unexplained Children: Basil Caroline Montagu and the Wordsworth Circle," turns to west-country England in 1795, where William and Dorothy Wordsworth, twenty-something siblings, cared adoptively for the three-year-old Basil Caroline Montagu, the maternal orphan son of a bastard son of a titled father, the Earl of Sandwich. This haphazard family on the remote coast puzzled the Dorsetshire locals, who surmised that they might be French, and thus up to no good. One Somersetshire observer recalled the disturbing presence of "an *unexplained child*," a phrase that pinpoints the stakes of identity in these untimely adoptive histories. Shuffled back and forth among multiple adoptive caregivers during his orphaned childhood and young adulthood, Basil Caroline Montagu suffered the diminishing whiplash of ever-shifting homes at an alarming rate. Especially because three years of that history—from the time when he was nearly three until he was nearly six—weave in and out with the lives of writers who were busy fostering the infancy of the Romantic child, the life of Basil Caroline Montagu as an adoptee speaks tellingly of the ambitions, shaky foundations, and subsequent costs of that hegemonic construct. Drawing on an adoption memoir left in manuscript by the relinquishing birth father, this chapter tracks the unhappy life story of the adoptee Basil Caroline in three stages. After grounding his birth culture and early infancy in the Rousseau-inflected Godwinian circles of oppositional London in the mid-1790s, I turn to the defining years of his adoptive care by the Wordsworth siblings in the west country of Dorset and Somerset from 1795 to 1798. The subsequent stages are the less familiar portion of Basil Caroline's story, including repatriated efforts to navigate the family chaos of his birth father's many married lives and children; failed navy service; a bitter falling-out and uneasy reconciliation with his adoptive Wordsworth family in Cumbria in his early twenties; and his retreat into illness and aimless London and Cambridgeshire life before his unheralded death in 1830. In the British book of the Romantic child, the historical child who most closely shadows the emergence of that illusory figure is this forlorn and severely diminished adoptee.

Chapter 6, "Found Children: Emma Isola and Charles and Mary Lamb," turns to one of the most remarkably ectopic families in literary Romanticism, launched in 1820 during the summer of Queen Caroline's adultery trial when a twelve-year-old orphan in Cambridge, Emma Isola, met a vacationing alcoholic essayist and London clerk nearing fifty and his intermittently mad coauthor and older sister. Through her marriage in 1833 to Edward Moxon and Charles Lamb's death in 1834, Emma Isola, Charles Lamb, and Mary Lamb performed a de facto adoption that balked interpretations of yet another unexplained child. The manifold surrogate diversity of the Lamb family unit disrupted the normative biologism that sustained dominant constructions of the family, tribe, and nation. Like a rich caricature, this trio both reproduced and parodied a bionormative family model: mother, father, child. Performatively, the trio queered the biogenetic props of both family and nation, in untimely alliance with Willy Austin on the royal stage. The chapter frames the multifamilial and political spaces where de facto adoptive care manifested itself in the first decades of the century. The first section sorts the multiple forms of de facto care shared between the Lambs in London and Emma's Cambridge family, measuring the costs to Emma, the doubly differentiated adoptee; to her adoptive caregivers; and to members of her birth family. The second section turns to Emma's history as a governess, which tracks the gendered fate of an adopted orphan of the middling classes, the threat Jane Fairfax confronts in Austen's *Emma*. In the final section, I return to the politics of adoption in 1820, when the commencement of the Emma Isola adoption doubled up oppositionally with the adultery trial of Queen Caroline, whose misbehavior trailed in its wake the untimely national discomfort of an adopted child.

In the conclusion, "Untimely Adoption," a tally of the diminished victims and survivors of Romantic-period adoption sets the stage for the explicit legal recognition of existing de facto adoption in a subordinate section of the 1926 Adoption Act, which for the first time established, imperfectly, an early form of de jure adoption in England and Wales. But instead of a Whiggish progressivism, the untimely adoptions of the Romantic period contribute to an adoption history in which bad outcomes repeat rather than reform. To end where these histories begin, this final chapter closes with the recently recovered history of the abandoned children of another Romantic-period writer, Letitia Elizabeth Landon, the wildly popular poet of the 1820s and 1830s known as L.E.L., who gave secret birth to and abandoned three children during her rapid ascent to literary fame. Unlike the unknown children of Thérèse Levasseur, these three children—Ella, Fred, Laura—survived, defined in common law as spurious issue, as bastards, as diminished individuals who passed as nonpersons. From the vantage of late Romanticism, Landon's secret history as an unwed relinquishing birth mother previewed from the culture of de facto adoption the modern de jure regime of secrecy and shame that dominated postwar adoption in the mid-twentieth century. Faced with such repeated failures, the ongoing work to reform necessarily imperfect systems of modern adoption might look to untimely Romanticisms, following Jerome Christensen's lead: "If we want to discover what possibilities for change remain open now, we might inquire into the untimely then, back at the beginning of the nineteenth century." In the details of these haphazard families, readers might discover "a principled frustration with the way things have turned out and a deliberate impatience to turn them right."[14]

---

14. Christensen, *End of History*, 12, 2.

The following chapters sort the children of de facto adoption in Romantic-period Britain into several sets, with a focus in each chapter on exemplary cases: lost children, national children, natural children, abandoned children, unexplained children, found children, and spurious children. Forerunners of the children of modern de jure adoption, these Romantic-period children form the first adoptee cohort in the burdened wake of Romantic childhood.

CHAPTER 1

The Burden of Romantic Childhood

The most widely circulated child in print culture in the British Romantic century was an adoptee, the boy known as "Little Charles" in *Lessons for Children,* Anna Letitia Barbauld's enormously popular reading primer, which first appeared in 1778. At her aunt's death in 1825, Barbauld's niece Lucy Aikin reported Barbauld's 1777 adoption of her brother John Aikin's third son, Charles, who was two: "The union of Mr. and Mrs. Barbauld proved unfruitful, and they sought to fill the void, of which in the midst of their busy avocations they were still sensible, by the adoption of a son out of the family of Dr. Aikin."[1] But in unpublished comments for a later family history, Lucy Aikin left a cooler judgment of this kinship adoption: "Not a good expedient, especially where the adopted has parents & brothers & sisters of his own! Jealousies *must* interpose. My aunt, with hers, kept herself, at least, continually on the fret."[2] Jane Austen would soon map the fraught territories of such kinship adoptions with the tales of Fanny Price in *Mansfield Park* and Frank Churchill in *Emma.*

---

1. Barbauld, *Works,* I.xxviii.

2. McCarthy, *Barbauld,* 188. McCarthy writes of this event as an adoption (185–89), but he also refers to Anna as a "foster mother" (37) and Charles as a "foster son" (440); elsewhere, Charles as "nephew" and Barbauld as "aunt" (437) also substitute biologically for, adoptively, "son" and "mother."

Writing in 1825, Lucy Aikin loaded the adoptee Charles with a burden of Romantic childhood, tasked with the impossible affective labor "to fill the void" of a pair of adults without children. But fifty years earlier, Anna Letitia Barbauld framed her pitch for the adoption as an Enlightenment calculation of cost and benefit, quantified. From her letter to her brother John, the parent of a surplus of children:

> I am sensible it is not a small thing we ask; nor can it be easy for a parent to part with a child. This I would say, from a number, *one* may more easily be spared. Though it makes a very material difference in happiness whether a person has children or no children, it makes, I apprehend, little or none whether he has three, or four. . . . We should gain, but you would not lose.[3]

In late Enlightenment fashion, Barbauld put little Charles immediately to work as a character in a book of instruction. The first sentence of her "Advertisement" to *Lessons for Children* announced that "This little publication was made for a particular child," and Charles Aikin as "Little Charles" appears in that name throughout, in dialogue on every page with "Mama," who as her modern biographer observes speaks the language of an Enlightenment *philosophe* let loose in the nursery.[4] In *Lessons,* Little Charles undergoes catechistic drills in the wonders of the natural world, the mysteries of cultural systems such as British coinage, and, fundamentally, the ways and means of counting, of quantitative method: "'Pray give me a raisin.' 'Here is one.' 'I want another.' 'Here is another. One two.' 'I want a great many. I want ten.'" Threatened by this excess of quantified desire, Enlightenment reason struggles to contain and underwrite both pedagogy and the adoption itself.

The method falters especially when the lessons turn to family history. After drills about days of the week and months and seasons of the year, *Lessons* shifts to genealogy on a patriarchal grid, anchored in the figure of the father, "papa." But Charles Aikin's status as an adopted child plays no part in the bionormative map of family in *Lessons.* The genealogy lesson opens with the stipulation that "Your papa's wife is your mother"—but in Charles's case, his papa's wife, who was caring for him adoptively, was, biologically, his birth father's sister, not his birth mother, and his "papa" was not a blood relation of any kind. The list of relatives then specifies that "Your mamma's brother and sister are your uncle and aunt"—but in Charles's case, his uncle and aunt—John Aikin and Martha Aikin, "your mamma's brother and sister"—were,

---

3. McCarthy, *Barbauld,* 188.
4. Barbauld, *Lessons.*

biologically, his birth mother and birth father. In *Lessons,* Little Charles is normalized genealogically, anticipating the form of a modern closed adoption overwritten with new birth records. In *Lessons,* Charles Aikin's birth identity disappears into his adoptive identity, which is instead figured as his natural-born self.[5]

In this chapter, I focus on constructions of Romantic childhood that emerge from late-Enlightenment culture to prepare the ground for the historical and narrated adoptees in the following chapters. As Lucy Aikin understands, tasking an adopted child to fill a void is not a good expedient, one of many forms of the burden of Romantic childhood that trail adoptees to this day. The first section unpacks a set of necessary preliminaries: the social contexts of Romantic-period childhood in Great Britain among the middling classes; the lexicon of Romantic-period British adoption, when adoption did not exist legally; and the legal history of Anglophone adoption in common law, especially in contrast to adoption in civil code traditions on the continent, particularly in France. The main section takes up the critical history of Romantic childhood and foregrounds the new inflection of Enlightenment exceptionalism defining childhood in this period, with telling effects on adoptee subjectivity. Phrased generally in summary preview, multivarious experiences of doubled differentiation yield for adoptees the diminishments of nonpersonhood. After calibrating the study of Romantic-period adoption with the performance and study of narrative, the chapter turns from the cultural figure of the Romantic child to what it would erase, the children of history.

THE SOCIAL, LEXICAL, AND JUDICIAL SURROUND

The social history of adoption in Great Britain in the Romantic century is a book that remains to be written. Most of the families in this book belong to the broad spectrum of the middling classes, ranging from mercantile and semiprofessional sets in expanding urban settings to the abundant families gathered about the landed gentry throughout the countryside, their offspring schooled for a century by tales of Little Charles in Barbauld's *Lessons.* But adoption remains offstage in the best scholarship devoted to the middling classes, such as Leonore Davidoff and Catherine Hall's pathbreaking *Family Fortunes: Men and Women of the English Middle Class, 1780–1850,* where families are exclusively networks of legitimate blood kin. Aristocratic and

---

5. Charles Aikin, who died in 1847, took a medical degree at Edinburgh and spent his career as a physician in London, in practice with members of his extended biological family; he was active in the history of smallpox vaccination.

laboring-class family dynamics necessarily inflect de facto adoption among middling-class families, which remain the primary focus in these chapters.[6] For example, Basil Caroline Montagu, whose adoptive story unfolds in chapter 5, was the hapless maternal orphan son of a London lawyer, also Basil Montagu, who was the acknowledged bastard son of the Earl of Sandwich, who cut him off when he married a pregnant younger daughter of a family too far down the social scale. Through primogeniture and marriage law, aristocratic families zealously guarded the blood-based landed-property system even as they spun off illegitimate offspring at a remarkable rate. Grim mortality rates and rising birth rates flung laboring-class families in shards against the boundaries of poor laws in remote rural parishes and teeming urban districts. Chapter 2 unfolds the history of William Austin, an adoptee whose story flips between class extremes in a bipolar spectacle that fed the tabloid appetites of the nation for twenty years. The child of desperately poor wartime laborers in London, the infant Austin was taken under the rowdy adoptive care of Princess Caroline in 1802 and stood weeping beside the deathbed of Queen Caroline in 1821, her residuary legatee. Displaying an adopted child in a dysfunctional family frame, the royal scandal of Caroline's life often captured the attention of numerous middling-class writers engaged with adoption in their own lives, including, in this book, Jane Austen, Mary Shelley, William Wordsworth, and Charles and Mary Lamb.

Because adoption does not exist in English common law, a brief bout of lexical housekeeping helps prepare the extralegal scene. Samuel Johnson's 1755 *Dictionary of the English Language* registers instrumental forms of adoption in narrowly patriarchal terms: "To adopt. To take a son by choice; to make him a son, who was not so by birth"; an "adopter" is "He that gives some one by choice the rights of a son"; "adoptive" signifies "He that is adopted by another, and made his son; he that adopts another, and makes him his son."[7] On this evidence, adoption at the front end of the period functioned strictly and normatively within a patriarchal property system, ensuring the transfer of wealth from fathers to sons, of whatever kind. Only in the definition of "adoption" does Johnson's text point to something disruptively nonnormative in the human action: "Adoption. The act of adopting, or *taking to one's self what is not native*" (emphasis added). Forget property: "taking to one's self" runs a risk of scrambling the identity cards of personhood, especially when what is

---

6. In her study of illegitimacy in the eighteenth-century novel, Lisa Zunshine observes that bastardy was a site of anxiety (and hence literary interest) especially for the middling classes because of the threats to the legitimacy of property; this anxiety was not shared to such a degree by aristocratic families (with locks on property) and laboring-class families (with little or no property); *Bastards and Foundlings*, 1–22.

7. Johnson, *Dictionary*.

added is by definition strange, "not native." The adoptee is now by definition the stranger.[8]

The stepchild of Johnson's historical method, the *Oxford English Dictionary*, plays it safe with its history of adoption. The primary definition of "adopt" in the *OED*, with abundant citations from the fifteenth century onward, is "To take (a child) and bring it up as one's own, (usually) assuming all rights and responsibilities from its biological parents *on a permanent, legal basis.*"[9] At odds with its own method, the *OED* creates a historical muddle: the final phrase, "on a permanent, legal basis," does not signify in England and Wales until legislation in the wake of World War I. Except for the faint (and parenthetical) "usually," the *OED* fails to distinguish, in its six-century span of quotations, between the long history of de facto adoption and the far more recent history of de jure adoption in the Anglophone world.

Jane Austen's fiction offers a better introductory map of the working vocabulary of de facto surrogate childcare in the period, and such a map guides my reading of Austen and adoption in chapter 3, "Natural Children."[10] In three instances in her published fiction, the word "adopt" refers to the care of a child, all in relation to kinship adoptions: once in *Mansfield Park*, about Fanny Price, and the other two in *Emma*, in connection with Frank Churchill—one of which moments casts a backhand glance at Rousseau. In contrast, three characters in *Emma* are defined by a phrase with much wider currency in Romantic-period culture for surrogate caregiving: a caregiver "takes the charge" of another person, a phrase applied once to Frank Churchill, twice to Jane Fairfax, and once to Harriet Smith; the phrase is often in the period bundled with "care" in the adoptive formula "charge and care." Emma Woodhouse's protégé Harriet Smith is as close as Austen's novels ever get to the word "bastard," which she never uses in the published fiction, but the euphemism "natural daughter" is twice applied to Harriet, and twice the problem of her status is pegged as "illegitimacy."[11] There are no "guardians" in

---

8. See Simpson, *Question of the Stranger*, although Simpson does not take up the topic of adoption or other forms of surrogate childcare.

9. *Oxford English Dictionary (OED)*, s.v. "adopt," https://www.oed.com/search/dictionary/?scope=Entries&q=adopt; emphasis added.

10. References to Austen's fiction throughout this book are to the volumes in the recent Cambridge University Press edition (2005–8): *Sense and Sensibility*, ed. Copeland; *Pride and Prejudice*, ed. Rogers; *Mansfield Park*, ed. Wiltshire; *Emma*, ed. Cronin and McMillan; *Persuasion*, ed. Todd and Blank; *Northanger Abbey*, ed. Benedict and Le Faye; *Later Manuscripts* (for *The Watsons* and *Sanditon*), ed. Todd and Bree.

11. The gossipy euphemism "natural daughter" also dogs Willoughby's conduct in *Sense and Sensibility*. Zunshine (*Bastards and Foundlings*) is wary of criticism in which "the bastard, the foundling, and the orphan all merge into one fuzzy category" (14); this book can be taken as a test of the idea that de facto adoptive care offers a meaningful category to collect these types.

the novels and only one (absent) "ward" in *Northanger Abbey*, nor does Austen deploy the available term "protection" to signify adoptive care.[12] Johnson's *Dictionary* limits guardians and wards to "care over orphans," which in equity did not include orphaned illegitimate children, who had no inheritance rights in common law. Austen denominates two characters as "orphans," Jane Fairfax in *Emma* (a legitimate child) and the first of the two (offstage) Elizas in *Sense and Sensibility*, who is illegitimate.[13] Twice in the fiction, once in *Mansfield Park* and once in *Persuasion*, Austen renders the Latin "*in loco parentis*" as "in the place of a parent." Curiously, Austen never uses any form of the word "foster," especially because Johnson's *Dictionary* records several columns of these forms: foster-child, foster-mother, foster-brother, foster-father, foster-sister, fosterage, to foster—an abundance that signals the widespread contingency of family forms in the period.

This map from Austen's fiction samples how British culture in the period deploys "adopt" among manifold associated terms, a century before its specific de jure signification. When I cite historical instances of the word "adopt" in this book, I embed them in this wider web of associated period-specific terms for de facto surrogate childcare. The word "surrogate" itself never appears among this network of period terms for childcare, either in Austen or elsewhere. During the period, forms of the word "surrogate" signified exclusively in a narrow judicial context, to designate a substitute judge or other temporary court officer.[14] Two centuries later, however, the primary senses of "surrogate" refer to the begetting of children, especially by high-tech means. In our laboratory days, the lexicon of ART—Assisted Reproduction Technology—summons genetic mapping, frozen eggs, sperm donors, frozen embryos, and wombs on generous loan or for hire, a legacy of the first "test-tube" baby, Louise Brown, born near Manchester in 1978. When I use the term "surrogate," it does not signify a temporary judge (the Romantic sense) or a petri dish (in the modern way), but functions ahistorically as a synonym for "substitute"—and a useful synonym because it now brings to mind children, who are, after all, a bundle of biology de novo, whatever else—significantly—they have already become.

***

12. For "protection," the *OED* offers the synonyms guardianship, care, and patronage. For "protection" in an adoptive context, see the details in Queen Caroline's will in chapter 2 and the birth father's memoir in chapter 5 on Basil Caroline Montagu.

13. "Orphan" now typically signifies the deaths of both parents. But "orphanhood" was a multivarious status in the period; for a good introduction to the various forms, see Nixon, *Orphan*.

14. *OED* senses A.1.a. and A.1.b.

It bears repeating: adoption does not exist in English common law. In 1889 the Earl of Meath introduced an "Adoption of Children Bill" in the House of Lords. The bill went nowhere, withdrawn in the face of immediate and forceful arguments that it was "contrary to the laws and institutions of this country."[15] As declared by the Lord Chancellor, "The Bill seeks to alter the whole law of England with reference to the right of parental control, one of the cardinal principles of our law." In the alarmed words of Lord Fitzgerald, "Adoption is wholly unknown to the law of England." It did not help the Earl of Meath to invoke adoption legislation as "a thing which has not been unnoticed in other countries," citing recent US laws in Illinois and New York and, far worse, France, where "children are made wards of the State." Against such a threat, the insular barriers of the island kingdom held firm. In the words of the Lord Chancellor, "The only principle I can find in the Bill is that the principle of adoption should be imported into the law of this country." Parliamentary action legislating de jure adoption in England and Wales waited another thirty-seven years, until the Adoption of Children Act in 1926, in the wake of war's devastation.

In book 1, chapter 16, "Of Parent and Child," the term "adopt" appears nowhere in William Blackstone's *Commentaries on the Laws of England* (4 vols., 1765–70), the landmark summary of law for the period and still influential, in terms of historical precedents, in Britain, the Commonwealth, and the United States.[16] Almost obsessively, Blackstone instead has much to say about "bastards" in terms of the blood-based patrimonial property system and inheritance law, what legal records in the period refer to as "the propinquity of blood."[17] Bastards are infamously "sons of nobody"; in Blackstone's words, "he can *inherit* nothing, being looked upon as the son of nobody; and sometimes called *filius nullius*." Emma Woodhouse aims a sidelong glance at this passage in Austen's *Emma* when she debates Knightley about Harriet Smith's status: "As to the circumstances of her birth, though in a legal sense she may be called Nobody, it will not hold in common sense."[18] In Blackstone, the laws governing guardians and wards apply to the care of legitimate children only (primarily orphans), whose status is locked in by their biological genealogy.

---

15. *Hansard,* House of Lords Debate, July 16, 1889.

16. Blackstone, *Commentaries.* Justice Samuel Alito cites Blackstone nearly a dozen times in his majority opinion in the US Supreme Court "Dobbs" decision on abortion in June 2022; Supreme Court of the United States, "Dobbs v. Jackson Women's Health Organization," June 24, 2022, https://www.supremecourt.gov/opinions/21pdf/19-1392_6j37.pdf. See Walker, "Abortion."

17. See Shakespeare, *Lear,* I.I.107–10, where Lear abandons Cordelia: "Here I disclaim all my paternal care, / Propinquity and property of blood, / And as a stranger to my heart and me / Hold thee from this forever."

18. Austen, *Emma,* 65–66.

In the absence of both common law principle and statutory definition of adoption, work-around schemes for adoptive care appear sporadically in the historical record. As Sarah Abramowicz details in her study of nineteenth-century English child custody case law, individuals "began to turn to contracts, as well as to other legal instruments, such as wills and deeds, to formalize their adoptive ties to other people's children."[19] These ad hoc arrangements highlight "the ways in which clients and attorneys struggled to articulate what adoption meant."[20] And with little or no success. As Abramowicz explains, "Victorian courts refused to enforce these private legal transfers of parentage," holding that "parental rights could not be transferred, even voluntarily, through legal instruments."[21] This record of custody disputes in equity courts underscores the fundamentally unsettled terrain of de facto adoption in England in the Romantic century.

In the words of the historian George Behlmer, "England's common law tradition early on developed an aversion to the idea that parenthood might be transferable."[22] In a European context, this English aversion is exceptional, in contrast to the civil code heritage of Roman law on the continent. Adoption was a legal tool of private family formation in Rome, and the related practice of adrogation (the adoption of an adult) was a public device of Roman statecraft.[23] This heritage of Roman jurisprudence shaped subsequent adoptive practice across Europe, especially in France. In revolutionary France in the wake of Rousseau, for example, the Assembly itself adopted orphans of the Terror in the name of the nation, joining them in the autochthonous siblinghood of *enfants de la patrie*.[24] In 1794 the English Francophile expatri-

---

19. Abramowicz, "Limits of Contract," 49–51. Abramowicz supplies an important Victorian prehistory to the 1926 Adoption Act; although some equity cases that she cites occur earlier in the century, Romantic-period culture is hard to recognize in her argument about an "environmental model of child development."

20. Abramowicz, 56.

21. Abramowicz, 38, 60. For the prehistory of modern de jure adoption, Abramowicz argues that the modern "best interests" standard of child custody begins to emerge in these equity cases.

22. Behlmer, *Friends of the Family,* 273. For a long-range account of adoption in a European context, see Goody, *Family and Marriage in Europe,* 71–75; Goody notes that "there is no entry for adoption in the whole of Sir William Holdsworth's multi-volume *History of English Law,*" which was published two decades before the first British adoption legislation in 1926.

23. Gardner, "Into the *Familia,*" 114–208. For Roman adoption, see also Shell, *Children of the Earth,* 130–42; and Stevens, *Reproducing the State,* 119–20. Comparing European adoption customs to Roman practice, Gardner comments that "among those most at variance [is] the law of England and Wales" (114).

24. For adoption in revolutionary France, see Kertzer and Barbagli, *Family Life,* 133–39; and Shell, *Children of the Earth,* 142–45. As Kertzer and Barbagli note, after the revolution adoption in the civil code soon shifted to more conservative forms; in modern France, there are two basic forms of adoption, "simple" (some ties preserved with birth family) and "plenary" (ties with birth family erased).

ates Helen Maria Williams and John Hurford Stone signed the guestbook of a Swiss library as "an adopted child of the French Republic" and "*filius adopti Repub. Gallicae.*"[25] British culture during the revolutionary decades coded adoption as French, to be viewed with suspicion or admiration, depending on your politics, a national and cultural rivalry that I address throughout this book. In the century since adoption became by legislation a formal legal practice in England in 1926, the United Kingdom has remained measurably insular about adoption when compared to other European countries. For example, the number of intercountry or "overseas" adoptions tallied annually is remarkably fewer in the UK than in other European nations. As reported by adoption demographers, "while France since the 1970s has been among the countries that adopt the most children from abroad, the UK engages in even fewer intercountry adoptions than much smaller nations like the Netherlands, Sweden and Norway."[26] Such numbers register a residual trace of the aversive common law tradition that governs surrogate childcare in Britain in the Romantic period.

THE LEGACY OF ROMANTIC CHILDHOOD

The Romantic-period adoptive lives in this book come to focus burdened by the figure of the "Romantic child," a critical construct with its own vexed history. Philippe Ariès's billboard claim in his 1960 landmark study *Centuries of Childhood*—"In medieval society the idea of childhood did not exist"—has long been pummeled on the score of its shaky evidentiary particulars, but his absolute claim also pointed to a big truth: something significant shifted between medieval childhood and modern childhood. Scholars of western childhood post-Ariès typically point to Romanticism as the locus of that shift, what the adoption scholar Claudia Nelson calls "the perennially interesting question of the Romantic and post-Romantic fixation on childhood" and what the Romanticist Alan Richardson registers as "the unprecedented cultural importance attributed to childhood at this time."[27] This habit of analysis has created its own handicap of familiarity, as Frances Ferguson observes: "It has so long been recognized that children had a special status in the Romantic

---

25. Information in email posting from Patrick Vincent of the Université de Neuchâtel to the NASSR-L listserv (North American Society for the Study of Romanticism), February 21, 2013.

26. Selman, "Global Trends," 1–17; see Mignot, "Full Adoption."

27. Nelson, "Review of *Strange Dislocations*," 123; Richardson, *Literature, Education, and Romanticism*, 24. For a survey of Romantic-period childhood based on the historiography of Lawrence Stone, see Richardson's section "Some Versions of Childhood," 8–25.

period that to say so is perhaps merely to rehearse a cliché."[28] In her 2012 study *Romanticism and Childhood,* Ann Wierda Rowland summarizes why the study of Romantic childhood remains necessary: "The ideas associated with childhood that emerged in the Romantic period, and the rhetoric and images that gave them shape, became foundational to the dominant cultural and historical paradigms of the nineteenth and twentieth centuries and thus to how, for a significant period of time, we have explained the world."[29] As phrased by others in a blunt echo of Ariès's hyperbole, the Romantics invented childhood.[30]

The fraught landscape of Romantic childhood supplies key territory for this book. The following map of critical arguments about that terrain stakes two claims. For students of Romanticism, to attend to adoptive personhood in Romantic-period culture is to open foreclosed accounts of Romantic childhood to new ways of understanding culturally mediated identity. For adoption studies, the critical history of Romantic childhood brings to focus modern adoptee subjectivity as inheriting, multivariously, untimely burdens of doubled differentiation. Because Romanticism marks the regnant elevation of children as primary engines of affective value—Zelizer's "sacralization of children" and Cunningham's "sanctification of childhood"—the adopted child in the shadow of Romantic childhood shoulders a weight of personhood at least twice over, born naturally into a new scene of high-stakes signification and then shuffled culturally, whereupon life deals the signifying cards all over again, and sometimes again.[31]

Soon after William Wordsworth began celebrating peculiar children—idiot boys who can't tell the moon from the sun ("The Idiot Boy") and grave-haunting girls who can't count ("We Are Seven")—this strand of Wordsworthianism when it geared up to epic scale was subject to takedown by gatekeeper critics: "This will never do."[32] The more influential form of Wordsworthian childhood took deep anchor in the poem that is widely known as the "Intimations Ode," which Rowland rightly calls "the period's manifesto of childhood."[33] Publishing the poem in 1807 under the plain title "Ode," Wordsworth immediately began burnishing its exterior to highlight its bottoms-up celebration of child-

---

28. Ferguson, "Afterlife of the Romantic Child," 215.

29. Rowland, *Infantilization,* 10.

30. Rowland keeps the inflated claim of invention at arm's length, but she is willing to risk a claim of discovery: "In the Romantic period, the child was 'discovered,' coming fully into its own as the object of increasing social concern and cultural investment" (5).

31. Zelizer, *Priceless Child,* 10; and Cunningham, *Children and Childhood,* 59.

32. "This will never do" is the cold opening phrase of Francis Jeffrey's review of Wordsworth's long poem *The Excursion* in 1814.

33. Rowland, *Infantilization,* 3. Cunningham, a historian of childhood, adds that "it is difficult to exaggerate the influence of Wordsworth's Ode"; *Children and Childhood,* 55.

hood.[34] For his 1815 edition, Wordsworth raided his own lyrics for the opening line of a new epigraph, now infamous: "The Child is Father of the Man." A new long title snaked its way to the closing keyword, childhood: "Ode. Intimations of Immortality from Recollections of Early Childhood." Soft readings of the poem have long recirculated lines that honor "Delight and liberty, the simple creed / Of Childhood." But other passages gave even sympathetic readers pause. Absolute celebrations of the child as "Mighty Prophet! Seer blest!" and "Thou best Philosopher" irritated Samuel Taylor Coleridge off the bat, especially when he noticed that this elevated child is counted as "A four year's Darling." In *Biographia Literaria* in 1817, Coleridge, long separated from his own three children and always eager to boost his credentials as a philosopher, sputtered about those lines: "What does all this mean? In what sense is a child of that age a *philosopher?* . . . Children of this age give us no such information of themselves."[35] In spite of Coleridge's objections to the elevation of this exceptional child, the "Intimations Ode" won the long game. Wordsworth's hyperbole prevailed, culturally, and the figure left long-standing on the field of Coleridgean contest was the Romantic child, most often in soft and sentimental focus.

Recent work in Romantic-period scholarship aims both to dismantle and repurpose the figure of the Romantic child. Rowland supplies a useful snapshot of the popularized figure: "The 'Romantic child' earns its sobriquet because it is essentially an idealized, nostalgic, sentimental figure of childhood, one characterized by innocence, imagination, nature, and primitivism, qualities associated with Romanticism that survive today in very few cultural figures, the child being one of the most enduring."[36] In *Romanticism and the Vocation of Childhood* in 2001, Judith Plotz filed a vehement brief against the influence of such a "relentless focus on an unchanging child forever fixed in childhood," what she terms "the embrace of the absolute child," including, notably, Wordsworth's fabrication of the "sequestered child . . . a world adequate unto itself."[37] Occluded by this dominant figure are what Plotz calls the "children of history": "The discourse of these children of history, children inescapably defined by their environment, is antithetical to Romantic discourse"; figures of the child in Charles Lamb's essays, for

---

34. Wordsworth, *Poems, in Two Volumes,* 269–77. In the many lifetime collective print editions of his poems, Wordsworth always gave pride of place to the "Ode," always placing it as the final text as the collections grew in size and number of volumes. As the figure of the Child is elevated in the text of the poem, so the poem itself is elevated in bibliographical prominence.

35. Coleridge, *Biographia Literaria,* II.138.

36. Rowland, *Infantilization,* 9.

37. Plotz, *Vocation of Childhood,* xiii–xvi, 69.

example, are "discontinuous with history."[38] A kindred body of work to disestablish a masculinist "Romantic child" tradition tracks in recent histories of women's writing in the period. Before her untimely death in 2001, the scholar of children's literature Mitzi Myers was among the most vocal champions of remapping children in the literature of the Romantic period. In her 1995 essay "De-Romanticizing the Subject" Myers argues that "the metanarrative of childhood that dominates the appropriation of Romanticism for juvenile literature and pedagogy is, literally, a master narrative—the Romantic story of the emergent male self," where "usually the Child turns out to be the Romantic boy."[39] Alan Richardson in his 1999 essay on "Romanticism and the End of Childhood" similarly laments the occlusion of "ethnographic children" in the "blind spot" of the Romantic child tradition, its "transcendental element" that underwrites sentimental and naive forms and elides the "social and material world."[40]

As a tool of analysis on the interpretive shelf, the overly familiar figure of the Romantic child now displays a warning label: well past its use-by date, this product is hazardous, historically and ideologically. But repurposed with caution, the figure offers significant leverage for adoption studies. The differentiated status carved out for children in the Enlightenment and Romanticism helps build a better picture of the intellectual history of adoption.[41] Especially because modern adoption regimes are the products of liberal politics, it is crucial to register the long segregation of the child in the history of liberalism, which inflects in complex ways the exceptionalism of Romantic childhood and its effects on untimely adoptions.

Arguing that difference determines both the subordinate status of modern adoption and, paradoxically, its utopian promise, Frances Latchford helps point the way to the place of Romanticism in the history of adoption, stipulating that "the institution of adoption consistently conflates the meaning of

---

38. Plotz, 38, 128.

39. Myers, "De-Romanticizing the Subject," 88–110.

40. Richardson, "End of Childhood," 180.

41. Most accounts of pre–twentieth century adoption foreground social or literary history instead of intellectual history. A recent exception is Frances Latchford's 2019 study, *Steeped in Blood: Adoption, Identity, and the Meaning of Family,* in which Latchford aims to establish "a genealogy of the modern bio-genealogical imperative" (14). In her shorthand summary, "the intersection of naturalism [for Latchford, Darwin and Freud] with individualism [for Latchford, Descartes and Kant] produces the modern experience of being 'adopted'" (124). For adoption history, I argue that Romanticism supplies a key bridge between her two genealogical panels. For a theoretical sketch of the project of adoption genealogy, see Rudy, "Anxious Kinship," notes 13 and 16.

adoption with difference."[42] A fundamental dilemma for modern liberal universalism—the principle that all human beings are created equal—is how to define and manage difference. From liberalism's tangled Enlightenment roots and well into the Romantic century, large-scale exclusions of race, gender, and class long worked and continued to work damage.[43] For adoption studies, the history of the differentiation of children forms an especially telling part of this history of exclusions, which begin to track in the Enlightenment prehistory of Romanticism. The scholarship of cultural and legal historians working on childhood, contract law, and age-of-consent law foregrounds the key principle of exceptionalism in the status of childhood in this long period.[44] In the pre-Romantic Enlightenment, the new exceptional child signifies the excluded child—the nonadult, nonrational human being. But this exceptionalism script gets flipped, famously: in Romanticism, the excluded child is now the elevated child, exceptionally.[45] Paradoxically, this new Romantic child remains excluded in difference (the not-yet-rational human) even while celebrated (the already-extraordinary). As the following chapters track the effects on adoption of this new hybrid figuration of childhood, this book does not traffic in old warehoused notions of Romantic childhood, in which unreason is recostumed as imagination. Instead, for adoption, this book tracks the perplexing, unsettling, destabilizing burden of childhood figured as segregated elevation (the strange new Romantic form of exceptionalism) when it encounters, in adoption, a second-order segregation of familial remove, an experience of multiplied difference.

---

42. With a Foucauldian model "that differentiation is an aspect or apparatus of normalization and subject formation" (*Steeped in Blood,* 10), Latchford builds a primary argument that "the differentiation of family ties in adoption discourse fundamentally sustains the superiority of biological ties over adoptive ties" (11). But the book's "final suggestion is that we fail our families and ourselves when we ignore the idea that *difference* as much as *sameness,* or in conjunction with it, is a basis for real and meaningful family bonds. . . . Indeed, adoption is a phenomenon wherein family bonds are founded upon difference every day" (309–10).

43. In 1997 Charles Mills argued in *The Racial Contract* that liberalism's segregating exclusions of race and gender were, in the words of Jennifer Szalai, "historically so vast that they weren't mere anomalies but clearly fundamental to it" ("Liberals Gone?"). As Mills puts the matter, "It would be a fundamental error . . . to see racism as anomalous, a mysterious deviation from European Enlightenment humanism" (*Racial Contract,* 26–27).

44. Abramowicz heads a section of her essay "Childhood Exceptionalism" ("Limits of Contract," 47); Brewer (*Birth or Consent*) tracks in detail the emergence of what she terms "meaningful consent."

45. Brewer, an Enlightenment historian, glimpses Romanticism over the horizon and renders it in plain summary: "Romantic writers maintained the same distinctions between childhood and adulthood as those of the Enlightenment, but reversed the characteristics that should be most honored"; *Birth or Consent,* 128.

The work of Frances Ferguson helps to unpack this vertiginous mix of Romantic childhood when it is experienced in adoption as a perplexing surplus of differentiated exclusions. In her 2003 essay "The Afterlife of the Romantic Child," Ferguson emphasizes the segregation principle inherited from the Enlightenment in the managerial engines of modern liberal politics: "I am claiming that the ability to treat children as different from adults is almost as fundamental to modern political thinking—of a more or less liberal cast—as any distinction we make politically."[46] Ferguson's Romanticism marks a moment in the history of modern liberalism when "the very distinction between childish unreason and adult reason comes to look like the paradigmatic instance of apportioning the world and segregating some persons from others."[47] For adoption studies, which specializes in how some persons become peeled off from others, the key takeaway is that the many engines of liberal difference that "segregat[e] some persons from others" are in the Romantic period brought to bear with new inflections upon the human subset of children. A striking feature of this phase of liberal segregation is that difference in this instance comes packaged with elevated exceptionalism rather than exclusionary erasure, as in segregated sets of race, gender, and class.[48]

In a later essay on "Rousseau, *Emile*, and Britain," Ferguson spotlights the early Romantic inflection of Enlightenment exceptionalism in Rousseau's educational project. Rousseau makes a "basic claim" in *Emile* "that children and adults speak different languages, and that most of their conversations are lies, in being differentially understood by parties to the exchange."[49] As Ferguson puts the matter in her earlier "Romantic Child" essay, "the introduction of a divide between adults and children insists that the two groups may use the same words but that the child will not mean what the adult does by them."[50]

---

46. Ferguson, "Afterlife," 222; the essay offers ambitious range, subtitled "Rousseau and Kant Meet Deleuze and Guattari." Framing segregated Romantic childhood at an epistemological turning point, her account of schizoanalysis centers on a contemporary debate about age of consent law, tracking how Deleuze and Guattari "address questions of the organization of thought rather than specific beliefs and opinions" (217).

47. Ferguson, 217.

48. Whether the noun "childism" maps post-Romantic human behavior honorifically or pejoratively seems to be up for grabs. In the wake of historians who speak of the Romantic-period "sanctification" and "sacralization" of children, "childism" inclines toward the honorific. But the psychoanalyst Elisabeth Young-Bruehl in 2012 proposed "childism" as a pejorative category of prejudice *against* children comparable to ageism, racism, and sexism (*Childism*).

49. Ferguson, "Rousseau, *Emile*, and Britain," 187–207. The key *Emile* passage appears in Rousseau's attack on catechistic method: "All the answers of the catechism are misconceived. It is the pupil who teaches the master. In the mouths of children these answers are really lies, since the children expound what they do not understand and affirm what they are not in a position to believe"; Rousseau, *Emile*, 378.

50. Ferguson, "Afterlife," 223.

Ferguson thus locates Romantic childhood within the tangled histories liberalism tells of itself, which leaves subjects epistemologically and existentially stranded: "Far from resolving itself into a simple idealization of childhood innocence or a commitment to potentiality, the classic liberal perspective treats the sense of childhood as a statement of the fundamental unactualizability of a knowledge of our own positions."[51] In pursuit of a larger argument about how "modern liberal toleration creates a new ground for politics in representation itself," Ferguson positions Romantic childhood at a high-altitude epistemological pivot, when "Rousseau and Kant relocate the questions of philosophy to replace perceptions and statements with the conditions of the possibility of perceptions and statements."[52] But for adoptees stranded down on the ground, such a shifting foundation of knowledge produces urgent ethical and existential effects. In such a contingent system of unstable subject positions, adoptees too often stall in the gaps between uncertain self-knowledge and the (in)ability to put such conditional knowledge into actual practice.[53]

In the representation of both children and adoptees in "the classic liberal perspective," as Ferguson frames the view, multiple contradictions collide. Misfiring on the launchpad, modern liberalism cannot precisely explain why it leans upon a claim that children are different from everyone else, as if that claim guarantees its other long-exercised regimes of segregation. Contemporary "biopolitical liberalism," argues Sayres Rudy, simultaneously works a derivative angle, upholding a bedrock claim of liberal universalism that there is no difference between adoptees and everyone else, but it cannot precisely explain why it insists on that claim, which strikes adoptees as suspicious:

> Adoptees in liberal democratic societies remain neurotically anxious about their full and equal inclusion in a surrounding normative order that explicitly offers all inhabitants full political rights and equal physical opportunities. As a result, adoptees who still complain of second-class status based on biology, blood, or genes again seem deluded, stuck in the past, narcissistic, or to confirm the no-win condition of "genealogical bewilderment." If adoptees cannot explain why they remain fixated on biological origins, despite

---

51. Ferguson, 232.

52. Ferguson, 217.

53. Formulated in an attempt to address modern adoptee dysfunction, the vexed psychoanalytic concept of "genealogical bewilderment" fails to historicize how foundationally differentiated Romantic childhood is paradoxically central to the illusion of liberal stability. For the primary marker for the phrase in 1964, see Sants, "Genealogical Bewilderment,"133–40; for an incisive critique of its legacy, see Leighton, "Addressing the Harms," 63–107.

the explicit norms of biopolitical liberalism, then they appear to desire their own suffering—a kind of madness.[54]

In the politics of adoption regimes, the special burden on adoptees of this legacy of Romantic childhood is that, having first been enrolled in a differentiated subset of humans, adoptees are then subject to a second segregation, suffering differentiation at least twice over, multivariously, a process whereby difference gears up from first-order exclusionary exceptionalism into new forms of separation and division, often traumatically. Adoption in the wake of Romantic childhood entangles the incongruous elevation of childhood exceptionalism with the abjection of familial dislocation.[55]

In his history of nonpersons in western societies and legal systems, Daniel Heller-Roazen helps bring to focus these forms of doubled differentiation as marks of qualitative difference: "In every community, society, and assembly, nonpersons are lesser ones—where 'lesser' points not to a quantity, but to a quality, which is intensely variable in kind."[56] Heller-Roazen tracks forms of "the diminished individual," where western social codes and laws have enforced "the formal judgment that a present person, while in appearance capable of language, may not lay claim to certain rights. This is a speaking body from which full personhood is missing: a nonperson conceived not by vanishing, but by lessening."[57] Such social and legal systems have long produced "an individual distinguished by the fact of being unfit for representation as a complete person."[58] In a chapter on "Rules of Diminution," Heller-Roazen details the historical means by which "the personhood of human beings may be lessened," the subjects of which processes have most often included, historically, foreigners, slaves, and women, all of whom "wear the masks of an infinitely variable lessness."[59] In the wake of emerging forms of modern liberalism, doubly differentiated adoptees suffer kindred forms of diminution at

---

54. Rudy, "Anxious Kinship," 209.

55. Elevation here signifies "to raise above the usual position, or above the level of surrounding objects" (*OED* II.2.a), with the effect "to hold up to view" (II.2.b); a synonym would be "singled out." In the context of adoption history, the term should not be mistaken, honorifically and necessarily, for exaltation (as, liturgically, in the "elevation" of the Host in the Mass). The modern clinical category of the "exceptional child" is capacious absolutely in its spectrum of forms of elevation, all held up to view as "special."

56. Heller-Roazen, *Absentees*, 7.

57. Heller-Roazen, 9, 78–79.

58. Heller-Roazen, 81.

59. Heller-Roazen, 83, 100.

The Burden of Romantic Childhood

tense odds with their exceptionality as heirs of Romantic childhood.[60] Reciprocally inflected, these two bundled sites of difference—Romantic childhood and adoption—yield multivaried forms of adoptive diminishment under both de facto and de jure adoption regimes. The following chapters provide exemplary cases of such imbricated forms of adoptive difference that emerge, untimely and post-Romantically, within the Romantic period, offering models of what Jerome Christensen terms "unrecognized possibility."[61]

Heller-Roazen confesses the temptation to see diminished individuals everywhere, a paradoxical form of erasure—the night in which all cows are black—which his model risks with universalizing models of Romanticism: "Those lacking in full personhood may be less the exception than the rule. Among the speaking beings who we are, diminishment is unceasing."[62] To map modern adoptee subjectivity, Romantic and post-Romantic adoption as a hybrid process of doubled differentiation supplies a more useful template than other closely related models of Romanticism, such as an existential condition of systemic loss, shared by all. Stanley Cavell describes this Romantic preoccupation with loss as "our worldlessness or homelessness . . . we conceive that some place elsewhere . . . must be what [R]omantics call 'home,'" what Martin Heidegger signifies with *Dasein* (among much else) as a zero-grade sense of abandonment.[63] Risking nostalgia, these apophatic models of loss exert leveling force: all humans are haunted by loss (sometimes everyone feels like a motherless child), and because everyone loses their own childhood, the child becomes the figure of the lost home of all humans, all conditioned by loss. Such a reading of Romanticism underwrites Carolyn Steedman's *Strange Dislocations: Childhood and the Idea of Human Interiority*, whereby the Romantic child as the figure of loss marks the invention of interiority, paving the proleptic way to Freud and psychoanalysis. From such a starting point, it is not a large leap to inflect the adoptee as the figure of the human: defined by

---

60. It helps to test the vexed comparability to adoption of at least one of Heller-Roazen's historically diminished categories, slavery. Brutal violence categorically marks an absolute divide between slavery and adoption (although adoption is far from innocent on the score of violence.) But there are grounds to explore the extent to which they are kindred forms, as Austen does in *Mansfield Park* (see chapter 3). See Orlando Patterson's discussion of "natal alienation"—a phrase resonant for adoption—in *Slavery and Social Death*, 5–7. Skeptical of intersectional theory, Sayres Rudy excludes adoptees from a remarkably narrow *desideratum* of exteriorized difference: "Adoptees are not identifiable as a physically distinct group" ("Anxious Kinship," 223).

61. Christensen, *End of History*, 11. See also Galperin, *Missed Opportunities*, 25.

62. Heller-Roazen, *Absentees*, 81.

63. Cavell, *Quest*, 9, 32; Cavell reads *Walden*, for example, as a Romantic text "propos[ing] human existence as the finding of ecstasy in the knowledge of loss" (171). Heidegger, *Being and Time*.

loss, abandonment, or diminishment, all are adopted—except all are not.[64] To conflate existence and adoption is to risk a trope for exiled and bewildered humanity that forgoes purchase on those who, both exceptionally differentiated and diminished in qualitative difference, are actually adopted. A model of manifold differentiation rather than universalized loss resists the leveling temptation to declare the adoptee as the figure of the human.

In his call to forgo the figure of the Romantic child, Alan Richardson also wishes to retain a "residue" of the discredited figure because it registers "decentered subjectivity," but his wish defaults to a set of sunny liberal postures: "the ingenuous, questing, unique, emotive, dynamic child of the Romantics."[65] The arguments of Ferguson and Rudy, which locate Romantic childhood and the modern adoptee within the history of liberalism's tangled self-constructions, bear in these pages upon a very different set of Romantic-period cases that dwell outside normative attitudes of liberal complacency. Chapter 2 unravels the spiral into madness of the adopted waif William Austin, unwelcome on a bionormative national stage; chapter 3 collects an abject set of gypsies, spinsters, orphans, and adoptees in *Emma*; chapter 4 tracks Victor Frankenstein's nightmare through the repatriated struggles of the widowed Mary Shelley, refusing to abandon her sole surviving child to the surrogate care of strangers; chapter 5 excavates beneath what has long become the popularized figure of the Romantic child the failed mourning and bitter melancholy of the adopted maternal orphan Basil Caroline Montagu. Chapter 6 recovers the distress of the orphaned Cambridge adoptee Emma Isola, who obsessed about how her Italian birth name—Isola—defined less her natal membership in a differentially exceptional tribe than her orphaned, adopted, and diminished difference, the bundled effect of which doubled inheritance bequeathed "the fundamental unactualizability of a knowledge of [her] own position." In her isolation, Emma Isola was ironically an untimely Romantic-period member of an emerging tribe assembling on the outside of liberal repose, what Rudy describes as "adoptees [who] still exist as a carnival, or perhaps a quiet kinship, of mad suspects," kin to the abject set of what Heller-Roazen describes as an "unruly multitude" of nonpersons.[66]

---

64. Interpreted through the lens of Pauline texts, adoption has long operated as a universalizing trope in Christianity.

65. Richardson, "End of Childhood," 175, 183.

66. Rudy, "Anxious Kinship," 223; and Heller-Roazen, *Absentees*, 8.

ROMANTIC CHILDHOOD, NARRATIVE, AND ADOPTION

A second front where Romantic childhood contributes to the work of adoption studies is narratological, specifically the ways in which modern adoption narratives shoulder the burden of the quest for origins, default to necessary strategies of invention, and suffer the travails of national fiction-making. The interpretive pressure to measure Romanticism as a condition of existential loss haunts all these scenes of narrative praxis, confounding the dilemma of adoptees negotiating the burdens of doubled difference.

Ann Rowland's work speaks to these points in her exacting account of how exceptional figures of children and infants functioned as synecdoches in Romantic-period historiography, where they were put to work as "the dominant rhetorical strategy for figuring origins," which is one of the most fraught tasks in adoption.[67] Promoting "the child as the figure of the primitive," early-Romantic Scottish writers such as Adam Ferguson and Dugald Stewart promulgated "the belief that the child represents the childhood of the race as a whole," foregrounding "the figure of a child who is simultaneously ancestor and progeny, past and future."[68] This prominent rhetorical maneuver in Romantic historiography, an early version of the "ontogeny recapitulates phylogeny" gambit, spotlights outrageous pressures on origin searches and origin narratives in modern adoption. In the long shadow of Romantic childhood, adoptees in search of origins also bear the impossible burden of representing the lost horizons of the pasts of everyone else.[69] Rowland measures the load this way: "The promise is that the child might repeat and experience in his own lifetime the full course of human history."[70] To a modern adoptee undertaking search, such an offer looms impossibly large as an imperious threat: that way madness lies.

Origins are infamously fugitive, whereupon invention steps up. Romantic-period historiographers called this shift "conjecture," which Rowland describes as "a strategy for what to do when the trail of history goes cold."[71] Such blind alleys and shuttered gates block searching adoptees on abundant trails; the subsequent tasks loaded on the child in Romantic historiography shadow the structures of modern adoption search narratives. Drawing on the work

---

67. Rowland, *Infantilization*, 34.

68. Rowland, 10, 32.

69. As Margaret Homans characterizes the pressure, "Adoptees are peculiarly burdened, in popular adoption culture, with this obligation to find, know, and grasp material origins"; *Imprint of Another Life*, 114.

70. Rowland, *Infantilization*, 60.

71. Rowland, 42.

on narrative in trauma theory, Margaret Homans argues that, in the wake of deconstruction's absolute skepticism about "the elusiveness and constitutive fictionality of origins," modern adoption narratives adopt fiction and invention as the very tools to reframe the fugitive past in ways that speak to present needs: "A different model for adoption narrative emerges, one in which claims to reveal the truth of the past are replaced by the narration of an emotionally satisfying but probably fictional story about the present."[72] When the pasts of adoptees are sealed away in any one of manifold ways, the narrative act itself takes up the heavy lifting. As Homans glosses the recuperative potential of the process, "origins may not be graspable, but they can be written."[73] Romantic childhood marks an early proving-ground of such ominously freighted narrative transactions.

Fictions of the past are collective as well as individual. Conjectural histories of origins in the Romantic period took as a primary object the nation, the burden again bearing down on children. In Rowland's phrase, the emergent presumption—spectacular in its encumbrance—was that "the past of the nation can be found in the present of the child."[74] The history of modern adoption offers abundant versions of how national narratives spin out by spotlighting, often blindingly, the children of adoption: the tribulations of postwar Korea, reproductive politics in China, the specter of lawlessness in Guatemala, the maltreatment of indigenous peoples of North American nations, the aftermath of war in Germany, illegitimacy and Catholicism in Ireland, and multiple tumults in the shifting self-images of US national identity.[75] Rowland is altogether too Whiggish about the process; in her view, Romantic childhood "enables new ways of narrating national continuity and progress, and new ways of making the past perpetually available to the present."[76] This book argues instead that Romantic childhood bequeaths to modern adoptees a harrowing inheritance of impossibly weighted narrative tasks. A standard progressive narrative of modern childhood affirms that after Romanticism, children were freed from constituting a labor pool and transformed into primary engines of affective value, what Zelizer frames as the shift from the "useful child" to the "priceless child."[77] In terms of adoption, I read that shift as

---

72. Homans, *Imprint,* 122.

73. Homans, 177.

74. Rowland, *Infantilization,* 60.

75. See also recent accounts of "coercive adoptions" and the manipulations of national image in Chile during the Pinochet regime, as reported in the *New York Times* in 2021; Londoño, "Stolen at Birth."

76. Rowland, *Infantilization,* 16.

77. Zelizer, *Priceless Child.*

THE BURDEN OF ROMANTIC CHILDHOOD　　　31

exchanging the burden of economic labor for the burden of affective labor. As a remix of famous lines in Wordsworth's "Intimations Ode" might put it, modern adoptees trail heavily freighted clouds of Romantic childhood.

These crossroads of narrative praxis, Romantic childhood, and adoption speak to why this book foregrounds narrative forms, both literary and biographical. As scholarship in critical adoption studies has richly demonstrated of late, the narrative act itself—its motives, forms, and effects—is a defining and necessary feature of adoptive experience in unique ways, distinct even from other forms of narratively mediated social praxis, such as marriage. Homans, for example, argues that origin narratives function in special ways in adoption. In origin stories generally, telos functions as both ongoing goal and finished conclusion. But in adoption narratives, telos as aim rarely becomes telos as conclusion, an accomplished and closed-off end point; the narratives remain open-ended. John McLeod details the narrative dialectic of "being adopted" and "adoptive being," the dialectic of bloodlines and what he terms "life lines," mediated narratively.[78] Marianne Novy works diachronically to map how adoption narratives over time navigate a structural set of origin, separation, and reunion narratives.[79]

After chapters on Austen and Shelley, which foreground some of the most famous novels from the period, I turn from the privileged narrative form of the novel to memoir and other nonfiction narrative forms such as essays and letters to mix genres, thereby hoping to reduce the risk that a book devoted entirely to novels might be misread as a backdoor route to empirical social history.[80] Aside from occasional references, I make no systematic attempt to correlate this handful of narrative texts with large sets of historical data. But while I hold history-in-numbers at arm's length, I regularly turn from literature to biography, a move that requires comment. In her close reading of bastard and foundling fictions in the eighteenth century, Lisa Zunshine is wary of paired attention to historical lives.[81] I work on the assumption that historical lives are necessary to the enterprise; these histories supply brakes to the extraliterary effects of literary form and in turn illuminate unique iterations of those very cultural forms. McLeod puts the risk of segregating literary texts in these terms: what too often results is "the freighting of adoptive units in

---

78. McLeod, *Life Lines.*

79. Novy, *Reading Adoption.*

80. See the historian John Boswell's magisterial *The Kindness of Strangers: Child Abandonment in Europe from Late Antiquity to the Renaissance,* for caution about leaning on fictional narrative for evidence: the abundant figures of orphans and foundlings in fiction and drama may be just as much (or more) evidence of narrative job work than social reality.

81. Zunshine, *Bastards and Foundlings,* 17.

symbolic terms with little sustained engagement with the painful histories and experiences which underscore their materialization."[82] Guided by such caution, and in advance of the unwritten book on the social history of Romantic-period adoption, throughout this book I pair primary literary texts with lived histories, painful and otherwise. I pair adoption in Austen's fiction with the history of her brother's kinship adoption; the tale of Victor Frankenstein with the history of the widowed Mary Shelley in England after 1823; the child in Wordsworth's poetry with the melancholy history of the maternal orphan Basil Caroline Montagu; Charles Lamb's dream children with the history of an adopted orphan teenager, Emma Isola. I surround these coupled literary and historical lives with the scandalously national story of the adopted waif William Austin, and I embed all these stories within the bleak records of the laundress Thérèse Levasseur's lost infants at one end of the Romantic century and, at the other, the poet Letitia Elizabeth Landon's abandoned children.

While this book hopes to contribute to exemplary projects about adoption narrative, I also aim to broaden both temporal and geographical fields, in alliance with Sayres Rudy's promotion of the work to "seek out the differential concept *adoption* by its nonuniversal emergence in discrete social and historical settings."[83] In his 2015 study *Life Lines*, McLeod, a British scholar, writes "to establish a centre-point for adoption literary and cultural studies happening outside of the United States," a goal that I wholeheartedly endorse.[84] One challenge that I hope to address by means of this book is that most of the examples typically cited to study adoption in British cultural history dwell outside the Romantic period.[85] Similarly, the developing social history of de facto adoption in Britain during the eighteenth and nineteenth centuries offers important work that is nevertheless clustered on either side of Romanticism. Scholarship on the earlier period takes its measure from the history of Thomas Coram's foundling hospital, which makes appearances in this book in

---

82. McLeod, *Life Lines,* 32.

83. Rudy, "Anxious Kinship," 224.

84. McLeod, *Life Lines,* 34.

85. McLeod's set of British and Irish texts, for example, are all contemporary. Although Homans's 2013 book *The Imprint of Another Life* includes an early chapter on George Eliot's *Silas Marner,* the bulk of her readings feature twentieth-century American texts. In her 2005 book *Reading Adoption,* Novy offers the most extensive work to date to map adoption in British literary history, with three chapters in sequence on Shakespeare, the "Developing British Novel," and George Eliot. When she turns to the novel, however, Novy's foregrounded British writers—Henry Fielding, Charlotte Brontë, Charles Dickens, and Eliot—bracket the outside of literature in the Romantic period.

the chapters on Jane Austen and Mary Shelley.[86] Scholarship in the latter half of the nineteenth century takes its cues from the more densely documented Dickensian world of annual parliamentary reports and acts, waifs and strays societies, emigration schemes, and key figures in the history of surrogate childcare closer to the time of de jure adoption, such as Thomas Barnardo.[87] There remains, however, a striking gap in the scholarship of Romantic-period adoption.[88]

THE CHILDREN OF HISTORY

It is time to turn from the Romantic child to what it would erase, the children of history. In addition to the work on childhood and children in the scholarship of women's writing, skeptical challenges to ahistorical "Romantic child" scholarship include pockets of research about children in laboring-class culture. In his heralded *The Making of the English Working Class*, E. P. Thompson in eight hundred pages made room for twenty pages on "Childhood." Acknowledging that "there was a drastic increase in the intensity of exploitation of child labour between 1780 and 1840," Thompson was chiefly concerned to argue that "the most prevalent form of child labour was in the home or within the family economy" instead of in the early industrial workhouse: "Above all, the work was within the family economy and under parental care."[89] In this drive-by account of children, Thompson did not pause to

---

86. The history of the London Foundling Hospital from 1739 anchors an extensive body of work on orphans, foundlings, illegitimacy, and infanticide in the middle decades of the eighteenth century; see McClure, *Coram's Children*; Evans, *Lone Mothers*; Nixon, *Orphan*; Jackson, *New-Born Child Murder*; Zunshine, *Bastards and Foundlings*; and Bowlby, *A Child of One's Own*.

87. Scholarship tracking child welfare from the 1860s through the 1926 Adoption of Children Act includes Keating, *A Child for Keeps*; Frost, *Illegitimacy*; Rose, *Massacre*; Wagner, *Barnardo*; Wagner, *Children of the Empire*; Parr, *Labouring Children*; Nelson, *Family Ties*; and Behlmer, *Friends of the Family*.

88. In her 2009 study of interwar adoption in England, Jenny Keating registers that she was "surprised to find how little had been published about the early history of adoption in the United Kingdom"; *Child for Keeps*, 8. Adoptive family forms, defined broadly, are missing from a recent history monograph focused on representations of parents in Georgian England (Bailey, *Parenting*). Whereas a comprehensive social history of Romantic-period adoption remains unwritten, there are excellent recent models in Victorian studies, including especially Nelson, *Family Ties*, with chapters on "The Extended Family" and "Stepfamilies and Foster Families."

89. Thompson, *English Working Class*, 331–34.

34   CHAPTER 1

unpack haphazard, nonnormative structures of "the home," "the family economy," or "parental care."[90]

Post-Thompson, the bulk of the scholarship about children between 1780 and 1900 still tilts toward post-Romantic social history in the second half of the nineteenth century.[91] A notable exception is the work of the British historian Hugh Cunningham. In addition to his broad contributions to the field, in his 1991 book *The Children of the Poor* Cunningham foregrounded a set of topics inflected in telling ways within the Romantic period, including child slavery and the abolitionist movement, the history of charity schools and the Holy Thursday spectacles, child theft and the climbing boys (chimney sweeps), and the figure of the child as (ignoble) savage.[92] Taking Cunningham's lead, in chapter 2 I add to the Romantic-period record of Plotz's occluded "children of history" the bizarre tale of the urban waif Willy Austin, born in desperate London poverty in 1802 and plunged, not down a chimney, but into a lifetime prolepsis of the fantasy of adoptive status elevation soon to come in Freud's tale of the family romance. Also in these pages, children of history who emerge from the shadow of the Romantic child include Basil Caroline Montagu, whose disruptively melancholy life resembles the tale of the unlamented lost sailor son Richard Musgrove in Austen's *Persuasion,* and Emma Isola, the orphaned daughter of an immigrant family on the margins of the Cambridge establishment. To launch those tales of adoption, I close this chapter with the remarkable story of a child abandoned at Coram's foundling hospital in 1757, who as a widowed adult adoptee witnessed firsthand the scandal of an adopted child on the royal stage during the Regency, the tumultuous second decade of the nineteenth century.

SABRINA BICKNELL, CHILD OF HISTORY

On the 24th of May, 1757, a female infant was deposited at the London Foundling Hospital and given the enrollment number 4579; she was subsequently tagged with an institutional name, Ann Kingston, and bundled two years later to a satellite establishment, a new Orphan Hospital at Shrewsbury. A decade

---

90. Thompson briefly flags urban evils such as the "climbing boys" (chimney sweeps), noting that one branch of Romanticism, in a form of "traditionalist social radicalism," deployed the figure of the Romantic child as a critique of such systems of abuse.

91. For example, post-Romantic family structures dominate a useful five-volume collection of excerpted primary documents from the long nineteenth century; Nelson, Strange, and Egenolf, *British Family Life.*

92. Cunningham, *Children and Childhood*; Cunningham, *Invention of Childhood*; and Cunningham, *Children of the Poor.*

later, when Ann Kingston was twelve, a young Oxford graduate, Thomas Day, showed up at Shrewsbury with a novel male scheme. Besotted with Rousseau's advice from the sidelines about child-raising, Day plotted to adopt a girl for a preconjugal experiment. Plucking Ann from a lineup and renaming her Sabrina Sidney, Day spirited her to France with another adopted orphan from the London hospital, Dorcas Car, to gauge their conjugal potential. It was a bizarre trial with a long train of untidy consequences, many of which migrated from gossip and correspondence into fiction in Maria Edgeworth's *Belinda,* published in 1801 and echoed on Box Hill in Austen's *Emma* in 1816. Eventually discarded by Day, Ann Kingston—foundling baby number 4579— was widowed as Sabrina Bicknell in 1787 and subsequently labored as the housekeeper for Dr. Charles Burney, the brother of the novelist Frances Burney, at his boarding school in Greenwich.[93]

In October 1811, a carriage from royal stables across Blackheath pulled up at the door of Dr. Burney's Academy at the foot of Croom's Hill near the Thames, as boys assembled for autumn term. Alert to the advent of a special new pupil, the housekeeper, Mrs. Bicknell, stepped out to greet Thomas Stikeman, the page of the Princess of Wales. Trailing behind him was a nine-year-old boy, William Austin, whose identity had been a gossipy mystery since a secret royal commission in 1806, widely known as the "Delicate Investigation." Rumored to be the natural child of the boisterous princess by any one of several lovers, or even by her hated royal spouse the prince regent, Austin was in fact the biological child of a pair of Deptford laborers, a laid-off dockworker and his laundress wife. But ever since his birth mother handed him over to Stikeman four months after his birth in July 1802, Willy Austin had been a puzzling fixture of life in the royal fast lane at Montague House, on the edge of Blackheath.

And now it was time for the adopted boy to be day-boarded at school down the hill in Greenwich, where Dr. Burney relied on the widowed Mrs. Bicknell to manage the bustling establishment. Among the annual routines of boarding school life, the arrival of a new boy with royal baggage turned the heads of many a kitchen maid and laundry worker. Before long, stringers from the national press began nosing about, keen for a conversation with "The Child," as they pitched him in the papers. As Mrs. Bicknell mulled the

---

93. The story summarized in this first paragraph is narrated in rich detail by Moore, *Perfect Wife*. My warrant for using the word "adopt" is Austen's adaptation of the history in *Emma* (see chapter 3). Day's success in taking the two girls under his charge and care was a tangle of lies, deception, and subterfuge, including a donation to the London hospital. For Day's Rousseauvianism, see his 1783 novel *The History of Sandford and Merton,* which is "A Work Intended for the Use of Children."

arrival of this royal surrogate child, she no doubt paused to ponder her own singular history, as the victim of one of the most infamous adoption episodes on recent record. Memory aside, Mrs. Bicknell set about sorting school life for a boy who for the next decade performed disruptively in a celebrity adoption, an outsider planted uncomfortably close to the bionormative bloodlines of royalty. I take up his story in chapter 2.

CHAPTER 2

National Children

The Madness of William Austin

In March 1845, a notice circulated in British newspapers of a "Commission of Lunacy on William Austin, the Adopted Son of the late Queen Caroline," as one provincial headline billed the item. This widely duplicated piece reported that a London jury in the past week "returned a verdict 'That William Austin was of unsound mind, and incapable of managing his affairs.' . . . The unfortunate gentleman was adopted when a child by the late Queen Caroline, and to him she bequeathed by will a portion of her property."[1] In this chapter, I track the history of William Austin to display how, in the wake of Rousseau, the figure of the child separated from consanguineous origins spotlights the fictiveness of the nation—a liberating spectacle in France but an alarming prospect for the British nation, whose power remained deeply rooted in the bloodline guarantees of biological genealogy. Such daunting stakes of national identity, played out in a riot of multiple narratives, fall upon the systemically manifold identities of surrogate children as superabundant burdens; it may be neurological bad luck that William Austin ended his life in a madhouse, but it is nevertheless richly symbolic. Because the history of William Austin also foregrounds class issues of a family of London laborers during the Napoleonic Wars and the decades after Waterloo, these earlier episodes preview vexed

---

1. *Hull Packet and East Riding Times,* March 14, 1845.

· 37 ·

38   CHAPTER 2

topics of class in post-Romantic adoption debates such as sexual license, illegitimacy, and eugenics.

Royal scandals ensnare attention scandalously, then as now. During the first two decades of the nineteenth century, the unspooling story of the spectacularly bad marriage in 1795 between the Prince of Wales and Princess Caroline of Brunswick featured stormy episodes about William Austin, a relinquished child of impoverished London laborers who was taken under the adoptive care of Princess Caroline as an infant in 1802.[2] Crisis episodes about this haphazard royal family included, early on, a secret royal commission in 1806, the "Delicate Investigation," which was charged to adjudicate the mysterious identity of "The Child," as Austin was styled. Most famously, what is known as the "Divorce Trial" of Queen Caroline erupted in 1820, after she returned to England from a rowdy self-exile on the Continent to claim her place as queen at the death of her father-in-law, George III, and the succession to the throne of her despised spouse as George IV. A year later Caroline was dead; after a pyrrhic triumph in the divorce trial in Lords, she was humiliatingly denied entrance to the new king's coronation in Westminster Abbey. Among those gathered at her royal deathbed was William Austin, adoptively her residuary legatee, the biological child of a desperately impoverished Deptford laundress, Sophia Austin, and her laid-off dockworker husband, Samuel Austin.

The noise attending a surrogate child let loose in this theatrically dysfunctional royal family speaks tellingly about the fiercely guarded redoubts of biocentric national power in the British Romantic century. An adopted child lurking around the throne triggered alarms especially during this early nineteenth-century moment in the fraught history of royal succession. To gain an introductory sense of the volume and intensity of the din around William Austin, it helps to detour—quickly—through the thickets of royal kin on either side of the life of Princess Caroline. Her father-in-law, George III, on the throne since 1760, attended to his "heir and a spare" duty in Olympian fashion: he and Queen Charlotte produced thirteen royal princes and princesses who survived into second-string adulthood. In Victoria's reign from 1837, succession was again superabundantly guaranteed with nine royal off-

---

2. In addition to abundant press accounts, there is abundant evidence in contemporary book publications that Austin was referred to as an adoptee. For example, in a memoir about George IV published in the year of his death in 1830, the author refers to "the charges" against Princess Caroline in the Delicate Investigation, "the principal of which was, that a child, whom the princess had adopted, and was bringing up, was not the offspring of a poor woman, named Austin, as alleged, but the Princess's own"; Lloyd, *George IV,* 277. Austin is sometimes styled the princess's "protégé" and, after her death, her "residuary legatee," which registers the looseness of "adoption" as a signifier during the period.

spring before the death of Albert in 1861. But between these two fecund royal generations with their oversupply of backup understudies, the nation faced a crisis of scarcity. Married grudgingly in 1795, the Prince of Wales and Princess Caroline quickly produced a single child, Princess Charlotte, and thereafter endeavored to keep as far apart as possible while sparring in a royal custody battle. Separated from her only child, Princess Caroline soon took the charge of an infant waif in her household, who for the rest of her life functioned as a peculiar substitute for her absent biological child. When in the celebratory wake of Waterloo in 1816 Princess Charlotte married in national celebration, her mother was abroad in Palestine, performing a parody of the royal family with William Austin and her Italian lover, Count Pergami. A year later, Princess Charlotte and her baby both died in childbirth.[3] The Prince of Wales was now without the prospect of a direct heir when he came to the throne in 1820. Although the king's agents tried to buy her off and keep her out of the country, Caroline insisted on returning to England as queen, with a rowdy entourage including the young adult William Austin.

Because the actors in this chapter of adoption history orbit centers of state power, the story of William Austin spotlights mutually constitutive relationships between the family and the nation. In his study of the Romantic-period novel, Ala Alryyes tracks how in the late eighteenth century children became "national raw material" especially in the France of Rousseau, where "familial-modeled national politics endowed children and childhood with great symbolic significance."[4] Hugh Cunningham adds how in Britain the status of children at this period began to emerge as "a story which reaches deep into the emotional experience of the nation."[5] In *Reproducing the State*, Jacqueline Stevens laments that "metaphors of family connections have been too frequently pushed aside in recent studies of the nation, largely because of a belief that, even if nations are not genetically homogeneous, families are, and therefore it makes no sense to turn to the family for ontological or historical (as opposed to psychoanalytical) understandings of the nation." To counter this trend, Stevens installs the traffic between family and nation at the center of her argument, tracking in contingent familial forms such as adoption "the metonymic subtleties of their interconstitutive patterns."[6] With similar aims, Lynn Hunt in

---

3. For a recent history of Princess Charlotte and her embattled parents, see Behrendt, *Royal Mourning*; the surrogate child William Austin goes unnoticed in this version of the family saga. See also chapter 6, "A Nation's Sorrows," in Schor, *Bearing the Dead*, 196–229: "In the nation's mourning for Princess Charlotte, the family became the moral measure of the state" (229). The adoptee William Austin is the only family member absent from Schor's account.

4. Alryyes, *Original Subjects*, 72–74.

5. Cunningham, *Children of the Poor*, 232.

6. Stevens, *Reproducing the State*, 107.

The Family Romance of the French Revolution points to "the centrality of narratives about the family to the constitution of all forms of authority." During the revolution, Hunt argues, "the most obvious material at hand for thinking politically was the family, not the family as some kind of modal social experience, but the family as an imaginative construct of power relations."[7]

In his chapter on "Rousseau and the National Child," Alryyes details how Rousseau "created the national child who does not naturally belong to the family" (76), a maneuver that Alryyes tags "his most brilliant outrage" (85). The family is most explicitly a contingent cultural construct when it cobbles itself together not in consanguineous but in surrogate forms, such as adoption. Narratives of the state become remarkably tangled when forced to grapple with mongrel and migrant family forms, with border-crossings of surrogate parenting. The dynamic reproduces what Stevens unpacks as the paradox of adoption in Roman social history, where the system of state formation toggled between an openness to contingency and a reflexive consolidation of closed, established power: "If adoption renders the alien a citizen, then kinship can be copied. . . . Although the practice suggests the possibility of evading the kinship system, it also underscores the power of that system."[8] In the history of William Austin, the metonymic traffic between a haphazard family form and biocentric national absolutism bobbed and weaved in disorderly fashion on the conspicuous stage of a dysfunctional royal family, upon which prominent platform adoptive contingency intermittently confounded closed absolutism.

Austin's history also provides an exemplary case of the narrative multiplicity that structurally defines adoption, often disruptively. During Austin's lifetime, at least half a dozen different stories of his parentage circulated at one time or another. Tracking these many tales and their media forms draws out a countervailing dynamic on the flip side of the narrative excess of adoption, where bionormal engines of silence and secrecy churn out reactive forms to the disruptions of narrative overabundance. In her work on sex scandals in late eighteenth- and early nineteenth-century Britain, Anna Clark argues that "scandals can democratize politics."[9] But the narratives of scandalously contingent family forms are double-edged, offering in their narrative multiplicity not only democratizing promise but also the threat of radical destabilization, a threat often rendered mute in the biocentric silence and secrecy that attend adoption. As Margaret Homans observes, adoption with its manifest fictional-

---

7. Hunt, *Family Romance*, 8–10, 196; see also Berlant, "Infantile Citizenship," 395–410: "The state of America can be read . . . in the centrality to national culture of an imaginary children's public sphere" (398).

8. Stevens, *Reproducing the State*, 119.

9. Clark, *Scandal*, 223.

NATIONAL CHILDREN 41

ity challenges essentializing narratives of family formation and nation-building, but that very fictionality also sponsors aversion and stigmatization.[10] In this chapter, I argue that the adopted child is the locus of a politically inflected narrative multiplicity that cuts conflicting ways: this clamorous multiplicity is potentially liberating and democratizing, but it is also destabilizing in its uncertainty, in its liability to doubt, fears of which are marked by silence and secrecy. Narratives of surrogate parenting in the early nineteenth century supply sites where the culture plays out anxieties about the nation.

The history of William Austin offers a trenchant series of narrative tangles, which circulate in multiple forms of print culture—journalism, the book trade, graphic satire—and multiple forms of public spectacle: the theater, trials, processions, weddings, funerals. I take up that history below in three parts. The first follows his adoption as an infant in 1802 to the crisis of the secret "Delicate Investigation" in 1806, which adjudicated competing narratives of his identity, and to the belated publication of the documents of that affair in 1813. The second tracks his scripted performances of multiple identity in Caroline's carnivalesque rambles on the Continent from 1814 to 1820, culminating in the explosion of the divorce trial in London in 1820 and Caroline's death in 1821. The last section takes up the valedictory shadow of Regency turmoil cast by his madness and disappearance into silence two decades later, on the cusp of the revolutionary eruptions across Europe of 1848.

ADOPTION, THE DELICATE INVESTIGATION, AND *THE BOOK,* 1806–1813

Samuel Austin, the biological father of William Austin, was a laborer from the west country in Somerset, "brought up to the woolen trade." As the British war economy expanded in the 1790s, an uncle lured him to London with the prospect of abundant work in the Deptford dockyards. Later remarks by wagon-circling royalists about William Austin's low origins dismissed his mother Sophia Austin, "a poor woman from Deptford," as a "washerwoman." During the Peace of Amiens in 1802, Samuel Austin lost his job in the temporary lull of war, and when a second child, William Austin, was born in July 1802, the family confronted bleak urban poverty. Although many alternative narratives subsequently disrupted the following set of facts, best evidence indicates that in November 1802, Sophia Austin and her four-month-old baby came begging for assistance to Montague House, where Princess Caroline

---

10. Homans, "Adoption and Essentialism," 257–74.

maintained, riotously, her own separate establishment on the edge of Blackheath at Greenwich.[11] Alert to their mistress's extravagant whims, Caroline's servants suggested that Mrs. Austin return the next day with the child to allow the princess to take stock of it. The baby was immediately taken under care at Montague House and became a permanent and puzzling fixture of life with Caroline in the royal fast lane.

Throughout her stormy career as Princess of Wales, Caroline decorated her court with charity children plucked from her surroundings, a royal habit that boasts a pedigree as old as Moses.[12] In Caroline's case, such typical royal practice was long interpreted as especially motivated by her enforced separation from her one biological child, Princess Charlotte, born in 1797. In the language of a late nineteenth-century account, "The maternal feelings of the Princess, being thwarted in this way, found vent in adopting children, and placing them out under care in the village, where she constantly visited them." But this account of time-honored royal practice emphasizes that William Austin was not only an example but also a singular exception to this rule: "Not satisfied with this, she subsequently had one of them, an infant of a few months old, named William Austin, removed to her own house, where she tended him with the greatest care and affection, an indiscretion she soon had cause to bitterly repent."[13] In the daily theater that was Caroline's household, some of these children were generic philanthropic supplements, a surplus signifying a venerable tradition of royal charity and royal patronage. But William Austin functioned in a unique way as a substitute, as a surrogate marker for a missing royal child.[14] William Austin stands out as a special case, his life the primary proving ground of the vertiginous stakes of surrogate identity, played uncomfortably close to the centers of bionormative power.

Especially because it exasperated her despised spouse, Caroline cultivated an air of mystery about baby William, known as Willikin or Willy. Amply proportioned, the princess was an infamously bawdy social ringmistress,

---

11. The most reliable set of facts about Austin is in a privately printed volume of royalist genealogy: Camp, *Royal Mistresses and Bastards,* with subsequent addenda on the author's website: http://anthonyjcamp.com/. The most reliable accounts in royal biography are scattered references throughout the two volumes by Hibbert, *George IV: Prince of Wales* and *George IV: Regent and King;* and in Fraser, *Unruly Queen.* There is a considerable amount of information about the 1802 events in the documentary record published in 1813 as *The Book.* The information about Samuel Austin is from a letter to *The Examiner,* 1813, 176.

12. Caroline had earlier taken into her household another infant, Edwardina Kent, whose name and troubled history also survive in the biographical record; for Kent's peculiar history, see Camp, *Royal Mistresses and Bastards.*

13. Molloy, *Court Life below Stairs,* 339.

14. For an example of how Austin was represented as different in kind from other children who were the beneficiaries of Caroline's charity, see *Bury and Norwich Post,* May 5, 1813.

which meant that a clandestine pregnancy was not out of the question. Gossip was not shy to speculate that the child might be the product of any one of her several rumored lovers, especially Sir Sidney Smith, Captain Thomas Manby, or the artist Thomas Lawrence. While these mysteries were spinning, the princess was not above keeping Willy's low origins in view as a competing narrative. The thought that the Royal Princess Charlotte on her rare visits to Montague House would spend sibling time with a dockworker's and washerwoman's child gave the Prince of Wales fits, as Caroline well knew. Midcentury memoirs from disgruntled survivors of Caroline's social circle traffic in unflattering snapshots of a child whom Lady Hester Stanhope in 1845 branded "a little, nasty, vulgar brat. . . . It was unpardonable in the P—ss to lavish her love upon such a little urchin of a boy, a little beggar, really no better."[15] A primary trace of Willy Austin's special status in these royal skirmishes—what Lady Hester calls "pure spite to vex the Prince"—is that at least two engraved early childhood portraits survive in the print collections at the British Museum and the National Portrait Gallery, a mark of status unbestowed on the other anonymous children encircled by Caroline.[16] In one of these prints, Austin is tagged as "The Protégé of the Princess of Wales." After Caroline's death in 1821, newspaper accounts regularly referred to Austin as her "adopted son," but during her lifetime a handful of euphemisms cloaked their relationship in public records: he was her protégé, or she was his protectress, his patroness, his benefactress. Only in off-the-record rumor and accusation was she often termed mother.

After three years of rumors about William Austin, the Princess of Wales quarreled flamingly with two of her society favorites, Lord and Lady Douglas, who began spreading toxic dirt. These gossipy grenades were also a high-stakes political game, which ignited a secret government investigation in 1806, popularly known as the "Delicate Investigation," focused on the identity of this mysterious male child. Lady Douglas indicated to the government her willingness to testify that not only was the child the illegitimate issue of the princess, which was trouble enough: adultery on the part of the Princess of Wales, if proven, would be treason.[17] But Lady Douglas piled a second fiction on top of the fiction of illegitimacy: she hinted that she might testify that the Princess of Wales to acquit herself was not unwilling to attribute paternity to none

---

15. Stanhope, *Memoirs*, I:308–10. Published in the year of Austin's lunacy hearing, Stanhope's volumes offer disdainful anecdotes of a spoiled toddler, several of which recirculate in modern biographies of Caroline.

16. These prints are readily available online: at the National Portrait Gallery, search item D38618; at the British Museum, in "online collections," search item 1980,U.1029.

17. According to the Treason Act of 1351.

other than the Prince of Wales. In a casual airing of this tale, the royal pair would be guilty of little more than yielding to a mutually repugnant hookup on one of the princess's rare visits to Carlton House, which in the logbook of royal self-indulgence would not make much of a stir, by itself. But if Caroline's story were to gain credence, the nation would of course have a new male heir on its hands, or an impostor, and a succession crisis of unprecedented scope would erupt.

Such high-stakes anxieties provided the Prince of Wales sufficient ammunition to persuade the king to instruct the government to undertake an official inquiry about the identity of "The Child" (as it was styled), although the prince's motives were fundamentally self-interested: he saw the Douglas conspiracy as a devoutly wished-for opportunity to find leverage to dump a hated spouse. The identity of a surrogate child provided an inviting platform to interrogate and stigmatize the sex life of the absent princess. As always when illicit sex is the brief, the prosecutorial machinery of the engines of state wallowed in proxy pleasures. The royal commissioners devoted special attention to stained fabrics and the servants who washed the bed linen. They pored over birth and baptismal records and, in the end, Princess Caroline wriggled her way out of trouble, even though the commissioners kept her entirely in the dark about the secret proceedings. In the language of the official verdict, biological certainty labored diligently to banish the doubt posed by the puzzle of a surrogate child:

> We are happy to declare to Your Majesty our *perfect conviction,* that there is *no foundation whatever* for believing that the child now with the Princess of Wales is the child of her Royal Highness, or that she was delivered of any child in the year 1802, nor has any thing appeared to us which would warrant the belief that she was pregnant in that year, or at any other period within the compass of our inquiries. *The identity of the child* now with the Princess, its parentage, the place and date of its birth, the time and circumstances of its being first taken under her Royal Highness's protection, are all established by such a concurrence both of positive and circumstantial evidence, as can, in our judgement, leave *no question* on this part of the subject. That child was, *beyond all doubt,* born in the Brownlow-Street Hospital, on the 11th day of July 1802, of the body of Sophia Austin, and was first brought to the Princess's house in the month of November following.[18]

"Perfect conviction," "no question," "beyond all doubt," "no foundation whatever": this is the language of dominant politics on the run from questions and

---

18. *The Book,* I:4; emphasis added.

doubt, which in spite of the commissioners' best efforts continued to surround the person of William Austin. By their cascading redundancy, these absolute phrases betray the desire to corral the multiple narratives of adoption into a single story. The anxious knowledge that this is an impossible task drives these documents to construe the identity of the adopted child as a fixed question with a single determinate answer, grounded in the body of the biological mother. The narrative multiplicity and contingency that necessarily define a surrogate child loom as threat rather than promise.

In terms of adoption and narrative dynamics, it is conspicuously ironic that this quasi-judicial investigation, instead of fixing the identity of William Austin in unequivocal form, only multiplied the manifold stories already in circulation. The Delicate Investigation worked entirely in secret, so the little information that percolated out in 1806 was exclusively rumor, gossip, and innuendo, which instead of putting to rest questions and doubts about "The Child" only gave fiction more fuel. The subsequent bizarre publication history of the investigation turbocharged the narrative energy generated by a secret proceeding about a mysterious child. Whereas a print record of the investigation would seem to serve the cause of certainty, the print product of the episode instead became another mysterious pawn in the rapidly shifting power formations of party politics. Having gained what felt like victory on the issue of sexual infidelity, Caroline's partisan political supporters decided to play an oppositional hand against the Prince of Wales and print all the documents, findings, and a long (ghosted) response by the princess in a volume that became known as *The Book,* a publication intended to embarrass the prince and his allies in the government in power at that moment. After Caroline's oppositional supporters stockpiled copies threateningly in advance of release, these same allies suddenly found themselves in charge of the government and, fearful of accusations of blackmail, pivoted with alacrity and burned all copies of *The Book* they could locate. These partisan gymnastics transformed *The Book* into an officially banned, censored, and clandestine object and placed the veridical claims of the investigation into the identity of "The Child" under larger clouds of suspicion.[19] In the world of print politics, the adopted child became not less but even more mysterious.

The battle between the royal parents from 1806 to 1813 continued to center on the care and education of Princess Charlotte, escalating sharply when the prince became regent in 1811. Disputes came to a very public boil in February 1813, with the newspaper circulation of an indignant letter of (ghosted) protest from Caroline to her husband, a document that caught Jane Austen's eye in Hampshire and accelerated a rising tide of sympathy for Caroline and dis-

---

19. Gray, *Spencer Perceval,* 84–90; McCalman, *Radical Underworld,* 41–42.

46 CHAPTER 2

dain for the regent. Pressing this advantage, Caroline's advisers exhumed *The Book* from its early grave and published it posthumously. The 1813 title page was typographically mischievous, placing the open figure of "THE CHILD" in the same all-caps bold font as "THE KING," the ultimate closed authority. The story of the surrogate child now circulated in a documentary record and sworn testimony; this is a print account, as the title page puts it, "Faithfully Copied From Authentic Documents." This veridical dynamic was most vividly captured in the transcribed voice of Sophia Austin, the birth mother, who testified on June 7, 1806:

> I know the child which is now with the Princess of Wales. I am the mother of it. I was delivered of it four years ago the 11th of July next, at Brownlow-street Hospital. I have lain in there three times. William, who is with the Princess, is the second child I laid in of there. It was marked in the right hand with red wine. . . . I did wean the child, and brought it to the Princess's house on the 15th of November, and left it there, and it has been with the Princess ever since. I saw the child last Whit-Monday, and I swear that it is my child.[20]

In spite of such decisive tone, forensic details from the 1806 proceedings labored against a multitude of competing accounts at their belated print appearance in 1813. Four hundred pages into the documentary record, a fly-title page offered "A Statement of Facts" about the identity of what remained, except in Sophia Austin's voice, an anonymous all-caps creature, "THE CHILD."[21] But instead of certainty, the surrogate child in *The Book* in 1813 appeared in an abstracted anonymity that offered a blank canvas upon which the culture busily projected multiple images of identity.[22]

In the long gap between the Delicate Investigation in 1806 and the publication of *The Book* in 1813, opposition culture generated even more tales about the peculiar child filling Princess Charlotte's place with her mother. With *The Book* officially banned, the hack writer and blackmailer Thomas Ashe cranked out from his Newgate cell a fictionalized version of events, published in 1811 as a scandal novel titled *The Spirit of "The Book,"* which cast itself as a series of letters from mother to daughter, from Caroline to Charlotte. Here is a taste of Ashe doing his Caroline impression, just after he introduced "the child":

---

20. *The Book,* II.220–21.

21. *The Book,* II.109.

22. The journalist William Cobbett added to the confusion about Austin in February 1813 by retailing a rumor that the mysterious Child was named "Billy Fawcett" (*Cobbett's Weekly Political Register,* February 20, 1813, 226); see also *Morning Post,* February 25, 1813; *The Examiner,* 1813, 176.

NATIONAL CHILDREN

The circumstances of my attention to the little boy, mentioned to you, my dear Charlotte, in my last letter, and other circumstances industriously buzzed about by report, aroused certain *conjectures*; these conjectures engendered *suspicion*; and in process of time the parentage of the little W——m was not merely *doubted*, but boldly *attributed* to me.[23]

"Conjecture," "suspicion," "doubt," "attribution": this oppositional language gleefully disrupted the dominant tale of absolute certainty, which in 1811 remained officially secret. The most remarkable feature of Ashe's clumsy plot is that, in its conclusion, it floated an entirely different tale of parentage. The narrative revealed that the lost love of Caroline's youth was a German nobleman who had taken up surreptitious residence in a cottage near her country estate; the boy W——m was revealed to be the orphan son of a clandestine marriage between Prince L——s and Melina, the childhood friend of Caroline. This lost lover had smuggled this orphan child from Germany and put it in the way of Caroline on her outings, and she took the bait.[24] Beyond the fact that this version erased William Austin's laboring-class origins, what makes Ashe's clunky plot especially interesting is that it put into popular print circulation yet another story about Willy Austin's identity—in brief, that he was the biological child of German nobility. Ashe's tale is worthy of special attention because it is a story that Caroline herself seems to have set spinning and a story that she repeated to witnesses at least twice in the last years of her life, once—dramatically—on her deathbed.

Bibliographers of the novel in this period have recently documented a remarkable spike in "scandal" fiction in the wake of the Delicate Investigation, so Ashe's example of representational practice can be multiplied, even to an entirely different order of sophistication in texts such as Jane Austen's *Emma*, published in 1815, which presents multiple adoption subplots and is anxiously dedicated to the prince regent—an argument that I turn to in detail in the next chapter.[25] The collision between surrogate children and national politics is also vividly on offer in satirical prints, which as popular graphic genre gleefully sponsored the narrative circulation of William Austin's figure post-Waterloo. Before I follow Caroline and Austin to the Continent, an 1813 print from the royalist periodical *The Satirist* supplies an especially telling example of how the figure of the adopted child circulated in national political discourse in the early years of the Regency.

---

23. Ashe, *Spirit of "The Book,"* III.225; emphasis added. Ashe's text went through multiple printings and was immediately reprinted in North America.

24. Ashe, III.268–69.

25. Garside and Schöwerling, *English Novel 1770–1829*, II.42–43.

FIGURE 1. William Austin satirical cartoon, 1813. Used with permission from the British Museum.

Published in the immediate wake of the much-publicized February 1813 letter from the princess to the regent, this print (figure 1) appeared at the same moment when *The Book* rose from a pulped grave, offering in its April Fool's Day images a loyalist send-up of oppositional politics in the guise of an absurd conspiracy.[26]

Henry Brougham, the ghostwriter of the letter from the princess, is the bewigged figure seated on the right (the book at his fingertips is "The Young Man's Complete Letter Writer"), engaged in horse-trading conversation with the radical MP Sir Francis Burdett. William Austin is the homunculus crawling out of the container before the cloven-footed Brougham, who offers this devilish deal to Burdett: "The interests of Billy Austin are entrusted to my care—he shall marry Your daughter by that Lady & dash for the—[image of crown]." Austin's container is inscribed with a detail from Austin's birth record, available in the testimony only now in print circulation in *The Book*: "from Brownlow Hospl Glass to be kept dry this side up." The opposite homunculus is if anything even odder, a female figure with her father's unmistakable profile—one of the bastard children of Burdett and Lady Oxford, who is the woman busy in the left corner with another lover; Lord Oxford is the cuckhold on the far right, who remarks "Oh! great joy! I shall be Foster-Father to a Q—n and

---

26. The term "Caput" in the title of the print signified loosely the governing "heads" of a university body, although historically the term signified more precisely at Cambridge (*OED*).

step-father to a K—G !!! how lucky it is to marry a ——Wife!"[27] Diminished as "Billy," Austin lunges for a royal crown that has tellingly slipped askew off its cushioned seat. The quasi-normative figure of an aristocratic bastard (Burdett's and Lady Oxford's daughter) strikes an attitude isomorphic with a figure whom the state has ruled is a legitimate child (William Austin, born in "Brownlow Hospl"), but a child who remains nevertheless a threateningly surrogate figure, scandalously plucked from a pair of laborers and planted in the courts of royalty. Beyond this primary class violation, surrogacy threatened more generally because it had the bad habit of reminding absolute power that the identity forms upon which power depended might be rendered contingent, in spite of the claims of blood.

Sufficiently anxious to deploy the weapons of ridicule to attempt to spin these multiplying stories to its advantage, established power envisioned these two little grasping bastards and their puppet masters as a farcical plot to knock state power off its soft seat. On April 6, the loyalist rag the *Morning Post* published a satirical "Letter from Billy Austin," addressed "To Mr. Whitbread" (the younger Samuel Whitbread, a leading advocate of Caroline's cause): "Yes, Sir, though you are so great a man, yet, as your origin, like mine, was also a little queer and obscure, I hope you will not be angry with me for writing you this letter."[28] What is at stake in these many skirmishes is "origin," plain and simple, any threatening forms of which bionormative power wishes to banish as "queer and obscure."

In spite of the state's best efforts, the identity of William Austin refused to remain fixed. Caroline's pleasure in bedeviling the question purrs teasingly on the cusp of her Continental journeys in a diary entry from 1814 by Lady Charlotte Bury:

> She swore to me as she was standing by the fire the other day . . . that Willikin was *not her* son. "No," said she, "I would tell you if he was. No," she continued, "if such little accident had happened, I would not hide it from you. He is not William Austin, though," added she; "but avouez-moi, it was very well managed that nobody should know who he really is, nor shall they till after my death." I replied, that I thought it was nobody's business who the boy was, and that I, for one, had no curiosity to know. "That is for why I tell you," replied the Princess. "Then somebody ask me who Willikin is de child of. De person say to me, '*Dey* do say, he is your Royal Highness's child.'

---

27. See the opening of chapter 3 for Jane Austen's take on Lady Oxford and Princess Caroline.

28. *Morning Post,* April 6, 1813.

50 CHAPTER 2

I answered, 'Prove it, and he shall be your king.' The person was silent after that."—I could not resist laughing, and the Princess laughed, also. She takes great pleasure in making her auditor stare.[29]

From 1814 to her death in 1821, when much of Europe and the British nation stared perplexed at Caroline, William Austin was nearly always a puzzling figure in the frame.

ADOPTION ABROAD AND THE DIVORCE TRIAL, 1814–1821

In 1814 Princess Caroline began her rowdy self-exile on the Continent, boosted by a padded annual allowance on the condition that she just go abroad and stay there. William Austin, now twelve, was her constant companion. She delighted in introducing him in European courts as "the Little Prince," which occasioned a great deal of diplomatic dyspepsia. In this far more public phase of his adoptive life, William Austin became an actor in multiple forms of theatrical spectacle: royal boxes at the theater, royal processions, urban parades, a state trial, a coronation, a state funeral. The most telling forms of evidence from this period are widely circulated graphic prints, several examples of which follow. But I begin with a different body of evidence, a set of letters from Austin to his birth mother that survive archivally.[30] Whereas biographers of Caroline and the regent glance at these documents as simple evidence that Austin was in no doubt about his parentage, I read them instead as the structural necessity for the adopted child to inhabit and perform multiple identities.[31] Austin's de facto adoption anticipates open forms of modern de jure adoption in this regular traffic between a surrogate child and his birth family.[32]

---

29. Bury, *Diary of a Lady-in-Waiting*, I:184–85. The diary was originally published in 1838, ed. John Galt, with authorship unattributed but widely assumed to be Lady Charlotte.

30. Goulding Papers (4.A.2.2.1–49), Lincolnshire Archives, Lincoln. My thanks to Dr. Mike Rogers, archivist, for kind assistance. Subsequent references are by date in the text.

31. Hibbert, *Regent and King*, 208; Fraser, *Unruly Queen*, 465. For multiple identities in adoption, see Lifton, *Twice Born*, which is a foundational classic of modern adoption studies.

32. William (born July 11, 1802) was the second child; a brother Samuel was born in 1800, and at least two other children survived, Job (born 1805) and Caroline (born 1815), although family letters suggest there were more children. In the servants' depositions in 1806, it is stated that "the father has now lost the use of his limbs" and that he now lives in the household of the princess's page Thomas Stikeman in Pimlico, "employed to turn a mangle" for Stikeman's wife, a laundress for the prince. The 1813 letter to *The Examiner* states that "the father, Samuel Austin, with Sophia, his wife, and family, now live on Tower Hill, and he is employed in the new West India Docks." According to an 1833 letter from the son Samuel Austin to John Thelwall,

NATIONAL CHILDREN

Although the bulk of these four dozen letters dates from the Continental travels and the months of the divorce trial, the earliest document, written from Kensington Palace on January 1, 1810, announces to his birth mother in an eight-year-old's labored script the theatrical theme that would increasingly define Austin's life: "I went to the play yesterday and saw Cinderella I was very much pleased." The palpably overdetermined irony of this event is that, like Cinderella, Austin the biological child of laborers was actually living the fantasy of status elevation that Freud famously posits is a developmentally necessary fantasy of adoption shared in childhood by all.[33] On the road with the Princess of Wales, the teenaged Austin found himself on display in the exalted public spaces of royal and titled boxes in the theaters and opera houses of Europe. Soon after Caroline's traveling circus pitched tents for the winter in Naples in late 1814, Austin addressed a letter to "My Dear Mother" on January 6, 1815:

> The Play House [phrase deleted.] The Opera House is very fine indeed at Naples the King and Queens box is in the middle very large and fine[.] There is a large chandeleer in the middle hung from the top[.] They give always in the month of January Masquerades in the Opera House every body that likes plays and [word missing] goes in[.] There is one on Sunday and I am going to see it, it will I dare say be very beautiful indeed.

Similarly, three years later, to "My Dear Mother" from Pesaro on February 2, 1818: "I amuse myself very much at Pesaro every evening almost there are theatres or balls and Masquerades." Such very public appearances were a primary theatrical venue for Austin's performance as proxy royal progeny in the bizarre improvisational show that was Caroline's court on the road, crisscrossing Italian sovereignties for five disreputable years.

The headline delinquency of these Continental peregrinations was Caroline's lusty attachment to Bartolomeo Pergami, the Milanese courier who quickly rose from new court functionary to randy ringmaster.[34] The prince regent and his government tracked Caroline fiercely, planting spies and bribing servants in clandestine surveillance that led to a rerun of the Delicate

---

"there was a situation procured for my father in the Customs"; one of William's 1817 letters to his London family is addressed to "Mr Austin Locker Up at the Custom House London." Samuel Austin the father died in 1832; Sophia Austin died in 1842. Samuel Austin the son, a clerk, became the public voice of the family in the 1830s and 1840s; for his many letters to the papers and the later history of the family, see the last section.

33. Freud, "Family Romances."

34. Contemporary English texts usually rendered the surname "Bergami." I follow Hibbert and Fraser in using Pergami's preferred form.

Investigation, the secret Milan Commission in 1818–19, which laid the rotten evidentiary footings for the divorce trial in 1820. But British travelers happy to volunteer the latest scandalized gossip eagerly supplemented this state-sponsored surveillance. A letter home from Lord Sligo in Rome on November 6, 1814, supplies a typical snapshot of how Austin's surrogate figure in the theater offended establishment sensibilities: "It was really abominable, there was the Princess . . . and *Billy Austin* sitting in front of the Box and all the English and most of the nobility of Florence standing behind her to pay their respect. Now really it was too bad to have that little bastard sitting in front while everyone else was standing up."[35] To established power and its many opportunistic supplicants such as Sligo, Caroline and her entourage were a transgressive horror.

Caroline's most elaborate extravaganza during her Continental interval was a ten-month journey to the Holy Land, which produced sharply competing images of William Austin. While London lavishly celebrated the wedding of her daughter Princess Charlotte to Prince Leopold in May 1816, the royal bride's absent mother shipped out with Billy Austin and Pergami via Athens on the way to Constantinople and an entry into Jerusalem in July, on Austin's birthday. In a widely reproduced print of that Jerusalem moment, produced by Caroline's supporters and staged to echo the Triumphal Entry of Jesus in New Testament narrative, Austin, Pergami, and Caroline are three becollared figures on horseback in the foreground, composing a defiantly parodic image of a nuclear royal family far from home, posed at just the moment when the newlywed Royal Princess Charlotte was primed to produce proper biological issue, in proper proximity to the throne.[36] The transgressions that pile up in the scene—a surrogate child, an adulterous lover, the absent mother of the heir to the throne—rest outrageously upon the framing transgression of the biblical narrative, wherein an itinerant prophet perched on an ass defied state power. This defiantly unorthodox tableau anticipates Caroline's riotous triumphal procession into London in June 1820, which oppositional stage managers smartly designed to echo these same heresies.

Allies of the prince regent loaded their satirical weaponry and recast Caroline's Levantine journey as devilishly unhallowed. A print attacking Caroline

---

35. White, "Lost Correspondence," 233.

36. Caroline commissioned a painting of the scene by Carloni, a Milanese artist, which was exhibited in London in August 1820 with a published key: *The Public Entry of The Queen into Jerusalem, Painted by Signor Carloni* (London, 1820). The print I discuss, which adapts the painting, also appeared as frontispiece to *The Royal Exile,* a book detailing Caroline's travels published in the wake of the divorce trial in 1821. A copy of the key is available online: British Museum, search "collection online," item 1873,0809.1561.

NATIONAL CHILDREN 53

relocated this unholy royal family in Egypt, ironically one of the few points not on this eastern Mediterranean tour. Whereas the sympathetic Triumphal Entry print piggybacked on the antinomian substructure of the Gospel event to justify the lawlessness of the modern performers, this loyalist print redrew the journey as raw blasphemy, framing another episode from Gospel narrative, the Temptation in the Wilderness.[37] The outrageousness of Caroline as a Christ figure becomes a wicked measure of her vast failures to resist temptation. The satanic tempter from biblical narrative is transfigured as a manic Mahomet, which rendered the scene for a contemporary British audience doubly beyond the orthodox pale. The print gleefully exploits the many sins of the flesh supplied by Caroline's and Pergami's example, but the stakes of the biblical temptation story ratchet up in seriousness from pleasures of the flesh to political power, as Milton in *Paradise Regained* had earlier spelled out for a British audience. Although the action in the right foreground of this print, featuring Caroline and Pergami, is all about sex and drink, pyramids in the left background remind a viewer that royal state power was simultaneously very much at issue. Near the center of the scene is wee Willy Austin, blowing soap bubbles, identified in the subtitle as "young Saint Austin," in the disreputable company of "Saint Caroline" and "Saint Bartholomew." Those bubbles marked the desire of established power to dismiss these lawless characters as inconsequential and ephemeral, but they also signified the recalcitrantly disruptive enigma of the surrogate child, whose performative identity is, like a bubble, both elusive and eye-catching.

For William Austin, the Jerusalem journey superscribed his birth identity, as he explained to his London mother in an anniversary letter from Rome on July 11, 1817: "To day is my birth day. . . . It is also a year that We entered Jerusalem and it will always be kept an Anniversary for that Great Voyage which we have made, and undergone the dangers of the Sea." After returning to Italy in late 1816, Caroline and company shifted restlessly from jurisdiction to jurisdiction, scuttling north to Germany and Austria in the spring of 1817, before settling down in Pesaro on the Italian coast for the last two years of her Continental sojourn. Two of the most pointed graphic attacks on Caroline hang on a visit to Vienna in the spring of 1817, which came off badly: the Emperor Francis I refused to receive Caroline, taking refuge in the fact that his court was still officially in mourning following the recent death of the empress. The first of these two prints drawn by the satirist George Cruickshank shows the gatekeepers at the British ambassador's residence refusing Caroline's party, while Caroline's herald demands extensive top-tier bedding ("Vite! Vite! 7 Lits

---

37. See online copy, British Museum, search "collection online," item 1935,0522.12.177.

54 CHAPTER 2

de Maitre—13—de Domestique—!!") for its many-rumored bedroom sports.[38] Willy Austin, who was now fifteen, peeks in profile from his privileged seat in the royal carriage, his low roots nevertheless underscored in a figure of an urchin and his canine mutts greeting the royal carriage in the left foreground. Pergami is an equally scandalous figure, an erect feather on his headgear a preparation for the even more outrageous images in a second print.

The accompanying print, "R-y-l Condescension," illustrates vividly how loyalist satire pitched Pergami and Austin as the two defining males in Caroline's outlaw ways.[39] In Vienna, Caroline introduces her motley crew to Prince Metternich, who bows in elegant contrast to Caroline's literal grossness: "Permit me, Sir Prince, to present to you my sweet [del] suite—." Metternich's reply ("Your R—l H—s is really too condescending!!") repeats with bald irony the attack in the print's title, "to condescend" signifying, in the words of Samuel Johnson's *Dictionary,* "to sink willingly to equal terms with inferiours." The class violations in the persons of Pergami and Austin morph hypersexually throughout the print. Pergami's sword hilt caressed by Caroline's hand is a wicked touch, and the embroidery on his trouser leg stands erect in anatomical salute. Cruickshank poses Willy with a firm grip on his own slender shaft, a riding crop, which is pointed shamelessly at his surrogate mother's crotch. The absent legitimate male member, the print thereby suggests, belongs to the prince regent. Tagging the main figures, the four prints on the wall underscore the sexual theme. Pergami is a stud horse ("Cock horse a favourite Stallion"), and to the right of Caroline's print ("A view in Wales"), above Austin's curly head, is an image labeled "Billy A—favourite mule—!!," captioned additionally as an ass who treads on Austin's birth turf, "Black-heath." The dwarfish Austin is simultaneously an overgrown infant and a budding adolescent male whose relationship with his adoptive mother the print sexualizes incestuously to compound her primary adulterous sins with Pergami.

At the death of George III in 1820, Caroline defiantly returned to London in early June to frenzied acclaim, the tumultuous crowds that greeted her as queen also hailing the eighteen-year-old Willy Austin as "Prince Austin."[40] Among its many tools during these wild months, radical opposition latched on to the figure of William Austin to help seize control of the narrative of political power, the open identity of the surrogate child providing London radicals another weapon to threaten Old Corruption (as state power was popularly known) with the idea that the public now possessed mobilized power

38. See online copy, National Portrait Gallery, item D17899.

39. See online copy, National Portrait Gallery, item D17897.

40. Most references to "Prince Austin" in the print record in 1820–21 are sarcastic jabs in the loyalist press.

NATIONAL CHILDREN

to declare which forms of power were legitimate.[41] A print attributed to Theodore Lane illustrates how the loyalist press counterattacked.[42] Welcomed by a radical throng in London, Caroline and her Continental train parade in from the storm-racked right, greeted on the left by a gallery of the queen's most notable supporters, including Henry Brougham, Sir Francis Burdett, and William Cobbett. Their train of braying asses anchors a send-up of Caroline's grand entrances into Jerusalem and London. Pergami and Austin, Caroline's two headline males in that history, yield the foreground to two local targets of loyalist scorn who escort the queen on either side, Alderman Wood ("Absolute Wisdom") in jester's cap and his son John Wood ("Young Absolute") on her left arm, who was pulling novice duty as the queen's chaplain. But the print's targets of ridicule signify that Pergami and Austin also threaten disruption in primary forms. The yellow-capped figure to the right of Young Absolute haunts the scene in the guise of Pergami, a ghost unnamed in the key (Pergami could not risk being physically present in Britain).[43] Austin is a red-capped dwarfish figure trailing Young Absolute while cradling two infants in his arms, labeled in the key below as "Billy By-Blow of Black-heath in charge of the Nursery." This figure cuts both ways: it attempts to defuse the figure of Austin by multiple diminishments of stature, chronology, and name, but at odds with this purpose the nursery figure also draws risky attention to the increasingly shaky fact that established power grounds its authority in the claims of birth and blood. At such a feast of power, which still stakes its ultimate guarantees in consanguinity, a surrogate child is an unwelcome guest.

In the uproarious year of Caroline's return and trial, a surrogate child was one among many offbeat sideshows in a widely pitched carnival of disruption. The debate in Lords on a Bill of Pains and Penalties against Queen Caroline on the grounds of adulterous intercourse ran from August through November, which included John Keats's last months in England. Diaries, notebooks, and letters document that this intense pitch of royal scandal proved irresistible across the literary spectrum, including the vacationing Charles Lamb in Cam-

---

41. Widely known as the "Divorce Trial," the government action against Caroline was officially a Bill of Pains and Penalties in Lords on the accusation of adulterous intercourse. The rich body of modern scholarship on this watershed event includes Laqueur, "Queen Caroline Affair," 417–66; Clark, "Queen Caroline," 47–68; Hunt, "Morality and Monarchy," 697–722; Wahrman, "Middle-Class Domesticity," 396–432; Fulcher, "Loyalist Response," 481–502.

42. See online copy, National Portrait Gallery, item D17900.

43. M. Dorothy George suggests that this unidentified figure is "perhaps Keppel Craven"; George, Catalogue, vol. 10, 1820–27. But the resemblance to other images of Pergami in wide circulation at the time is remarkable, and the absence of any reference to the figure in the key is consonant with the fact that Pergami had returned to Italy after escorting Caroline to the channel crossing in June 1820. The loyalist press fanned rumors that Pergami was in England clandestinely; see, e.g., Morning Post, November 29, 1820.

bridge during the weeks when he and his sister Mary met the teenaged orphan Emma Isola, whom they would take under adoptive care.[44] Transcripts of the quasi-judicial proceedings fed the maw of scandal, wherein the puzzling identity of Austin frequently pops up, one among many odd dishes on a very large menu of the peculiar. Here is a typical moment in one servant's testimony:

> Did the Princess and Bergami commonly dine alone or with some other person? *Sometimes they dined alone; sometimes with Wm. Austin, who was reported to be the son of the Princess.* How was Wm. Austin called, either by the Princess or in her presence? *Some called him "William," some called him "the young Prince," and sometimes I have seen the Princess when he was going to bed give him some token of affection as a mother would give her child.*[45]

Here is testimony from another servant about sleeping arrangements at Naples, where the prosecution alleged the queen's affair with Pergami commenced:

> Do you recollect a young person of the name of William Austin, being with her Royal Highness? *Yes.* Before the Princess arrived at Milan, where was William Austin in the habit of sleeping generally? *Generally he slept in the room of her Royal Highness.* Do you recollect where her Royal Highness slept, at what house, on the night before she entered the city of Naples? *In a country-house.* Do you recollect whether her Royal Highness slept in the room of William Austin in that country-house? *I cannot positively say about that night; but, generally, he was in the habit of sleeping in the room of her Royal Highness.* Had her Royal Highness about that time any communication with you about the place of sleeping of William Austin? *Her Highness told me, during that evening, that William Austin had become too big a boy to sleep in her room, and he must have une chambre particuliere.*[46]

Here is Austin in judicial transcripts, there is Austin in a victory procession to St. Paul's, here is Austin with the queen at the theater and the races, there is Austin in Home Office surveillance records of the queen's Hammersmith headquarters.[47] The first sympathetic image of Austin as an adult was pub-

---

44. Henry Crabb Robinson, for example, left diary records of conversations about the queen in 1820 with (on separate occasions) William Wordsworth and Samuel Taylor Coleridge.

45. Smeeton, *Important and Eventful Trial,* 131.

46. Smeeton, 133. The *Morning Post* on November 18, 1820, rendered explicit in doggerel ("Original Poetry") the sexual subtext of this testimony.

47. In the wake of the withdrawal of the bill targeting Caroline, there was a widely noticed procession to a Thanksgiving service at St. Paul's on November 29, with Austin logged in prominent place among the queen's triumphant party. In a letter to his Austin mother on June 8, 1821, he notes that he has just returned "from the races with the Queen."

NATIONAL CHILDREN 57

lished as a print in London on September 22, 1820, as interest in the trial surged toward its November crest when, faced with tumultuous popular support for the queen, the king's government abandoned the bill.[48] In the flush of parliamentary success, one of Caroline's most fervent supporters, Joseph Nightingale, floated the best published words ever bestowed on Austin:

> Young Austin, who, of course, is now (December 1820,) in his nineteenth year, is still with his royal and generous protector. With her he has travelled over a great part of the European continent, and through many of the most interesting districts of the eastern world. He has been the subject of conversation in all parts, and bids fair to form materials for an important chapter in the future history of England.[49]

How such an impossible chapter might have played out is anyone's guess.

At the queen's death nine months after her victory, Austin resumed an unsettled place at the center of the show, now inscribed within a new legal narrative that trailed him the rest of his days. After her humiliating exclusion from the king's coronation in July 1821, Caroline's health failed precipitously until her death on August 7, surrounded at the end by Lord and Lady Hood, Lady Anne Hamilton, Alderman Wood and son, five physicians, two lawyers—and William Austin, "overwhelmed with grief."[50] Later on the day of his surrogate mother's death, Austin wrote to his birth mother:

> Dear Mother[,] You must undoubtedly have heard the horrible News[.] I cannot find words to express them. But we must at all times submit to the Almighty. Wait with Patience till you hear from me again as I have not strength to see you for some time but do not come to see me or any of you till I desire you[.] I am your sincere son WAustin.[51]

Austin's adoptive mother is dead and he holds his birth mother at a distance: this moment dramatizes the existential plight of an adopted child, who experiences mothers both as surplus and as absence, simultaneously.[52] Rushed into

---

48. See online copy, National Portrait Gallery, item D38616.

49. Nightingale, *Memoirs of Queen Caroline*, 142–43.

50. Huish, *Memoirs of Her Late Majesty*, II.713.

51. A trace of Austin's exposure to religion is an octavo copy of an 1817 printing of the Bible "presented to W. Austin by Queen Caroline" in the British Library (C.129.M.9). See also *Morning Post*, November 29, 1820.

52. Although Austin corresponded with his birth family and met them in London (but in third-party locations), it is clear that there were limits to his knowledge of his blood relatives. In his birthday letter to his birth mother on July 11, 1820, explaining that he cannot be with his family "for the reasons I told you before," he adds: "Two women came this morning saying that

print while Queenite fervor still lingered, the many published accounts of the queen's last days foregrounded "Her Majesty's Last Will and Testament," the primary beneficiary of which was William Austin. The main document, signed four days before her death, directed her trustees to sell all her property, invest the proceeds, and "pay the principal of the whole of the said trust property to William Austin, who has been long under my protection, on his attaining the age of 21 years; and, in the mean time, to pay the interest and proceeds of the same, or so much thereof as to them may seem meet, towards the maintenance and education of the same William Austin."[53] This well-publicized document defined William Austin's identity in the final period of his life. A figure such as Austin was more legible to this culture in a discrete inheritance narrative honoring property instead of a wild array of competing narratives transgressing biology, especially and ironically because biology remained the dominant determinative ground of the system of property and power. Billy Austin bedding down near the Princess of Wales was a thought beyond the pale, but "the maintenance and education of the same William Austin" is language that had a chance to gain the traction of legitimacy. After the queen's burial in her native Brunswick, a routine item in *The Times* on September 17 is telling in how it enumerates the band of final mourners returning to England: "Lord and Lady Hood, Lady Anne Hamilton, Count Vasali, Captain Hesse, Dr. Lushington, Mr. Wm. Austin, Lord Yarmouth, and other persons of distinction, arrived at Dover on Friday by the *Rob Roy* steam-packet from Calais."[54] In person and in print, Austin the dockworker's and washerwoman's son and primary legatee of the queen now traveled as "Mr. Wm. Austin" in the company of "other persons of distinction." Another mark of his elevation from infantilized target of satire to a figure of adult record—however ambiguous— is that several more engraved portraits survive from the time of her trial and

---

they were my aunts but as I never knew that I had any aunts I thought it [wiser?] to desire Mr. Hieronymous to say so."

53. Huish II.729–31. In three codicils over the next four days that attended to subordinate details of property, Austin was again specified in several instances, but the estate was effectively insolvent at her death. Austin's income for the rest of his life (very modest annual interest) depended on separate instruments that Caroline had executed a few years earlier concerning her property at Blackheath. The labyrinthine details of these funds were hammered out in Chancery in July and August 1823, upon Austin's majority; there are lengthy accounts from the vice-chancellor's court concerning "Her Late Majesty Queen Caroline In Re Austin" in *The Times* on July 23, 1823, and August 8, 1823. Austin's will administered at his death in 1857 is dated August 17, 1824 (Camp, *Royal Mistresses and Bastards*).

54. *The Times*, September 17, 1821. Austin had internalized royal manners; his will, dated August 17, 1824, specified "10 guineas each for rings to Lady Anne Hamilton, the Hon Anne Seymour Damer, Lord and Lady Hood, Dr. Lushington, Mr Serjeant Wilde, [and] Mr Alderman Wood" (Camp, addendum 2019).

death.[55] Instead of "Billy Austin the little bastard," the portraits present, in the language of *The Times*, "Mr. Wm. Austin," poised on the cusp of his majority. Whatever democratizing promise might have been lurking in his scandalous history only fleetingly materialized, however, because his last decades instead rapidly succumbed to the doubt and uncertainty that also attend the figure of the surrogate child, an individual who must ever and always navigate multiple forms of identity. In William Austin's case, these displacements arrived at a sad spectacle of derangement and, at the end, silence.

AFTERMATH: THE MADNESS OF WILLIAM AUSTIN

As the news of the terms in the queen's will spread in 1821, a royalist letter to the editor of the *Morning Post* on August 17 fiercely attacked "that nondescript, BILLY AUSTIN." The noun "nondescript"—a signifier recently coined in biology for new, undescribed specimens—had just in these years also shifted from science to culture to signify diminishment, pejoratively: "insignificant; undistinguished." The word now carried additional senses of a mystery or a puzzle, a thing "not easily classified; that is neither one thing nor another; hybrid" (*OED*).[56] A hybrid identity that defies classification describes precisely the case of William Austin, a surrogate national child whom establishment culture instinctively thought of as something mysterious and unfortunate like street muck on the soles of its boots. At just this moment when engines of law and press fixed Austin in a legal narrative as Caroline's principal heir with marks of distinction in a potentially redeemable cultural currency, other media machines stirred up yet again the old question of his biological parentage, rendering his identity once more a topic of mystery and speculation. The deeply biocentric suspicion that a figure such as Austin threatened established order with counterfeit claims rebounded with new force within weeks of Caroline's death. Until his death in the middle of the century, Austin's life after Caroline punctuated the public record at regular intervals with unsettling reports of doubt, dispute, and, finally, madness.

In the wake of the queen's death, the puzzle of Austin's identity entangled the old speculation that she was his biological mother with the surmise that he was instead the biological child of German nobility, a tale that had been in quasi-fictional circulation as early as the publication of Ashe's *The Spirit of "The Book"* in 1811. Modern biographers of George IV and Queen Caroline

---

55. See online copies at National Portrait Gallery, items D38615 and D38617.

56. "Nondescript" does not appear in Samuel Johnson's 1755 *Dictionary*; Todd's 1818 revision of Johnson adds "nondescript" as a term in biology and comments "a Modern word."

briefly log the evidentiary residue of this story, which survives in two primary sources in the archival record. In brief, the tale—little different from Ashe's purportedly fictional version—is that the boy known as William Austin was the illegitimate biological son of Prince Louis Ferdinand of Brunswick, the lost love of Caroline's youth. After taking in the Deptford baby named William Austin in 1802, Caroline conspired to have the German infant switched for the English child (and no version of the story attends to what happened to the English baby, or the German mother). The first of these two sources is in March 1819 correspondence from James Brougham, who was with Caroline in Italy, to his brother Henry in London, a key political supporter of Caroline: "She has told me all about *W. Austin* who is not ye son of Austin, but quite another person, and also about the Manby business. *Nobody* knows anything of these matters. She told Percival, Eldon, and yrself that W.A. was not her son, wh. *was true,* but tho' old Austin and his wife both believe him to be their son, he is not."[57] James Brougham's details of the story in March 1819 accord with a second account forty years later, in an 1858 letter from Stephen Lushington, the queen's lawyer and coexecutor, again to Henry Brougham, in the wake of Austin's death in 1857:

> I will tell you all I know as to W. Austin. The Queen on her deathbed informed me that W. Austin was not the person he purported to be, that he was in truth a son of a brother or friend of Brunswick who was dead and that he had been clandestinely brought over from the continent. She then explicitly declared that W. Austin was not her own child. She did mention who the mother was but indistinctly. When attending the funeral I was on board a vessel in the Elbe commanded by Capt. Fisher, W. Austin being with him, a German nobleman or General (I do not remember which) asked for permission to see W. Austin; he immediately said you know his history and to my great surprize repeated in substance what the Queen had said to me respecting W. Austin's birth and parentage and he then added that Austin bore a great resemblance to his reputed father. I have no recollection of the name of this Consul or General. The enquiries made for him afterwards by Lord Liverpool produced no result.[58]

My interest in these details is simply to emphasize an important fact that scholarship has skated past: rather than fading into consensus or indifference, the question of William Austin's identity erupted again in public immedi-

---

57. Aspinall, *Letters of King George IV,* II.282.

58. Hibbert, *Prince,* 217; see also Waddams, *Stephen Lushington,* 152.

ately after Caroline's death, with renewed speculation. The Queen's ultimate tale-spinning about Willy Austin was news that hit the street the moment it occurred, in predictably garbled versions. While Caroline's final attendants were still in Brunswick for her burial, the *Morning Chronicle* on August 27, 1821, launched a Queenite attack on a "calumny of a most atrocious nature" published a few days previously in the most aggressive loyalist vehicle, *John Bull*:

> It is alleged that the QUEEN disclosed to Dr. LUSHINGTON, in the presence of *four other persons,* that WILLIAM AUSTIN was her own son, and that this disclosure was communicated by Dr. LUSHINGTON to the Earl of Liverpool. . . . In another paragraph the falsehood is stated even more circumstantially . . . Dr. LUSHINGTON is at this time out of the country,—and the vile calumniator has availed himself of his absence, in the hope that before the lie can be contradicted by him, it may obtain an extensive circulation.[59]

Regardless of the contradictory details, what matters is that the newspapers immediately sniffed out that multiple stories about Willy Austin still percolated. What continued to "obtain an extensive circulation" was not an impossibly unequivocal single truth about his identity but a renewed superabundance of narratives.

When Austin's birth family subsequently asserted inheritance rights, Lushington as executor played the mystery identity card to turn aside their importunities. Austin's older brother Samuel, a clerk in a London office, maintained an often testy correspondence on behalf of the birth family with Caroline's executors, and he periodically took these disagreements to the papers. In December 1839, in the wake of the most recent dispute about Austin's legacy, *The Times* printed a lengthy complaint from Samuel Austin, which ended by outing Lushington's tactics:

> Upon my threatening to apply to the Court of Chancery, [the executors] indirectly insinuate that the individual in question is not my brother, for that her late Majesty on her deathbed made an important communication to Dr. Lushington, which, in the event of an application to the court, he should be obliged to divulge, and thereby deprive the family of the property, but that, if the family remained quiet, and permitted my brother (still calling him my brother) to remain where he is, they (the executors) would, in the event of his decease, divide his property amongst them, and would enter into

---

59. *Morning Chronicle,* August 27, 1821.

62   CHAPTER 2

any agreement, or sign any understanding to do so. I can clearly prove the William Austin in question to be my brother, but, being in humble circumstances, am unable to compete with the executors, and it is only by bringing the matter before the public that I shall succeed.[60]

Three decades after the "Delicate Investigation," the identity of William Austin still circulated in public in plural forms, contesting for priority and subject to competing claims of proof.

In the Austin family management of the story, Samuel the older sibling became the proxy advocate because mental illness silenced William, who remained the impecunious family's best hope for a meal ticket.[61] After Caroline's death, William Austin lived primarily in Italy, where, according to Samuel, "he could make his income go twice as far." He revisited England in 1823–24 (at his majority) and again in 1827–28, both times in failed hopes that Chancery proceedings about the queen's will would yield better terms. The first public notice of his illness, a brief piece in *The Times* on November 10, 1832, is remarkable on several counts.

> We have received a letter from SAMUEL AUSTIN, the brother of WILLIAM AUSTIN, who, it will be recollected, was humanely brought up by QUEEN CAROLINE in her deserted state, whose humanity her base and cruel enemies attempted to turn to her ruin. The young man is at present in a madhouse at Milan, and but moderately provided for, where he has been for three years. The circumstances which affected his understanding were, we learn, the sufferings of his magnanimous benefactress, and the indignation conceived at seeing THEODORE MAJOCCHI, of *"non mi ricordo"* memory, and others of that stamp, living in affluence on British gold, the fruits of their perjuries, whilst himself, and other faithful servants of the Queen, were left to starve. His mother and the rest of his family are here in England, in great distress. The humane may hear of them at No. 4, Jamaica-row, Bermondsey.[62]

This paragraph lobbed a salvo of residual Queenite sympathy into the old Regency fray a dozen years after the fact. Pugnaciously, it politicized the very

---

60. *The Times*, December 10, 1839. In the provincial press, these details were recirculated under headlines such as "A Strange Court Story—Queen Caroline's Protégé" (*Staffordshire Gazette*, December 21, 1839).

61. See note 32 for Austin family history.

62. *The Times*, November 10, 1832. The item's sympathy was immediately challenged in a notice in the *Brighton Gazette*, reprinted as far north as Aberdeen (*Aberdeen Journal*, November 28, 1832).

NATIONAL CHILDREN

madness it made public: the letter blamed William Austin's mental illness on the old attacks on Caroline and the unjustly rewarded conduct of government agents in the divorce trial. Three months later, in February 1833, the aging radical John Thelwall wrote to *The Times* about an unspent subscription fund intended for a monument to Caroline. Samuel Austin wrote privately to Thelwall the next day, arguing that the unspent fund belonged by right to his brother William and soliciting Thelwall's assistance: "Is not my brother a living monument of her memory and her wrongs?"[63]

Four months after the passage of Reform in July 1832, *The Times* report of Austin's madness also mapped the adoptee in his birthplace among the poverty-stricken and the dispossessed, the birth family who claimed him now suffering in the Bermondsey precincts that would soon become infamously Dickensian. Throughout Austin's adopted life, establishment culture stigmatized him as inescapably vulgar, coarse, and ill-bred. Press accounts of Austin's birth family subsequently underscored the association of adoption with social abjection, a theme prominent in adoption debates later in the century. On January 15, 1833, *The Times* reported that Mrs. Sophia Austin, recently widowed, had appeared before the authorities:

> Among the persons who applied on Friday last to the overseers of the parish of St. Mary, Whitechapel, for parochial relief, was Mrs. Austin, the mother of William Austin. The latter, it will be recollected, had become very conspicuous, some years ago, in consequence of the notice of him by the late Queen Caroline, who had made him her *protégé*, and concerning whose birth, parentage, &c, an inquiry before the Privy Council was instituted. From the statement of the applicant, it appeared that her husband had for some years held a situation in His Majesty's Customs, but, being of most extravagant and profligate habits, he lived, if not beyond, at least up to his income, and having died a short time since, left the applicant and his daughter, a girl of 15 years of age, in great distress.[64]

The alleged "extravagance" and "profligacy" of Austin's birth father point to the dissolute character of this unwholesome set. Tagged with such base associations, the Austin family also endured a spotlight on licentiousness and wantonness. An item in the *Leeds Intelligencer* on November 29, 1826, reported

---

63. *The Times*, February 1, 1833; Samuel Austin's letter (from Thelwall's papers) was published in *Notes and Queries*, 3rd ser., XI, May 1867, 51–52.

64. See also *Leicester Chronicle*, January 19, 1833; *Worcester Journal*, January 17, 1833; and *The Times*, January 24, 1833 (a letter of protest from Samuel Austin).

64 CHAPTER 2

the court appearance of "William Austin's Mother" on charges of assaulting a young woman:

> A fat, portly, consequential looking lady, who proved to be no less a personage than Mrs. *Austin,* the mother of Wm. Austin, the protégé and residuary legatee of the late Queen Caroline, was brought up on Monday . . . charged with having, while under the influence of the "green eyed monster," inflicted divers assaults on the person of Miss Dorothea Manck . . . whom she suspected of having engrossed more of Mr. A's affections than the code of morality countenanced. After hearing the case, bail was given for the mother of the *Prince* of *Como,* and she was discharged.

Such records indicate how the popular press bundled Austin's adoption narrative with salacious tales illustrating the unwholesome unruliness of the urban poor. Adoption debates leading up to the 1926 Adoption Act also struggled with the fraught question of eugenics, in which these suspect populations of adoption risked definition as threateningly degenerate and biologically ill-bred.[65] In the final chapter of Austin's story, he appeared center stage as a lunatic, an anticipatory image of the opprobrium later haunting adoption debates.

In a madhouse in Milan, William Austin had at least two absent mothers, the "one who brought him up humanely," now dead, and a second who was alive but also separate from him, "in England, in great distress." Distress defines the tale of William Austin to its end. In 1845 Caroline's executors, Lushington and Sir Thomas Wilde, acting as guardians, arranged for his return from Milan to London and commitment to Blackland House, Chelsea, an asylum run by Dr. A. R. Sutherland.[66] Manuscripts in the Royal Archives at Windsor preserve a flurry of clerkly correspondence on this occasion about the person most often referred to in the documents as "the lunatic," whom Sutherland evaluated as always in "the same lost and fatuous mental condition. . . . He occasionally appears cheerful and attempts to sing but never enters into conversation."[67] At Austin's return, a solicitor's clerk wrote to Samuel Austin to put the Austin family on notice of the removal and the impending legal proceedings to have him declared insane. On March 7, 1845, William Austin made his final public appearance, at a Commission of Lunacy

---

65. Keating, *Child for Keeps,* 33–35.

66. Caroline's most recent biographer misreports this event on two counts: "It was his brother Samuel Austin [it was Lushington and Wilde] who rescued him in 1846 [1845] from a Milan lunatic asylum to which he had been committed" (Fraser, *Unruly Queen,* 465).

67. The Royal Archives, Windsor. My thanks to Pam Clark, registrar, and her staff for their kind assistance.

National Children

in a London court. In full or variously excerpted, the following account in *The Times* was reproduced throughout the nation, in other London papers, and in Carlisle, Hull, Bristol, Kendal, Lancaster, Leicester, Lincolnshire, Manchester, Newcastle, Reading, Cornwall, and Sheffield, headed in some papers "Queen Caroline's William Austin," in several (and in *The Times* source text) "William Austin, the Adopted Son of the Late Queen Caroline," and in one "Commission of Lunacy on the Celebrated William Austin."[68]

These last images of a severely aphasic and disaffected Austin, "the unfortunate gentleman," remain vivid and unsettling. The audience of his final performance included "Mr Commissioner Winslow and a special jury of 17 gentlemen of the county, at the Sheriffs' Court, Red Lion square," assembled as a "commission *de lunatico inquirendo* to inquire into the state of mind of 'William Austin, late of the city of Milan, but now residing at Blackland House, Chelsea, gentleman.'" The officers of the court opened with a summary snapshot of Austin's deterioration in Milan: "The unfortunate gentleman became completely imbecile, and his imbecility was so absolute as to amount almost to idiotcy." The Italian keeper who accompanied him from Milan then testified: "He would eat, drink, and sleep, but never spoke. During the three years he never spoke once. When spoken to, he never answered, and was incapable of doing anything. He was very much attached to a piece of stick, which never leaves his possession night or day. He never gave any reason for his attachment to the stick."

At this point, the court proceeding tripped over an awkward moment. Attempting to take the measure of Austin, the "Learned Commissioner" from his presiding chair "thought they should know something of his early life." The prospect of such noisy and scandalous history stumped the house: "There appeared to be some objection to answer, upon which the Learned Commissioner said, it was not necessary, certainly." The loud echoes of Regency unrest could still baffle a courtroom, which plainly preferred quiet order. It was more prudent to produce William Austin himself, safely speechless, who then discomposed a theater for the final time. The "unfortunate gentleman" was escorted into the court:

> He was attired in a long rifle-green great coat, thickly trimmed with fur, with a cap *en suite,* red and black cross-bar trousers, and a similar waistcoat. In height he is about 5 feet 6 inches, and rather stoutly made. He is a good-looking man, with a most intellectual countenance, and having a remarkable high forehead. In his hand he held a small piece of grape-vine stick, which

---

68. *The Times,* March 13, 1845.

66   CHAPTER 2

he kept twirling round, totally unconscious of all that was passing. The Commissioner spoke to him three or four times, but he took not the slightest notice. He, however, on the bidding of the keeper, stood or sat down, but beyond that all with him was blank. On the Commissioner giving the order for him to withdraw, he followed the keeper out as docile as a lamb. It was a most painful sight.

Once this disturbing human form was again out of sight, the press narrative took refuge in judicial order: "The jury immediately returned a verdict 'That William Austin was of unsound mind, and incapable of managing his affairs.'" The final sentence of the account ventured in its first clause the equivocal term "adopted" to describe Austin's identity but retreated in the second clause to the safer ground of property law: "The unfortunate gentleman was adopted when a child, by the late Queen Caroline, and to him she bequeathed by her will a portion of her property."

The history of this adoptee is the history of a recalcitrantly enigmatic life that refuses to fit in a series of national frames: "The Child" who is a mysteriously anonymous absence in the secret court of the Delicate Investigation; Billy Austin the little bastard and favorite boy, transgressively out of place in royal theater boxes; William Austin the Deptford boy who accompanies Caroline entering Jerusalem; Billy Austin the protégé and prince, an absent witness who hovers nearby throughout the royal divorce trial; William Austin the nondescript who is also the queen's residuary legatee; William Austin the adopted son of the queen, a wordless spectacle in yet another London courtroom summoned on his account. The press report of his insanity hearing ends by attempting to define him in terms of the queen's property rights, wherein he has indeed faded legalistically into a footnote in the historical record.[69] But especially in these final images, the strangeness of his figure and conduct defies such assimilation and erasure. Silently fingering that peculiar piece of stick, occasionally breaking into song like a mad George III wandering the halls of Windsor, he lingers in mind as a quintessential misfit, the "unfortunate gentleman" indeed, always and everywhere the adopted stranger, doubly differentiated and diminished.

William Austin's life was nearly always loud and noisy. From the hubbub of *The Book* and the Delicate Investigation through the rowdy years on

---

69. After the reports of the 1845 insanity hearing, a record of Austin's life disappears until his death certificate and burial record in 1857. In the middle decades of the century, his story circulated in memoirs and biographies of Regency principals; e.g., an obituary of Lord Denman in *The Times* on September 27, 1854, and a response in the *Daily News* on September 29; "Life of Lord Eldon" in Campbell's *Lives of the Lord Chancellors*, VII.177 (London, 1851).

NATIONAL CHILDREN 67

the Continent to the riots of the divorce trial and the death of Caroline, turmoil defined large stretches of his life. These rackets mark threats of disruption—ethical, political, existential. The din registers how adoption, nominally a private, domestic action, necessarily turns up the public volume on family formation, sometimes clamorously. When the family on the adoption stage is royal, the metonymic traffic between family and nation moves in a tight, tense circle. When one party to such prominently public surrogacy is a laboring-class family, systems of biocentric hierarchical order must shift and rebalance to stabilize. The many stories of William Austin by their very multiplicity supplied vehicles of revolutionary threat. As late as 1833, the French theater in Paris flipped off the British establishment with a rowdy melodrama, *Bergami*, in which Castlereagh (the British foreign minister) is shot in Lords during the queen's trial, Caroline is poisoned by an agent of the king at the king's coronation banquet, and Bergami stabs the agent to close the curtain with revenge and justice. And what of Billy Austin? Not the child of Sophia Austin, not the child of Caroline by any one of numerous fathers, not the child of German nobility, he is now the biological son of a friend of Bergami's, the firebrand hero. These scrambled French narratives served a threatening theme, noted with dry amusement in the London press: "An immense insurrection of an indignant people takes place."[70] That dry amusement is also nervous laughter, the dismissive doing double-duty defensively.

But William Austin's loud life also brims with silence and secrets. Often the scene of public controversy, adoption as a social practice offers on the flip side a vexed history of secrecy and silence, memorably marked in modern British culture by Mike Leigh's 1996 adoption film *Secrets & Lies*.[71] Austin the individual was silently absent from the first two quasi-judicial proceedings that interrogated his identity, the Delicate Investigation and Caroline's divorce trial. Judicial process carefully segregated Austin offstage, a place where secrets multiplied. When Austin finally appeared before a court in person, his insanity hearing in 1845, he was literally speechless, exhibiting an aphasia that is a peculiarly overdetermined image of the stakes in play. Such hush registers the reflexive reaction to the threats adoptive contingency posed to absolutist, bionormative forms of family and nation. Silence is the sound of power consolidating, as when Stephen Lushington in 1839 advised the Austin family to keep quiet about their demands. When Austin died in 1857, twelve years after his last courtroom performance, the newspapers were entirely silent about his life. That silence is peculiar, given the press and popular appetite for royal gos-

---

70. *London Standard*, July 3, 1833. The play was staged at the Porte St. Martin.

71. *Secrets & Lies*, directed and written by Mike Leigh, October Films, 1996; winner of the Palme d'Or at the 1996 Cannes Film Festival.

sip. Any storytelling about Austin was now off the record. Henry Brougham and Stephen Lushington, both now in positions of prestige at safe distance from their advocacy for Caroline in 1820, corresponded about Austin in the wake of his death, but privately.[72] The history of William Austin either offers too many stories or withdraws into silence, a silence that muffles the risks of contingent identity. As the commissioner of the London court in 1845 was given to understand when he asked to hear more about William Austin, the less said the better. The reaction to the hubbub of his adoption proved very effective. After his life, very little has ever been said about William Austin.

Austin died in Blacklands House asylum in Chelsea on February 11, 1857, from "general decay and debility. For several weeks there was great difficulty getting him to take any food"; he was buried on February 16 in a private grave in the nearby Brompton Cemetery.[73] With baby farming scandals in the 1860s leading to the 1872 Infant Life Protection Act, national debates about surrogate parenting now began the long run-up to the Adoption of Children Act of 1926, negotiating troubled social waters of illegitimacy, infanticide, eugenics, and child emigration schemes, social pressures that led to the National Children's Home and Orphanage in 1869, the Church of England Waifs and Strays Society in 1881, and the many schemes of Thomas Barnardo, who opened his first home for London nondescripts such as Billy Austin in 1870. In Romantic-period Britain, the narrative multiplicity of adoption mixed untimely with deep-seated biocentric narratives of the nation, so that the national figure of a surrogate child such as William Austin posed a threat rather than a promise. In the Brompton Cemetery, the section containing his grave is in our day untended and densely overgrown, an impenetrable thicket.

72. In 1857 Lushington was at the peak of his judicial career as a judge on the High Court of the Admiralty and on the cusp of his appointment as Dean of Arches in 1858. Brougham, who had served as lord chancellor from 1830 to 1834 and was Baron Brougham of Brougham and Vaux from 1830, was granted a second peerage in 1860.

73. There has been confusion on this point; in his 1935 biography of George IV, Roger Fulford notes that Austin "died in 1849," but he doesn't cite a source for this information (*George the Fourth*, 236). Hibbert and Fraser subsequently cite this 1849 date, with Fulford as source. Information supplied by archivists at the National Portrait Gallery reports the GRO Death Certificate, the probate record of his will (TNA: PROB 11/2247, pp. 124–25), and the Register of Burials of London Westminster Cemetery, Earls Court, Old Brompton (TNA WORK/97/19/, 1857).

CHAPTER 3

Natural Children

Jane Austen and Adoption

On February 16, 1813, Jane Austen wrote to her lifelong friend Martha Lloyd, front-loading local news from her Chawton circle in rural Hampshire. Toward the end of the letter, Austen turned to national news. On February 10, a letter from Princess Caroline—ghosted by her adviser Henry Brougham—to her estranged husband the prince regent splashed into very public view in London newspapers. The text of the long letter was reprinted in the *Hampshire Telegraph* on February 15; in her letter to Lloyd the next day, Austen takes up the royal topic:

> I suppose all the World is sitting in Judgment upon the Princess of Wales's Letter. Poor Woman, I shall support her as long as I can, because she *is* a Woman, & because I hate her Husband—but I can hardly forgive her for calling herself "attached & affectionate" to a Man whom she must detest—& the intimacy said to subsist between her & Lady Oxford is bad.—I do not know what to do about it;—but if I must give up the Princess, I am resolved at least always to think that she would have been respectable, if the Prince had behaved only tolerably by her at first.[1]

---

1. Austen, *Letters,* ed. Le Faye, 208. For Lady Oxford and William Austin, see figure 1 in chapter 2.

The latest salvo of protest at her enforced separation from her biological daughter Princess Charlotte, Caroline's letter included an appeal to "the feelings of every woman in England," which tipped Austen's ballot toward Caroline ("because she *is* a Woman") in the bad choice between two disreputable royal figures. Bundled with her blunt antipathy toward the regent ("I hate her husband"), Austen's perplexity—"I do not know what to do about it"—chafed at her again in London in late 1815, during her anxious negotiation of the dedication of *Emma* to the man himself, "His Royal Highness."

Austen's letter to Lloyd is the most explicit trace of her everyday attention to the haphazard royal family politics on exhibit in the previous chapter. Princess Caroline's 1813 letter, over which "all the World is sitting in judgement," included a long paragraph of complaint about the 1806 "Delicate Investigation," which interrogated the identity of the adopted child William Austin:

> He who dares advise your Royal Highness to overlook the evidence of my innocence, and disregard the sentence of complete acquittal which it produced—or is wicked and false enough still to whisper suspicions in your ear, betrays his duty to you, Sir, to your Daughter, and to your People, if he counsels you to permit a day to pass without a further investigation of my conduct. I know that no such calumniator will venture to recommend a measure which must speedily end in his utter confusion. Then let me implore you to reflect on the situation in which I am placed; without the shadow of a charge against me—without even an accuser—after an Inquiry that led to my ample vindication—yet treated as if I were still more culpable than the perjuries of my suborned traducers represented me, and held up to the world as a Mother who may not enjoy the society of her only Child.[2]

Because Brougham the ghostwriter needed to lock down on the primary purpose of the letter—the bitterly disputed care of the one legitimate royal child, Princess Charlotte, "her only Child"—his paragraph carefully maintains an unspoken subtext about the adopted child William Austin. In that quasi-judicial proceeding, Caroline's "innocence," "complete acquittal," and "ample vindication" was of the charge of being, adulterously, the biological mother of William Austin, who dwells unnamed just below the surface of Caroline's very public complaint. Such is the way Brougham's artful style would have been understood by "all the World" of the readers known to Austen.

At the moment of these February 1813 letters, *Pride and Prejudice* had been published a month previously. As Austen pondered "what to do about"

---

2. *Morning Chronicle,* February 10, 1813.

this royal scandal and its contested history of parenthood both biological and adoptive, she was at work full speed on *Mansfield Park,* quickly followed by *Emma,* two novels that offer a superabundance of adoption tales and form the focus of this chapter, following an account of the adoption Austen knew best in her own family, the kinship adoption of her older brother Edward Austen. Austen's abandoned fragment of a novel from 1804–5, *The Watsons,* experiments with a foregrounded repatriation plot, a form of adoption narrative that Austen then deploys in both *Mansfield Park* and *Emma.* Across all three fictional narratives, Austen explores forms of diminished abjection suffered by women, adoptees, and, in various elliptical moments, slaves.

In one of the most substantial accounts to date of adoption in Austen's fiction, Clara Tuite argues that in *Mansfield Park* kinship adoption (which starts the novel) and cousin marriage (which ends it) pair off as complementary, mutually enforcing means of endogamous family formation, underwritten by blood and thus naturalizing both adoption and marriage, actions that otherwise threaten to appear contingent and fictive, exogamously. The Austen of this ambitious reading duplicates in updated garb the normalizing, conservative writer of long tradition. I read Austen instead as an oppositional writer whose representation of adoption pushes in just that contingent and fictive direction, unsettling with untimely forms both blood kinship and the marriage settlement by rendering manifest the performative inventedness of human kinship.[3] That counterargument is best on view in *Emma,* which I argue is Austen's centerpiece adoption novel. The book offers a remarkable oversupply of adoption narratives, the cases of Harriet Smith (a "natural child"), Jane Fairfax (an orphan), and Frank Churchill (a kinship adoptee), a disruptive surrogate set which lines up with other creatures on the margins of Highbury: old maids, widows, governesses, and a band of "gipsies." The redundancy of surrogate identity in *Emma* supplies a generalizing force that suggests that all family narratives begin to look like adoption tales; at the level of form, surrogacy operates in the novel as a figure for the novel's own fiction-making procedures, which are doubled up by the busy narrative machines of both Emma Woodhouse and the narrator. These features come to a head in the Box Hill episode in volume 3, where an adoption palimpsest layers the outrageous adoption history of Sabrina Sidney already refashioned narratively in Maria Edgeworth's *Belinda,* behind which tale lurks Rousseau, the (un)exemplary figure of Romantic parenting. In brief, my argument is this: in Austen, surrogate parenting in its figurative and narrative

---

3. Tuite, *Romantic Austen,* 104–10. For a polemical argument that kinship is culture all the way down, see Sahlins, *Kinship.*

forms works oppositionally to hold open the radical contingency of human kinship forms, especially those that labor to pass themselves off as necessary and primary because natural—but "natural" only in privileged, officially sanctioned biocentric terms. To borrow a strong claim about disability from David Mitchell and Sharon Snyder's pathbreaking study *Narrative Prosthesis*, adoption, like disability, "services an unsettling objective in literary works by refusing its desired cultural return to the land of the normative."[4]

Kinship or familial adoptions have long straddled borders between biological and contingent family forms. In the long view, the term "adoption" is a net too large to sort all practices of shared family caregiving as old as procreation itself. In the British Romantic century, kinship surrogate care comes into focus as recognizably adoptive along class lines, specifically in instances when members of the landed gentry, balked by biology, forge alternative chains of inheritance. One marker of such adoptive practice is geographical distance: whereas laboring-class children shuffled among physically proximate kin, the act of transporting a male child of the gentry from one propertied location to another inevitably inflected geographical distance as familial difference, regardless of kinship ties. The exigencies of the property regime transformed uprooted biological sons of the gentry into uncanny forms of adoptive kinship, simultaneously familiar and strange.

In Austen's fiction, the closest model of such a male kinship adoption is the subplot of Frank Churchill in *Emma*, transferred from his biological Highbury roots as Frank Weston to the Yorkshire estate, Enscombe, of childless Churchill relatives. In Austen's life, this model was intensely familiar, in multiple senses: the adoptive transfer of her older brother Edward from the Austen home in Hampshire to childless Knight relatives in Kent. In Austen studies, these two paradigmatically male kinship adoption tales, one fictional and one biographical, measure tellingly in company with the most prominent kinship surrogate removal in the fiction, the adoptive transfer of Fanny Price— a daughter instead of a son—to the estate of Bertram relatives in *Mansfield Park*. Because both the Fanny Price and Frank Churchill fictions are shaped foundationally by the family biography of Edward Austen Knight, I begin with that brief history before turning to the case of Fanny Price and kinship adoption generally in *Mansfield Park*. The adoptee Frank Churchill bides his time until he joins the adoptive cast in *Emma* in the final section, much as the novel long delays his repatriated visit to Highbury, whose insular residents claim the adoptee by right of birth.

---

4. Mitchell and Snyder, *Narrative Prosthesis*, 8.

EDWARD AUSTEN'S KINSHIP ADOPTION

A silhouette drawn in 1783 by the artist William Wellings bids to be the defining icon of Romantic-period adoption (figure 2). The image pictures the adolescent Edward Austen, Jane Austen's older brother, being handed by his father to Knight family members, chiefly his adoptive mother Catherine Knatchbull Knight, who turns to them from a gaming table with her sister, and her husband, Thomas Knight, on the right. Notably absent is Edward's birth mother, Mrs. George Austen.

FIGURE 2. Edward Austen adoption silhouette, 1783. Used by permission of Chawton House Library.

Now available as an image on a tea towel or in a packet of postcards in the gift shop of Jane Austen's last home, Chawton Cottage, the silhouette is a family heirloom that long hung on a bedroom wall of nearby Chawton House, the Knight family ancestral home. After an early 1901 reproduction in a Janeite collection of images,[5] scholarship began taking notice of the image only in the 1980s, but it now introduces recent crossover books such as Paula Byrne's *The Real Jane Austen: A Life in Small Things*. Byrne foregrounds the Wellings

---

5. Hill, *Jane Austen: Her Homes & Her Friends,* between pp. 48 and 49. Hill comments that "Edward, Jane's second brother, had been adopted, when a child, by his cousin, Mr. Thomas Knight" (49). Edward was actually Austen's third older brother; the second, George, who was mentally impaired and was boarded out for his lifetime, is not mentioned in many early biographies.

silhouette as the book's frontispiece and devotes much of her first chapter, "The Family Profile," to adoption: "It should not come as a surprise that Jane Austen's novels show more than a passing interest in adoption."[6]

Now familiar to both scholarship and souvenir hunters, the silhouette disrupts the record and interpretation of Romantic-period adoption even as it illustrates the topic. When Byrne, for example, describes the image as commissioned by Thomas Knight II "to commemorate his formal adoption of his nephew, Edward Austen," the muddle is twofold: although kin, Edward Austen was a cousin, not a nephew (a minor issue), and the phrase "formal adoption" is, historically, a contradiction in terms (an issue): the image is indeed formal, stylistically, but the event is not a "formal adoption," if by "formal" Byrne implies "official" or even "legal," a reading she shares with many others.[7] The contemporary American novelist Lorrie Moore, an adoptive mother, coughed up one of the most garbled accounts of the Edward Austen adoption in the *New York Times* in March 2020. Responding to an interviewer's question for an example of an "interesting fact" from her recent reading, Moore offered this: "Jane Austen's mother allowed Jane's young brother to accompany a strange couple who were about to embark on their honeymoon and who had taken a fancy to him. Later Mrs. Austen allowed the couple to adopt him. Isn't this shocking?"[8] Certainly not a warm celebration, the Wellings silhouette in its cool poise is impossible to read as a shocked disavowal of child relinquishment. But perhaps Moore is on to something, in spite of her description of the Knight kin as "a strange couple." In her account, the guilty party is the birth mother, Mrs. Austen, and Mrs. Austen is missing from the silhouette. Is that absence a silent mark of disavowal of the event?

My point is that the image is hard to read. Our iconic age multiplies cloud-based images of defining life moments: engagements, gender reveals, births, weddings—and adoptions. Romantic-period adoptions left no such iconic records, except this one silhouette, which to modern eyes beckons anachronistically like a handoff photo at a Children's Welfare Institute or a Catholic Social Services office, or at an airport, a lawyer's office, a hospital, or family court, after the papers are signed. Silhouette-based readings of the Edward Austen adoption as "formal" or "official" incorporate into the reading of the

---

6. Byrne, *Small Things,* 15.

7. See, for example, Tomalin, *Jane Austen: A Life,* 38, where Edward Austen is "officially adopted" by the Knights.

8. Moore, *New York Times Sunday Book Review,* March 29, 2020, 8. With "shocking," Moore channeled Emma Woodhouse's city sister Isabella Knightley, who scorns the Frank Churchill adoption in *Emma*: "There is something so shocking in a child's being taken away from his parents and natural home!"; Austen, *Emma,* 104.

NATURAL CHILDREN   75

pictured event the fact that Edward Austen changed his name to Edward Knight, glossing over the untidy fact that the name change did not occur until 1812, twenty-nine years after the 1783 image—but adoption paperwork can sometimes be like that. To prepare for Austen's representations of untimely adoptions in her fiction, it helps to assemble in brief summary the facts of her older brother's kinship adoption, which resist concentrated collapse into a single iconic image. In an appendix, I document how the Edward Austen story was subsequently represented in Austen family biographies, where it was always referred to as an adoption, but never "formal," "official," or "legal."

In 1779 a cousin of Jane Austen's father, Thomas Knight II of Godmersham in Kent, and his new bride, Catherine Knatchbull, called at the Austen home at Steventon in Hampshire and invited the third Austen son, Edward, then age twelve, to accompany them on their travels (Jane Austen was six years younger than Edward). Edward the schoolboy subsequently spent some school holidays with the Knights in Kent. Supported by Knight money, Edward Austen subsequently made a tour of the continent from 1786 to 1790 and married Elizabeth Bridges of Goodnestone near Godmersham in Kent in 1791; they resided in a nearby Bridges family property, Rowling. The childless Thomas Knight II made an elaborate will in 1792, which ultimately rendered Edward Austen the heir to Knight estates in Kent (Godmersham) and, crucially for Jane and Cassandra Austen and their mother, in Hampshire (Chawton). Thomas Knight II died "without issue" in 1794, survived by his wife Catherine, who then held life interest in the Knight estates, under the care of trustees. In 1797 Catherine Knight took an annuity settlement from the estate and moved from Godmersham to nearby Canterbury; Edward Austen and his wife and children then moved from Rowling (a Bridges property) to nearby Godmersham, the crown jewel of the Knight properties, where Jane and her sister Cassandra were frequent guests, helping to care for their many nieces and nephews. When Catherine Knight died in 1812, Edward Austen inherited both the Kent and Hampshire estates. A provision in a chain of Knight family wills from the late seventeenth century required him to change his surname to Knight in order to inherit the Chawton portion of the Knight bequest (the name change was not tied to the Godmersham property). On November 10, 1812, a Royal License was granted to Edward Austen to henceforth use the surname of Knight. Whereas Edward Austen's oldest child Fanny, then nineteen, fiercely lamented the change ("How I hate it!!!"), Jane Austen coolly off-loaded her own response onto the performance of her handwriting: "I must learn to make a better K."[9]

---

9. Austen-Leigh, *Jane Austen: A Family Record,* rev. Le Faye, 196.

The Chawton portion of the Knight estate was especially beneficial to the material good fortune of Edward's younger sibling the novelist, giving her a place to live and write in the last decade of her life. But precisely because Edward Austen was adopted, the security of that very Chawton home was seriously at risk while Jane Austen lived and wrote there. In October 1814, six months after the publication of *Mansfield Park* and while *Emma* was underway, a "writ of ejectment" from the Chawton estate was served upon Edward Austen Knight by a local family, who contested his inheritance rights to Knight family property in Hampshire.[10] Instead of the kind of security generated by an (unavailable) de jure adoption, the disruptive threat of losing her Chawton home shadowed Jane Austen's life until her death in July 1817. A serious threat, the claim came with a steep final price tag; Edward Austen Knight settled the claim a year after his sister's death for £15,000, which cost his Chawton estate a substantial body of harvested woodland to raise that not unsubstantial sum, a late charge upon his adoption, three decades after the Wellings silhouette.

Modern inflections of the Edward Austen story that foreground the adoption as a settled identity swap—Edward Austen becomes in 1783 a new person, Edward Knight—obscure the main plotline in the history, which is a tangled tale of land and property, frequently at risk, spread over decades. Especially as repatriation narratives, a form that Austen first explored in the abandoned fragment *The Watsons,* the Fanny Price and Frank Churchill adoption fictions in *Mansfield Park* and *Emma* rehearse adoption scripts not of settled certainty but of burdened risk.

MANSFIELD PARK, SLAVERY, AND ADOPTIVE REPATRIATION

Was Fanny Price abandoned? Adopted? Cognitive literary studies answers yes to both questions, in those terms. In *Jane on the Brain,* a recent trade book about Austen and evolutionary biology, Wendy Jones treats Fanny's kinship transfer at age ten as an abandonment by her impecunious birth family and as an adoption by her wealthy Bertram relatives: "The adoption feels more like an abandonment than an opportunity, and all young mammals fear

---

10. As distant Knight relatives, the Hintons of Chawton Lodge and their nephew Mr. Baverstock, a local brewer, rested their claim to the Chawton portion of Edward Austen's inheritance on tangled maneuvers in the series of Knight wills half a century earlier. The foundation of their claim was that, because of a set of legal errors and oversights in those maneuvers, they had claim to the property as a proper bloodline of "heirs male" instead of Edward Austen who, adopted, was not an "heir of the body."

NATURAL CHILDREN

abandonment."[11] Austen's language, however, dwells at a distance from this mammalian template. In this section, I first map the language Austen employs to launch her narration of this kinship adoption; the book, for example, never uses the word "abandonment" (or obvious synonyms), and it withholds the word "adopt" until the term sums a prior set of alternative phrases for surrogate care, including a term with special inflections in this novel, "patronage." With a brief spotlight on the three "Ward" sisters whose surnamed identities open the book, I turn to the topic of proper names in the novel, tracking the important recent arguments about race and slavery tethered to the historical figure of Lord Mansfield, whose own haphazard adoptive family speaks to the dynamics of race in Romantic-period adoption. Finally, the figure of Fanny Price as stranger brings to focus the most overlooked and remarkable feature of her adoption story, her double estrangement. Fanny's adoption launches with her removal at age ten to a place where, although kin, she is a stranger. But startlingly, Fanny suffers a second hard removal eight years later at age eighteen. Deep into the book, Sir Thomas Bertram unlovingly ships Fanny back to her birth family where she is now a stranger to her family of origin, a fraught form of adoption narrative—repatriation—that Austen earlier explored in the unfinished fragment known as *The Watsons*.

The opening chapter of *Mansfield Park* quickly narrates the transfer of ten-year-old Fanny from her rough Portsmouth naval home—eight siblings, a harried mother, and a hard-drinking father—to her wealthy Bertram relatives at the estate of Mansfield Park (Fanny's birth mother and Lady Bertram are sisters). This move is clearly kinship surrogate care, but the book launches that general structure with a primary difference: the dominant male inheritance motive of such adoptive transfers among the gentry does not apply. Sir Thomas Bertram, Fanny's uncle, is not on the hunt for an heir, having already achieved "male issue" (two sons) and two daughters, all of whom are older than Fanny. The prime mover of Fanny's relocation is instead Mrs. Norris, the third and oldest Ward sister, who, without children of her own to manage at Mansfield, is not shy to organize the offspring of her two younger sisters. When Fanny's mother Mrs. Price writes to her Mansfield sisters asking for help as "she was preparing for her ninth-lying in," Mrs. Norris puts what the novel will later call a "scheme" in motion:

> Mrs. Norris was often observing to the others, that she could not get her poor sister and her family out of her head, and that much as they had all done for her, she seemed to be wanting to do more: and at length she could not but own it to be her wish, that poor Mrs. Price should be relieved from

---

11. Jones, *Jane on the Brain*, 209.

the charge and expense of one child entirely out of her great number. "What if they were among them to undertake the care of her eldest daughter. . . . The trouble and expense of it to them, would be nothing compared with the benevolence of the action."[12]

Two custodial terms, "charge" and "care," initiate the Bertram family debate about adoption.[13] Whereas "care" etymologically signifies mental effort, "charge" etymologically signifies a material load and immediately becomes the governing term in the deliberations. Mrs. Norris initially tries to duck the question of who will foot the bill for Fanny by cloaking "charge and expense" as benevolent relief (a burden removed from someone else) rather than the assumption of responsibility (a burden taken up by themselves). But the narrator calls her bluff immediately ("Mrs. Norris had not the least intention of being at any expense whatever in her maintenance") (6), and Sir Thomas is given to understand that "it would be totally out of Mrs. Norris's power to take any share in the personal charge of her" (6–7). Years before the novel opens, Mrs. Norris, the oldest Ward sister, suffered the sororal insult of watching her younger sister, Lady Bertram, marry first out of the gate—and marry serious money and property at that. In the first chapter, her retaliatory labor takes the form of an interfamily adoption scam. Sir Thomas is left holding the bill for benevolence; both Mrs. Price the birth mother and, even better, Mrs. Norris the aunt are "relieved from the charge and expense" of Fanny. For Mrs. Norris, these kinship adoption charges are explicitly and intensely "personal," but the person whose welfare is at risk is most certainly not the adopted child.

The term "charge" shapes the second custodial skirmish between Mrs. Norris and Sir Thomas in the third chapter. The action fast-forwards five years; Mrs. Norris is now a widow, which removes one of her token objections to taking Fanny into her own home at Mansfield, and Sir Thomas is newly anxious about money, to the point where "it became not undesirable to himself to be relieved from the expense of [Fanny's] support" (21). Five years earlier, Sir Thomas had been cautious about the undertaking from the start: "It was a serious charge" (4). But the earlier-bundled term for adoptive burden, "charge and expense," has now become for Sir Thomas narrowly and explicitly monetary: "expense." For the larger adoptive family, however, the wider

---

12. Austen, *Mansfield Park,* 3. Subsequent references are by page number in the text.

13. As I track in the next section, the custodial term "charge" marks the adoptive relationships in all three adoptee narratives in *Emma.* See the *Oxford English Dictionary* sense of "charge," n. 13: "The duty or responsibility of taking care of (a person or thing); care, custody, superintendence" (*OED*).

load signified by "charge" remains the defining term. Fanny's cousin Edmund endorses the new scheme to shift Fanny to Mrs. Norris: "Mrs. Norris is much better fitted than my mother for having the charge of you now" (23). But Mrs. Norris persists in ducking the adoptive burden, protesting to Lady Bertram: "What possible comfort could I have in taking such a charge upon me as Fanny!" (25). Sir Thomas remains no match for Mrs. Norris and surrenders again to her design to off-load all the labor and expense of kinship adoption. Mrs. Norris's urgent concern for her own "comfort" alone measures tellingly her obliviousness to emergent child-centered adoption standards.

Before the book explicitly refers to Fanny's case as an adoption at the close of this second skirmish, Austen supplements "charge" and "care" with a third term for surrogate oversight in the first three chapters. An adoptive term that strikes most modern ears as anachronistic, "patron" appears in the opening chapter of *Mansfield Park* and registers the place of power and money in Romantic-period adoption. In contrast to Mrs. Norris's fecklessness, the narrator poses Fanny's primary custodian in benign terms: "Sir Thomas was fully resolved to be the real and consistent patron of the selected child" (6). The term appears only once more in the novel, in prominent place in the final sentence, which maps Fanny's valedictory satisfaction: her married residence with her cousin Edmund "soon grew as dear to her heart, and as thoroughly perfect in her eyes, as every thing else, within the view and patronage of Mansfield Park, had long been" (432). With this formulaic and ironically "perfect" exit, Austen tethers two fraught topics: the practice (and abuse) of adoptive care (Sir Thomas as patron) and the management (and abuse) of wealth, both legitimate and illegitimate (the patronage system that is the Mansfield Park estate). Both lexical moments are unusual in Austen, because the terms "patron" and "patronage" elsewhere in Austen's fiction typically signify in narrowly ecclesiastical contexts: a patron is someone who controls a church living and steers it to a male cleric by means of patronage, which were the primary senses of the words in Austen's time.[14] Unlike Maria Edgeworth, who attacked the widespread abuses of the system in her 1814 novel *Patronage*, Austen risks a benign inflection of patronage as benevolent adoptive action enabled by wealth in the opening portrait of Sir Thomas, briefly framing him as a forerunner of a virtue-besotted modern celebrity

---

14. Such cases in Austen are abundant and familiar: in *Sense and Sensibility*, for example, Colonel Brandon's gift of the Delaford parish living to Edward Ferrars; in *Northanger Abbey*, the living controlled by his father that awaits James Morland; in *Pride and Prejudice*, the satire of ecclesiastical patronage in the persons of Mr. Collins and Lady Catherine de Bourgh and the darker picture of church patronage offered and abused in the backstory of Wickham's double-dealing with Darcy's family.

80 CHAPTER 3

adopter. But the final marker of "patronage" as guiding principle of the estate in the novel's closing sentence puts both words under severe Edgeworthian ethical pressure on two fronts, yoking adoption and slavery. The novel as a whole calls into question the web of Bertram wealth and slavery just as it calls into question Sir Thomas's cold decision as adoptive patron to return Fanny to her birth family.[15]

Near the end of the third chapter of *Mansfield Park,* as Sir Thomas readies his anxious Atlantic journey to attend to his West Indies properties, the book collects its multiple terms for Fanny's kinship load—charge, trouble, expense, care, patron(age)—under the umbrella term "adopt," a rare lexical moment in the novels. Before departure, Sir Thomas confesses his bewilderment at Mrs. Norris's scheming; he "could not but wonder at her refusing to do any thing for a niece, whom she had been so forward to adopt" (26). In Austen's fiction, there are only two other instances of "adopt" that signify the surrogate care of children, both in *Emma,* and both in the Frank Churchill narrative, which I discuss in the next section. In a simple empirical tally, this handful of Austen items supplies raw evidence that Romantic-period writing employs "adopt" and "adoption" to signify the surrogate care of children, a century before the terms carry statutory legal significance. But Austen's larger lexical practice is where the interest dwells: her fiction works the wide field of de facto surrogate care and its wide vocabulary to explore an extensive range of human motives and consequences bound up in the manifold historical practices collected under the heading "adoption."

Especially since Edward Said's chapter on *Mansfield Park* in *Culture and Imperialism* in 1993, a contemporaneous historical practice, chattel slavery, beckons as one of the novel's most urgent topics.[16] The brief passage that puts slavery unquestionably at issue appears in a conversation between Fanny and Edmund early in the second volume, in the wake of Sir Thomas's return from his sugar plantations in the West Indies. Fanny replays with Edmund a family discussion the previous evening: "'Did not you hear me ask him about the slave trade last night?' 'I did—and was in hopes the question would be followed up by others. It would have pleased your uncle to be inquired of farther.' 'And I longed to do it—but there was such a dead silence!'" (178). The best Austen criticism now understands this passage as the anchor of a narrative that, oppositionally, lines up plantation slavery with multiple forms of patri-

---

15. Echoing the *Mansfield Park* precedent, the term "patron" bled into family accounts of the Edward Austen adoption. The 1911 family biography puts the adoption of Edward in these terms: "But his adoption by his patrons must have been a gradual affair." In the 1913 biography: "On the death of Mrs. Knight—his kind and generous patron and friend—in October of that year, Edward and all his family took the name of Knight." See the appendix for the details of these family biographies. Queen Caroline was often styled William Austin's "patroness."

16. Said, "Jane Austen and Empire," 80–96.

archal oppression and abuse on the home front. To this set, I want to add the abuse of adoptive care manifest in Sir Thomas's "medicinal project" to return Fanny to her birth family as a stranger. A number of strong readings of the novel explore the homology of women and slaves that was widespread in early feminist polemic in the period, including Christopher Stampone's recent claim that the novel "marks Fanny Price as the text's representative slave."[17] Fanny's abjection, a function of this structural homology, protests most vividly in her fate as adoptee.

Before turning to the narrative of Fanny's repatriation, it helps to review the signifying effect of proper names in the novel, which brings to even sharper focus the traffic between slavery and adoption. Readings of the "deep silence" about slavery that Fanny registers at Mansfield often suggest that Austen hid the topic in plain sight in the novel's title, citing the famous judicial decision of Lord Mansfield in 1772—the Somerset case—which ruled, narrowly, that the case of slave ownership before the court could not be enforced in English common law. John Wiltshire, the most recent editor of the novel in the (currently) authoritative Cambridge edition, is judiciously skeptical of the claim that Austen intended this explicit link between her novel and the case history of slavery in English courts. But separate from case law about slavery, there is a more explicit link between the novel, slavery, and the Mansfield name in Lord Mansfield's history as an adoptive parent. At their Kenwood House estate on the north edge of Hampstead Heath, Lord and Lady Mansfield cared adoptively for Lord Mansfield's two young great-nieces, one of whom was a mixed-race child of West Indian slavery, Dido Elizabeth Belle, the daughter of an African slave and a British naval captain, Sir John Lindsay, who was Lord Mansfield's nephew.[18] Dido Belle was taken under the charge and care of Lord and Lady Mansfield as a young child; Austen personally knew the other adopted niece, Dido's companion and cousin Lady Elizabeth Murray, who in her married life as Lady Elizabeth Finch-Hatton was a neighbor of Edward Austen in Kent. Austen was thus certainly familiar with the adoptive history of the two cousins in the Mansfield family, including a child of slavery; Austen refers to Lady Elizabeth, unflatteringly, several times in her correspondence, and it is not unlikely that she is a model for the insipid Lady Bertram in *Mansfield Park*.[19]

---

17. Stampone, "Mental Slavery," 197–212.

18. Dido's life was the subject of the 2013 film *Belle* by Amma Asante; see also Jones, "Ambiguous Cousinship."

19. August 24, 1805: "I have discovered that Ly Eliz:th for a woman of her age and situation, has astonishingly little to say for herself" (*Letters* 107); November 1813: "Lady Eliz. Hatton and Annamaria called here this morng;—Yes, they called,—but I do not think I can say anything more about them. They came & they sat & they went" (*Letters* 253).

82   CHAPTER 3

In addition to thus repositioning the Mansfield name under a double sign of adoption and slavery, I want to register the act of naming that opens the novel under a sign of surrogate care. Austen launches *Mansfield Park* with the capsule backstory of the three sisters who, married, become Lady Bertram (the middle sister), Mrs. Norris (the oldest), and Mrs. Price (the youngest). Prenuptially, those three siblings are surnamed "Ward" in the opening paragraph, the only time Austen ever uses that surname. To name a set of blood sisters "Ward" is to move blood kinship a degree (or three) off the fixed and stable.[20] Although it may seem questionably helpful to add that the three Ward siblings who launch the novel are not styled the three "Blood" sisters (which was an available surname, if a bit too Welsh or Irish), I submit the following piece of evidence. Late in the novel, a letter arrives for Fanny in Portsmouth from Lady Bertram, whose pampered life depends in part on the proceeds of West Indian slavery. Mrs. Price is entirely uninterested in the news from her wealthy sibling, and the narrator frames this broken relationship between Ward sisters in terms of failed biology: "So long divided, and so differently situated, the ties of blood were little more than nothing" (496). In *Mansfield Park,* even biological kinship is from the very first located under a sign of surrogate care.

A full account of adoptive being in *Mansfield Park* must tally this: Fanny Price is uprooted not once but twice. Fanny's abrupt repatriation occurs in the last third of the novel, after she has seriously displeased Sir Thomas by refusing an offer of marriage to a suitor, Henry Crawford, whom he considers to be a prime catch.[21] Sir Thomas coldly rules that Fanny must suffer consequences; she is to be returned for a time to the misery of her birth family, which his language divides from her adoptive family as "her own family" (425), a phrase that limits "family" to only one of the two families Fanny as adoptee must always toggle between. Tagged by the narrator as a "scheme" and an "experiment," Sir Thomas's actions manifest the patriarchal power of a plantation lord engaged in a form of malign control that sounds like a Swiftean parody of mad science: "It was a medicinal project upon his niece's understanding, which

---

20. A "ward" in Samuel Johnson's 1755 *Dictionary* is (among other definitions) "one in the hands of a guardian; the state of a child under a guardian." A "guardian" is "one that has the care of an orphan; one who is to supply the want of parents." In the published fiction, Austen uses this sense of "ward" only once, in the opening chapter of *Northanger Abbey*: "There was not one family among their acquaintance who had reared and supported a boy accidentally found at their door—not one young man whose origin was unknown. Her father had no ward, and the squire of the parish no children"; *Northanger Abbey,* 9. So much for Tom Jones and his ilk.

21. Rachel Bowlby offers a useful reading of the Henry and Mary Crawford sibling history as the novel's "second case of quasi-adoption"; *Parental Stories,* 172–74.

NATURAL CHILDREN

he must consider as at present diseased" (425). The narrator's blunt summary measures the bleak distance between Sir Thomas's action and an oft-invoked goal of modern adoption: his scheme to ship Fanny back to Portsmouth had "nothing at all [to do] with any idea of making her happy" (425).

Repatriation occasions fraught debates in modern adoption policy, as in the question of whether adopted-out indigenous children are better served returned to tribal care.[22] Fanny's plight in the third volume of *Mansfield Park* manifests the deep unease baked into adoptive lives that ricochet among multiple settings.[23] Fanny herself at first imagines that her return to her birth family will cure a wound she suffered at adoption: "The remembrance of all her earliest pleasures, and of what she had suffered in being torn from them, came over her with renewed strength, and it seemed as if to be at home again, would heal every pain that had since grown out of the separation" (426). The novel devotes a long paragraph to these hopes, but they soon become tangled up with Fanny's guilt and self-reproach about her adoption. Fanny is tasked with arranging her own return:

> The next step was to communicate with Portsmouth. Fanny wrote to offer herself; and her mother's answer, though short, was so kind, a few simple lines expressed so natural and motherly a joy in the prospect of seeing her child again, as to confirm all the daughter's views of happiness in being with her—convincing her that she should now find a warm and affectionate friend in the "Mamma" who had certainly shewn no remarkable fondness for her formerly; but this she could easily suppose to have been her own fault, or her own fancy. She had probably alienated Love by the helplessness and fretfulness of a fearful temper, or been unreasonable in wanting a larger share than any one among so many could deserve. Now, when she knew better how to be useful and how to forbear, and when her mother could be no longer occupied by the incessant demands of a house full of little children, there would be leisure and inclination for every comfort, and they should soon be what mother and daughter ought to be to each other. (428)

---

22. For debates about repatriation and indigeneity that surround Barbara Kingsolver's novels *The Bean Trees* (1988) and *Pigs in Heaven* (1993), see the discussion and notes in Homans, *Imprint*, 131–36. In 2023 the US Supreme Court ruled against the most recent challenges to the 1978 Indian Child Welfare Act (ICWA), the federal legislation at the center of these debates.

23. Marianne Novy reads Fanny's return to Portsmouth as a failed "reunion" rather than an abusive repatriation; her emphasis on the novel as a whole is to locate Fanny in a "tradition of good adopted girls"; *Reading Adoption,* 119, 97.

Predictably, the fantasy of recuperative return is elusive; the Price home is instead again "the abode of noise, disorder, and impropriety" (450). The chief agent of Fanny's new dismay is the other (absent) patriarch in her life, her birth father, Mr. Price, who is loud, abusive, and supremely self-centered: "Fanny, with doubting feelings, had risen to meet him, but sank down again on finding herself undistinguished in the dusk, and unthought of" (438). Fanny's brother William tries to bring his sister to her birth father's notice, but Fanny proves invisible to him: "But here is my sister, Sir, here is Fanny. . . . It is so dark you do not see her" (439). At such an unwelcome, "Fanny was almost stunned" (441), which translates into renewed abjection: "What right had she to be of importance to her family? She could have none, so long lost sight of!" (442). "None" does double duty here; Fanny laments her lost "importance" while the novel, out ahead of her, laments her lost "family."

Fanny's abjection then takes extreme form in a recovered memory of a dead sister: "As she now sat looking at Betsey, she could not but think particularly of another sister, a very pretty little girl, whom she had left there not much younger when she went into Northamptonshire, who had died a few years afterwards. There had been something remarkably amiable about her" (445–46). The psychic violence of Fanny's repatriation loads her double grief at the loss of both her birth family and her adoptive family onto the grieved self-image of this dead sister, whose small deathbed gifts to her siblings now cause unruly, petty quarrels among Price siblings. When Fanny at last returns to Mansfield, Sir Thomas's medicinal project has both disciplined and punished her; Fanny's birth home and her own previous self, like her sister, are now dead to her: "When she had been coming to Portsmouth, she had loved to call it her home, had been fond of saying that she was going home; the word had been very dear to her; and so it still was, but it must be applied to Mansfield. *That* was now the home. Portsmouth was Portsmouth; Mansfield was home" (499). But the novel suggests that this renewed attachment to her adoptive home is itself fundamentally disordered. When her unwelcome at Portsmouth stuns Fanny, she retreats into a hyperbolically impossible picture of her adoptive home at Mansfield, a picture belied in every phrase by events of contrary evidence throughout the book: "At Mansfield, no sounds of contention, no raised voices, no abrupt bursts, no tread of violence was ever heard; all proceeded in a regular course of cheerful orderliness; every body had their due importance; every body's feelings were consulted. If tenderness could be ever supposed wanting, good sense and good breeding supplied its place" (453). Not so, on every count. Fanny Price is now homeless, estranged from both Portsmouth, her birth home, and Mansfield, her adoptive home.

NATURAL CHILDREN 85

I leave Fanny the adoptee suspended there, before she is overtaken by the marriage plot that drives the final pages of the novel. To round off the account of Fanny Price as an adoptee instead of a marriage suspect, I turn to a text that Austen herself abandoned, a fragment of a novel composed in 1804–5 and titled *The Watsons* when published in a family biography in 1871.[24] *The Watsons* offers a rehearsal for the Fanny Price adoption story in the person of its central character, Emma Watson, "who was very recently returned to her family from the care of an Aunt who had brought her up" (79). Like Fanny Price, the story of Emma Watson is an adoption tale; now nineteen, she has spent fourteen years under the kinship adoptive care of an aunt and uncle, since the death of her mother when she was five. And like Fanny Price in the third volume of *Mansfield Park,* Emma now suffers a second removal, a repatriation that opens this earlier narrative. (We learn later in the tale that at the death of her caregiving uncle, her caregiving aunt has remarried, and the new husband—a fortune-hunting Irish captain—wants nothing to do with the care and charge of Emma.) Emma's birth family is impecunious, with an invalid clergyman father and abundant siblings; Emma's older brother Robert drops in for a visit and welcomes her home with the cheerful thought that she has been "sent back a weight upon your family" (122–23). Like Fanny at Portsmouth, repatriated Emma suffers abjection and guilt:

> The change in her home society, and stile of Life in consequence of the death of one friend [her uncle] and the imprudence of another [her aunt] had indeed been striking.—From being the first object of Hope and Solicitude of an Uncle who had formed her mind with the care of a Parent, and of Tenderness to an Aunt whose amiable temper had delighted to give her every indulgence, from being the Life and Spirit of a House, where all had been comfort and Elegance, and the expected Heiress of an easy Independence, she was become of importance to no one, a burden on those, whose affection she could not expect, an addition in an House, already overstocked. (135)

Austen's brother Edward Austen Knight seems to have moved among multiple family settings without much turmoil of record. Adoption in Austen's fiction instead regularly stages multiple "homes" as necessarily agonistic events. Fictional adoptees such as Fanny Price and Emma Watson wrestle with dislocations that are at the very least unsettling and at worst traumatic, effects that we

---

24. Austen, *Later Manuscripts,* 79–136. Subsequent references are by page number in the text. Laura Wade has recently adapted the story for the stage, with its premiere performance in Chichester in November 2018, directed by Samuel West.

86 CHAPTER 3

will also see in evidence in the Frank Churchill and Jane Fairfax repatriation narratives in *Emma*.

A rehearsal for the Fanny Price narrative, the earlier fragment, lightly revised on the fly, foregrounds Emma as a stranger, in repetitive draft language. At Emma's return, the social event that looms in the opening pages is of course a dance; Emma, reluctant, insists that "I am a stranger here" (85). The narrative doubles up birth family and local community in Emma's insistence that "you know they will all be strangers to me" (86), a prediction confirmed in the event: "They were therefore all but Strangers to her" (88). After the dance, withdrawn into the narrower family circle, the narrator underscores that "an absence of fourteen years had made all her Brothers and Sisters Strangers to Emma" (118). Robert, the visiting sibling who considers Emma a returned "weight" on the family, belabors the point: "You are quite the Stranger at home" (122).[25] Robert then helpfully observes that her long absence in kinship adoption by her uncle and aunt "must do away all natural affection among us" (123).

But Austen also launches a more experimental form of representation to register the adoptee Emma Watson as an estranged outsider. One of the most striking experiments in Austen's final fragment *Sanditon* (unfinished at her death) is the late and tantalizingly brief introduction of a mixed-race character with West Indian connections, Miss Lambe, who is described as "half mulatto."[26] In a rich contextualization of this fleeting moment in Austen, Sara Salih observes that Miss Lambe is Austen's "only 'brown' character," which overlooks the presentation of Emma Watson.[27] Before introducing an explicitly mixed-race character in *Sanditon,* Austen explored a related form of chromatism to separate out the adoptee Emma: "Emma Watson was not more than of the middle height—well made and plump, with an air of healthy vigour— Her skin was very brown, but clear, smooth and glowing" (95). Throughout Austen, complexions that deviate from an ideal of whiteness are most often markers of male class difference, signifying manual labor or military service, as in Sir Walter Eliot's fastidious disdain in *Persuasion* for "a certain Admiral Baldwin, the most deplorable looking personage you can imagine, his face the colour of mahogany, rough and rugged to the last degree."[28] That convention also appears in *The Watsons,* when a neighbor remarks that Emma, the

---

25. "You are *returned upon their hands* without a sixpence" (123; emphasis added). He is the one other character who uses this somatic idiom for care in Austen's fiction, with Mrs. Norris in *Mansfield Park* and Mrs. Jennings in *Sense and Sensibility.*

26. Austen, *Later Manuscripts,* 202.

27. Salih, "Silence of Miss Lambe," 329–53.

28. Austen, *Persuasion,* 22.

returning stranger, resembles her brother Sam, whose "complexion has been rather too much exposed to all weathers" (90). This introductory attention to a brown Emma is not a fleeting gesture, because the fragment continues to set Emma's appearance apart. Her unsisterly sister Margaret tries to sell Emma to a male who is circling all the Watson girls on the marriage market: "Did you ever see anything more perfectly beautiful? I think even *you* must be a convert to a brown complexion" (129). But he isn't buying: "Your Sister's complexion is as fine as a dark complexion can be, but I still profess my preference for a white skin" (129). Emma's visible darkness marks her difference as a repatriated adoptee.

The fragment *The Watsons* anticipates an emerging homology of difference in Austen marked by race, gender, and adoption. Whereas the prevailing chromatic discourse of complexion in Austen's time depended on visibility, Austen in *Mansfield Park* registers a figurative darkness of the female adoptee that renders her invisible. Returned from her adoptive home to her birth home, Fanny Price "sank down again on finding herself undistinguished in the dusk" (438). Fanny's brother William attempts to bring her to the notice of her biological father, but "it is so dark you do not see her" (439). In the completed novel, the invisibility of the darkened adoptee lines up with the "dead silence" that earlier unwelcomes Fanny's attempt to jump-start a conversation about slavery with her adoptive patron, the questionable caregiver of her charge and expense within the questionable patronage of Mansfield Park.

EMMA, ADOPTION, AND NARRATIVE FORM

Emma is a novel famous for its many puzzles, riddles, games, and conundrums, so I begin with an unremarked puzzle that dwells off the beaten track.[29] Late in the novel, Emma tries to figure out what hot piece of news Mr. Weston withholds, forcing her to wait to hear it from her old friend Mrs. Weston. Emma speculates that the news must have to do with the recent death of Mrs. Churchill at Richmond, the adoptive mother and aunt, by marriage, of Frank Churchill, whose birth father is Mr. Weston:

> Emma found that she must wait; and now it required little effort. She asked no more questions therefore, merely employed her own fancy, and that soon pointed out to her the probability of its being some money concern—some-

---

29. For an incisive reading of riddles in *Emma* as "local events of form" (44–47), see Ferguson, "Novel Comes of Age," 37–63.

thing just come to light, of a disagreeable nature in the circumstances of the family,—something which the late event at Richmond had brought forward. Her fancy was very active. Half a dozen natural children, perhaps—and poor Frank cut off![30]

Here's the puzzle: who is the imagined father of these imagined natural children? And why are natural children—bastards—suddenly at issue at this point in the novel? And why so many? A profligate tale-spinner who really should be a novelist, it's actually Emma who produces this superabundant set of illegitimate offspring, so paternity may be the wrong question.

As an adoption novel in full scale, *Emma* offers precisely such superabundance. Austen braids three adoption narratives throughout the book: the stories of Frank Churchill, a kinship adoptee; Jane Fairfax, an orphan under surrogate care; and Harriet Smith, a "natural child"—a bastard farmed out to the care of a boarding school. This unusual surplus gives redundancy signifying force: surrogate families rival consanguineous sets in the world of this novel. The untimely contingencies of adoptive families run unsettlingly counter to the constraints of the closed systems of blood kinship that underwrite identity and power in manifold ways in Austen's world. In this section I offer an argument that, at the level of form, adoption functions as a primary figure for the novel's own fiction-making procedures.

After an introductory review of the lexicon of adoption in the novel, I turn to the 2009 film of the novel by Jim O'Hanlon, from a screenplay by Sandy Welch, which vividly foregrounds the stakes of surrogate identity in the book. In both film and novel, narratives of adoptively abject women—Jane Fairfax and Harriet Smith—open the novel out to a wider human set of outsiders, strangers, and nonpersons in Highbury, including widows, old maids, and "gipsies." A kinship adoption, the Frank Churchill narrative supplies the primary thread connecting *Emma* to both the Edward Austen family narrative and the Fanny Price story in *Mansfield Park*. Collecting all these adoption narratives and characters, the famous Box Hill episode in the third volume casts the shadow of Rousseau over isomorphic forms of adoption and marriage in Austen's fiction. Both adoption and marriage in Austen's practice unsettle settled forms, tilting them off their foundations. I aim at this analogy: as adoption decenters the consanguineous family, so an Austen novel simultaneously embraces and turns its back on marriage.[31] To poach an idiom favored by

---

30. Austen, *Emma*, 429; subsequent references are by page number in the text.

31. For Austen's oppositional representations of marriage, see Walker, *Marriage, Writing, and Romanticism*.

NATURAL CHILDREN 89

Austen, in both structures—the biological family and marriage—the normative center both signifies and, crucially, does not signify.

Here, briefly, is the set of adoptive lexical anchors for the three adoption narratives in *Emma*. As in *Mansfield Park*, the noun "charge" signifies the de facto load of adoptive care in all three cases. At the death of Frank Weston's mother, his Churchill relatives "offered to take the whole charge of the little Frank" (14); the "natural child" Harriet Smith is boarded at Mrs. Goddard's school by "whoever may have had the charge of her" (66); and at the death of her parents, Jane Fairfax "became the property, the charge of" military friends of her father, the Campbells, who committed to "undertaking the whole charge of her education" (174). But like its larger roster of adoptive characters, the language of adoption in *Emma* also exceeds the adoptive lexicon of *Mansfield Park*. Harriet Smith is as close as Austen's novels ever get to the word "bastard," which she never uses in the published fiction, but twice the euphemism "natural daughter" is applied to Harriet (22; 64) and twice the problem of her status is tagged explicitly as "illegitimacy" (65; 526).[32] Just as Harriet Smith is one of the very few bastards in Austen's published fiction, Jane Fairfax is very nearly the only orphan, one of only two characters in the published fiction so identified (the other is the first of the two back-story Elizas in *Sense and Sensibility*): "Jane Fairfax was an orphan, the only child of Mrs. Bates's youngest daughter" (174).

Beyond the single use of "adopt" to signify surrogate care in *Mansfield Park*, only two other instances of de facto "adopt" occur in the published fiction, both in *Emma*. Early in the book, in the history of Mr. Weston (Frank's birth father), the narrator explains that "as to Frank, it was more than being tacitly brought up as his uncle's heir, it had become so avowed an adoption as to have him assume the name of Churchill on coming of age" (15). Late in the book, on Box Hill, in Austen's most eye-catching use of the term, Frank commissions Emma to create a wife for him, bringing Rousseau and the Sabrina Sidney narrative into the book: "Find somebody for me. I am in no hurry. Adopt her, educate her" (406). In a different gear, Austen also deploys an overdetermined topographical detail to signal the central place of adoption in the book. Emma's London relatives—her sister Isabella, her brother-in-law John Knightley, and their five children—live (where else?) in Brunswick Square, a location mentioned a dozen times, which was a new town development next to the Foundling Hospital and named after—who else?—Princess

---

32. The other "natural daughter" reference in Austen's fiction points to Colonel Brandon and "Miss Williams" in *Sense and Sensibility* (78).

90   CHAPTER 3

Caroline of Brunswick, the adoptive caregiver of Willy Austin, among her other performances.[33]

The novel scatters the narrative backstories of the three adoptions in multiple locations. The Frank Weston / Frank Churchill backstory comes early, in chapter 2; details about Harriet Smith emerge in a heated debate about her status between Emma and Mr. Knightley in the eighth chapter; the novel delays the Jane Fairfax backstory until the second chapter of the second volume. The 2009 film of *Emma,* directed by Jim O'Hanlon from a screenplay by Sandy Welch, dramatically rearranges these details to launch its narrative with an intense focus on adoption.[34] Instead of opening in lockstep with the novel's chronology (the marriage of Emma's governess Miss Taylor to the widower Mr. Weston), O'Hanlon and Welch foreground in their opening images a different set of very dark events—the deaths of three mothers—from the novel's various backstories, none of which is directly narrated in the novel: the death of Emma's mother, the death of Frank Weston's mother, and the death of Jane Fairfax's mother.

The film narrates these three opening moments as traumatic separations, starting with the death of Emma's mother. The film begins with a shot of a very young Emma Woodhouse beside her mother's coffin, her hand resting on its top. The warrant for such a surprising image is the book's opening focus on how Emma and her father grieve the death-by-marriage of Emma's governess and companion Miss Taylor, who is now Mrs. Weston. The film proposes that this grief replays the death of Emma's mother more than a dozen years earlier, which frames Emma as a maternal orphan in need of adoptive care and charge.[35] Fast on the heels of this foundational sorrow, the film cuts to an image of adoption from the book's backstory material. Mr. Weston is at the bedside of his dying wife; their young son Frank is at the door with his aunt, Mrs. Churchill, who will now, in the language of the novel, "take the whole charge of" Frank (14), who grows up not as Frank Weston but as Frank Churchill. These backstory events in the novel are geographically distant from Highbury, the dominant village setting of the book. While serving in the military in Yorkshire, the young Mr. Weston (a native of Highbury) married a local girl, Miss Churchill, and Yorkshire is where Frank grows up at his new adoptive home, Enscombe, the Churchill family seat. But the O'Hanlon/

---

33. See Kaplan, "Brunswick Square," 236–47.

34. O'Hanlon, *Emma.*

35. From the novel's second paragraph: "Her mother had died too long ago for her to have more than an indistinct remembrance of her caresses, and her place had been supplied by an excellent woman as governess [Miss Taylor], who had fallen little short of a mother in affection" (3).

Welch film locates the Frank Churchill adoption episode in Highbury itself, and these narrative rearrangements immediately yoke a bereaved childhood Emma and a bereaved childhood Frank. The effect of this pairing in the film is to subordinate the marriage plot that will soon entangle these adult characters to a prior and primary adoption plot. As Frank Weston disappears into the carriage in which he exits Highbury to take up his new identity as Frank Churchill, the camera frames his face staring through a rain-drenched window at his tearful father bidding him farewell, Frank's hand raised to steady himself as the carriage lurches forward a visual echo of the young Emma's hand on her mother's coffin.

Immediately following these images of the death of Emma's mother and the death of Frank Churchill's mother, the O'Hanlon/Welch film foregrounds a third piece of the novel's backstories, the death of Jane Fairfax's mother. The novel delays this narrative background until the second chapter of volume 2, when Colonel Campbell makes the offer "of undertaking the whole charge of her education" (175), which translates into a de facto adoption of the orphaned Jane from her Highbury kin, Miss Bates (her aunt) and Mrs. Bates (her grandmother). Once more the film frames an adopted child conveyed away from Highbury in a carriage, and Frank Weston and Jane Fairfax are now joined visually by the occasions and modes of their leave-takings. The O'Hanlon/Welch film delays the many complications of the novel's generically primary marriage plot to foreground an anterior set of traumatic adoption plots, teasing out a powerful but generically subordinated dynamic in the book. For these three bereaved children, their futures are immediately and urgently at stake. The contingencies of adoptive identity—not only its dire necessities but also its fragile possibilities—will fall upon them a second time as adults in the contingencies of marriage.

And what of Harriet Smith, the illegitimate child who is missing from the film's opening tally of dead mothers and children under surrogate care? Harriet Smith's unknown and entirely unreferenced mother is the most abjectly absent mother in the book, an outlier even from the film's set of maternal bereavements. What little information the novel later offers about Harriet's "parentage" is all about her father, which is the way the cards are played about bastards in Austen's culture. Like the history of Edward Austen, the tale of Frank Churchill's kinship adoption is a status tale of material good fortune. In the adoption narratives of Harriet Smith and Jane Fairfax, who both dwell precariously on social margins, Austen inflects the abjection of these two female adoptees as signposts of an even wider set of outsiders and outcasts.

Early in the book, the narrator introduces Harriet as "the natural daughter of somebody. Somebody had placed her, several years back, at Mrs. Goddard's school, and somebody had lately raised her from the condition of scholar to that of parlour-boarder. This was all that was generally known of her history" (22). Emma, a matchmaking machine, hopes to break up Harriet's wish to pair off with one of Mr. Knightley's tenant farmers, Robert Martin; she can do better, Emma asserts, but Mr. Knightley objects: "What are Harriet Smith's claims, either of birth, nature or education, to any connection higher than Robert Martin? She is the natural daughter of nobody knows whom, with probably no settled provision at all, and certainly no respectable relations" (64). Emma parries, echoing the legal language of Blackstone about illegitimacy as it circulated widely: "As to the circumstances of her birth, though in a legal sense she may be called a Nobody, it will not hold in common sense. She is not to pay for the offense of others, by being held below the level of those with whom she is brought up.—There can scarcely be a doubt that her father is a gentleman" (65–66). In Emma's view, the (conjectural) status of Harriet's father settles the question; Harriet's mother simply does not signify.

Harriet serves as a comic pinball in Emma's matchmaking schemes for the full course of the novel. After squelching Harriet's attraction to the tenant farmer Robert Martin, Emma tries to pair her off with the clergyman Mr. Elton and then with Frank Churchill, and then discovers to her dismay Harriet's infatuation with Mr. Knightley. But there is a limit to the novel's investment in Harriet's character; Emma regularly casts about for "the charm of an object to occupy the many vacancies of Harriet's mind" (197). At the end of the novel, Harriet needs a bad tooth tended to in London and dwells briefly in proximity to the many "natural children" gathered for decades at the Foundling Hospital; lodging for dental care with the Isabella Knightley family, "Harriet was safe in Brunswick Square" (492). In the book's final tally of the overarching marriage plot, Harriet lands safely with her first love, Robert Martin. The putative stability and certainty of marriage is enabled by the disclosure of her birth identity, but it is only a partial discovery: "Harriet's parentage became known. She proved to be the daughter of a tradesman, rich enough to afford her the comfortable maintenance which had ever been her's, and decent enough to have always wished for concealment" (526).

The apparent closure of this narrative moment instead marks a failure to close off the story of Harriet Smith, a refusal of the desired cultural return to the normative known. Knightley had earlier stigmatized "the mystery of her parentage" (68), and now her "parentage became known." But what kind of knowledge is produced? These two phrases from *Emma* are the only two instances in Austen's fiction of the word "parentage," and that word needs to give modern readers pause: it signified to Austen's readers not "parents" but

Natural Children

"the *rank* of the parents."[36] What is at issue in the term "parentage" is not biological genealogy but a cultural construct, which depended on the status of the father: whether Harriet's male biological parent is, as Emma earlier asserts, a "gentleman" (66) or, in this late version, a "tradesman" (526).[37] Harriet's mother remains entirely absent from this narrative, abjectly stigmatized; beyond the boundaries of the novel's end, her erasure invites its own untold story, open to Harriet's discovery or invention. Expressing relief at the apparent resolution by normative marriage of Harriet's story, Emma—emphatically not Austen—remains locked inside the biocentric system of patriarchal privilege: "—Such was the blood of gentility which Emma had formerly been so ready to vouch for!—It was likely to be as untainted, perhaps, as the blood of many a gentleman: but what a connexion had she been preparing for Mr. Knightley—or for the Churchills—or even for Mr. Elton!—The stain of illegitimacy, unbleached by nobility or wealth, would have been a stain indeed" (526). The tautological circle of the final sentence betrays the empty patriarchal values bracketed in its center.[38]

Harriet Smith's abjection is defined by her illegitimacy, which is a status category that in Romantic culture sweeps up both males and females, although the stigma plays out in very different gendered scripts. The abjection of the orphan Jane Fairfax, on the other hand, whose deceased parents are clearly known, is a function of gendered impoverishment. Her backstory early in volume 2 explains that the only capital she inherits from her military father, killed in action abroad, is a debt of military friendship. After the death of her mother from "consumption and grief" soon after her father, the three-year-old orphaned Jane first lives in de facto adoptive care with her maternal family—her grandmother Mrs. Bates and her aunt Miss Bates—who are themselves impoverished: "She belonged to Highbury." But then a devoted friend of her father, Colonel Campbell, returns to England with a daughter Jane's age:

> Before [Jane] was nine years old, his daughter's great fondness for her, and his own wish of being a real friend, united to produce an offer from Colonel Campbell of undertaking the whole charge of her education. It was accepted;

---

36. In Samuel Johnson's 1755 definition in his *Dictionary*, "parentage" is "extraction; birth; *condition with respect to the rank of parents*" (emphasis added). Although Johnson nominally includes both parents in the algorithm, the rank of the father would be the determinative fact in almost all such calculations.

37. In the 2020 film of *Emma* by Autumn de Wilde, Harriet's father is not only a "tradesman," as in the novel, but he is from Bristol and sells galoshes, and he is said to be coming to visit her.

38. It is a peculiar sentence in Austen in terms of diction: this is the only form of the word "bleach" in the published fiction, and "stain" only appears in a very few instances.

94 CHAPTER 3

and from that period Jane had belonged to Colonel Campbell's family, and had lived with them entirely, only visiting her grandmother from time to time. (175)

Jane's identity is a function of sequential "belongings," first to the genealogical home of her extended birth family and then to her adoptive family. Because there is no money to support her on the marriage market, either from her birth family or her adoptive family, Jane is prepped to be a governess: "The plan was that she should be brought up for educating others" (175).

What the novel terms Jane's "path of duty" looms as a grim prospect, however; the narrator frames it as the end to her life: "With the fortitude of a devoted noviciate, she had resolved at one-and-twenty to complete the sacrifice, and retire from all the pleasures of life, of rational intercourse, equal society, peace and hope, to penance and mortification for ever" (176). When Jane discourages the village busybody Mrs. Elton from attempting to find her a job, a remarkable conversation follows that defines the gendered abjection of this orphan adoptee—life as a governess—in terms of prostitution and slavery. Jane labors to brush away Mrs. Elton:

> "When I am quite determined as to the time, I am not at all afraid of being long unemployed. There are places in town, offices, where inquiry would soon produce something—Offices for the sale—not quite of human flesh—but of human intellect."
>
> "Oh! my dear, human flesh! You quite shock me; if you mean a fling at the slave-trade, I assure you Mr. Suckling was always rather a friend to the abolition."
>
> "I did not mean, I was not thinking of the slave-trade," replied Jane, "governess-trade, I assure you, was all that I had in view; widely different certainly as to the guilt of those who carry it on; but as to the greater misery of the victims, I do not know where it lies."[39] (325)

Anchored at this moment in the abjection of the adoptee Jane Fairfax, the calculus of the "misery of the victims" nets a wide set of characters who suffer precarious lives on the margins of the establishment culture that Highbury represents. Illegitimacy, orphanhood, and gender stack the deck against Harriet Smith and Jane Fairfax, who is at one point, like Harriet, a literal nonperson, a "nothing" (417). A vivid snapshot of a kindred set of outsiders occurs

---

39. The Cambridge editors in a note read Jane's language as a reference to prostitution rather than slavery.

when Harriet is waylaid by a band of begging "gipsies," "trampers" whom Emma quickly reports to the local magistrate, Mr. Knightley (of course), supplying "notice of there being such a set of people in the neighbourhood" (362).[40] In the relentless patter of Miss Bates, the novel offers glimpses of the bottom rungs of those tolerated in the neighborhood, such as her scattered account of "old John Abdy" who is now "bed-ridden" and needs "relief from the parish" (416).

Miss Bates and her mother Mrs. Bates are precariously close to those bottom rungs of the village population. Mrs. Bates is the aging widow of a parish vicar; Miss Bates is her older daughter, outrun for marriage by her younger sister, the deceased mother of Jane Fairfax. The stereotyped figure of the "old maid" in numerous marriage debates in the novel, Miss Bates is humiliated by Emma's clumsy attempt at humor in the Box Hill episode, prompting Knightley's sharp rebuke to Emma:

> How could you be so unfeeling to Miss Bates? How could you be so insolent in your wit to a woman of her character, age, and situation?—Emma, I had not thought it possible. . . . She is poor; she has sunk from the comforts she was born to; and, if she live to old age, must probably sink more. Her situation should secure your compassion. It was badly done, indeed! (407–8)[41]

These exchanges in the Box Hill episode—a day outing to a local sightseeing spot—highlight Knightley's patriarchal supervision of not only privileged Emma but the full microcosm that is Highbury, policing boundaries that exclude vagabond trampers but include, charitably, the unthreateningly vulnerable such as Miss Bates. Mr. Knightley holds the power to define and enforce what counts as belonging. The alien whose character Knightley is most suspicious of at Box Hill and throughout the novel is the adoptee Frank Churchill, precisely because, as adoptee, Frank once belonged by birth to Highbury but now belongs elsewhere, by adoption. He is no longer a native but now, threateningly, a stranger.

Before the narrative reveals their secret engagement near the end of the novel, the stories of both Frank Churchill and Jane Fairfax unfold, structurally, as repatriation adoption narratives, the form that Austen utilized in the *Watsons* fragment and in the final section of *Mansfield Park*. Neither character shows up in Highbury from their adoptive homes until the second of the nov-

---

40. "The gipsies did not wait for the operation of justice; they took themselves off in a hurry" (364).

41. Emma is in turn humiliated: "Never had she felt so agitated, mortified, grieved, at any circumstance in her life. She was most forcibly struck" (409); see Fraiman, *Unbecoming Women*.

el's three volumes. Frank's much-anticipated return to his birth father's home village becomes a running joke throughout the first volume: "He was looked on as sufficiently belonging to the place to make his merits and prospects a kind of common concern. Mr. Frank Churchill was one of the boasts of Highbury, and a lively curiosity to see him prevailed, though the compliment was so little returned that he had never been there in his life. His coming to visit his father had been often talked of but never achieved" (15–16). The opening sentence of the final chapter of volume 1 is flatly and drily anticlimactic: "Mr. Frank Churchill did not come" (155). The first repatriated adoptee is instead, surrogately, Jane Fairfax, whose forthcoming is announced in the second chapter of volume 2: "Certain it was that she was to come; and that Highbury, instead of welcoming that perfect novelty which had been so long promised it—Mr. Frank Churchill—must put up for the present with Jane Fairfax, who could bring only the freshness of a two years absence" (177). In Highbury, surrogate substitutions are always less than the real thing.

Like the treatment of Emma Watson's prior adoptive life in *The Watsons*, *Emma* supplies details of the adoptive families of Jane Fairfax and Frank Churchill in distanced and fragmented backstories. Their foregrounded adoption narratives instead supply their repatriated experiences of a community, Highbury, where biological ties define them as novel objects of fantasy and as secretive and suspicious outsiders. The two sets of adoptive parents in the backstories appear in sharp contrast. The narrator sketches the Campbells as exemplary caregivers for Jane: "She had fallen into good hands, known nothing but kindness from the Campbells, and had been given an excellent education" (175). There is actually very little said about the Campbells, and all of it is honorific, except for Emma's eagerness to invent a romantic rivalry for Mr. Dixon between Jane Fairfax and her adoptive Campbell sister. The Churchills, on the other hand, and especially Mrs. Churchill, present a threat, framed in a pejorative portrait of adoption as a suspicious elsewhere from the biocentric viewpoint of insular Highbury.

Echoing the Edward Austen family history, the wealthy Churchills at their Enscombe estate in distant Yorkshire, "having no children of their own, nor any other young creature of equal kindred to care for" (14), undertake the charge and care of their three-year-old nephew Frank Churchill as heir, a de facto adoption that, again like the Edward Austen history, unfolds by degrees: "As to Frank, it was more than being tacitly brought up as his uncle's heir, it had become so avowed an adoption as to have him assume the name of Churchill on coming of age" (15). The major difference between Frank's tale and the Edward Austen history is that the Frank Churchill adoption is occasioned by the death of Frank's mother, which groups him in the book adop-

NATURAL CHILDREN

tively—as foregrounded in the 2009 O'Hanlon film—as a maternal orphan with Jane Fairfax and Emma herself.[42]

In the Frank Churchill adoption, the novel splits open a spatial divide between biocentric identity and adoptive identity. Of Highbury and its biocentric claim on him, Frank "had never been there in his life" (16). Mr. Weston, Frank's biological father, reveals of Frank's adoptive home at Enscombe that he has "never been at the place in my life" (130).[43] This spatial divorce is undergirded by a bedrock biocentric suspicion of adoption, most starkly expressed by Emma's sister Isabella Knightley, a Highbury native who has ironically removed to a London address within shouting distance of the Foundling Hospital: "There is something so shocking in a child's being taken away from his parents and his natural home! I never can comprehend how Mr. Weston could part with him. To give up one's child! I really never could think well of any body who proposed such a thing to any body else" (104). Who were the agents of this adoptive mess? From the point of view of Highbury, all are punished.

This Highburian stigmatization of adoption as a disruptive threat to biocentric order discharges itself most energetically in a barrage of slights and insults directed at the absent figure of Frank's adoptive mother, Mrs. Churchill. Everything is gossip and rumor, and there is a great deal of such second-hand opinion. The abuse begins quietly in the second chapter—she is "a capricious woman"—but at the Christmas Eve dinner at the Weston home near the end of the first volume, the hosts and guests unload on her, in the wake of the news that Frank's promised visit to Highbury is not going to happen. Mr. Weston observes that Mrs. Churchill "has no more heart than a stone to people in general, and the devil of a temper" (130). Emma picks up the tune; Frank's visit "seems to depend upon nothing but the ill-humour of Mrs. Churchill, which I imagine to be the most certain thing in the world" (131), a point endorsed by the new Mrs. Weston: "Mrs. Churchill rules at Enscombe, and is a very odd-tempered woman" (131). Mrs. Weston then frames the issue of Frank as adoptee as a contest for possession between adoptive parents and birth relatives: "I am still afraid that some excuse may be found for disappointing us. I cannot bear to imagine any reluctance on his side; but I am sure there is a great wish on the Churchills' to keep him to themselves. There is jealousy. They are jealous even of his regard for his father" (132). In the second

---

42. In the adoptive backstory, Emma Watson in *The Watsons* was also adopted by her aunt at the death of her mother. The invisible and absent mother of Harriet Smith in *Emma* recalls the iconographical construction of the Edward Austen adoption, where Austen's mother is erased in the silhouette narrating her son's passage into adoptive care.

43. "He saw his son every year in London, and was proud of him" (15).

volume, Mr. Weston doubles down on Mrs. Churchill's outsider status. She is not only, illegitimately, a mother only by adoption, but she is not even a blood relative in the kinship adoption (Frank's biological relative is Mr. Churchill): "Her pride is arrogance and insolence! And what inclines one less to bear, she has no fair pretense of family or blood. She was nobody when he married her, barely the daughter of a gentleman; but ever since her being turned into a Churchill she has out-Churchill'd them all in high and mighty claims" (335). The "nobody" in this sentence lines up Mrs. Churchill, an adoptive mother, with the bastard Harriet Smith and the orphaned Jane Fairfax, soon to become a governess. In the world of Highbury, (legitimate) blood rules. Although his biological father lives there, Frank Churchill no longer belongs.

Mr. Knightley makes his disdain for Frank abundantly clear in a remarkable exchange in the final chapter of volume 1, where Emma and Mr. Knightley stage an extended and heated debate about Frank's character as an adoptee. Almost all the evidence is secondhand: neither Emma nor Mr. Knightley has ever met Frank or his adoptive family. As they discuss the news that Frank is unable to come to Highbury as promised, the topic of disagreement becomes what an adopted son owes his adopted family versus what he owes his birth father and his birth father's new wife. Mr. Knightley is vehemently prejudiced against Frank, whom he blasts as "a chattering coxcomb," "the most insufferable fellow breathing," and a "puppy"—"his letters disgust me" (161–62). In his summation, Mr. Knightley insists that Frank reject the claims of his adoptive family to honor his biological roots: "It is Frank Churchill's duty to pay attention to his father" (157). Against her instincts, and to give Mr. Knightley an oppositional run for his money, Emma finds herself arguing the case for the adoptive Churchill family, defending "all their claims on his gratitude and regard . . . those, whom as child and boy he has been looking up to all his life" (159). This brief remark is the single moment in the novel when the Frank Churchill adoption does not appear pejoratively, but it is undercut by an aside: "To her great amusement, [Emma] perceived that she was taking the other side of the question from her real opinion" (156). Mr. Knightley's rule goes without real challenge; he erases Mrs. Churchill's identity as an adoptive mother by replacing her with Frank's birth father's new wife in Highbury, the second Mrs. Weston, who is now "standing in a mother's place" (160). By following the wishes of his adoptive mother in Enscombe, Frank, bewildered adoptee, has offended this new mother—his third—in the guarded precincts of Highbury.

I make no claim that Mrs. Churchill is in fact warmhearted and worthy of a forgiving hug; all the book's testimony is otherwise. My claim is that these secondhand reports of her character both exhibit and take advantage of the

Natural Children

culture's deep-seated suspicion of adoption to stigmatize her. Similarly, the novel again and again gives Frank the Knightley treatment, especially on the score of his secretiveness and fondness for mystery. In notably early anticipation of Mike Leigh's 1996 adoption film *Secrets & Lies,* Mr. Weston frames in just such terms his biological son Frank's adoptive family, the Churchills: "There are secrets in all families, you know" (129).[44] Adoption violates the norms of Highbury by trafficking in rewritten truths and, at an extreme, invented truths, which according to Highbury rules are by definition untruths. Frank generates numerous minor-key secrets, such as the mysterious delivery of a pianoforte for Jane Fairfax at the Bates home. But much of the plot of *Emma* rests upon a large secret about marriage between the two adoptees; the big reveal comes late in the third volume, the "secret engagement" (476) between Frank and Jane Fairfax. Mrs. Weston, distressed, pulls back the curtain for Emma: "There has been a solemn engagement between them ever since October—formed at Weymouth, and kept a secret from everybody . . . engaged since October,—secretly engaged.—It has hurt me, Emma, very much. It has hurt his father equally" (430–31). Mrs. Weston and Emma immediately condemn what Mrs. Weston labels "a system of secresy and concealment" (434), and what Emma quickly shuns as "a system of hypocrisy and deceit" (435). Divorced from these deep-rooted prejudices of Highbury, the novel as a whole risks the surmise that another name for such a system of contingency and invention is adoption, an engine of fiction-making.

Frank's suspiciously erratic behavior comes to a head in the Box Hill episode in the final volume, where, strikingly, Austen pairs the marriage plot driving the novel with adoption: Frank Churchill commissions Emma to find him a wife by adopting her. In the wake of Emma's embarrassing remark at the expense of Miss Bates, this verbal match immediately follows another awkward exchange between Frank and Jane Fairfax, the code of which is still hidden from the rest of the party because of their secret engagement:

> [Frank] made no answer [to Jane]; merely looked, and bowed in submission; and soon afterwards said, in a lively tone,
>
> "Well, I have so little confidence in my own judgment, that whenever I marry, I hope somebody will choose my wife for me. Will you? (turning to Emma). Will you choose a wife for me?—I am sure I should like any body fixed on by you. You provide for the family, you know (with a smile at his father). Find somebody for me. I am in no hurry. Adopt her, educate her."

---

44. Leigh, *Secrets & Lies;* for an incisive critique of the much-awarded film's representation of race and transculturalism in the context of adoption, see McLeod, *Life Lines,* 44–57.

100   CHAPTER 3

> "And make her like myself."
>
> "By all means, if you can."
>
> "Very well. I undertake the commission. You shall have a charming wife."
>
> "She must be very lively, and have hazle eyes. I care for nothing else. I shall go abroad for a couple of years—and when I return, I shall come to you for my wife. Remember." (406)

In this scene, Austen rings changes on one of the most infamous episodes in Romantic-period adoption history, when in 1769 Thomas Day, after ingesting far too much Rousseau on how to raise children, adopted two teenaged orphan girls from branches of the Foundling Hospital and took them to France to see which would turn out to be the better wife.[45] Austen knew this story, if not at first hand, then in a surrogate form, in Maria Edgeworth's 1801 novel *Belinda,* which Austen calls out for praise in *Northanger Abbey.*[46] In *Belinda,* Day's bizarre experiment is fictionalized as the subplot of Clarence Hervey; after reading "the works of Rousseau," Hervey "formed the romantic project of educating a wife for himself."[47] In *Belinda,* Hervey's project concludes with a happy ending. For the children of history, Day's experiment issued in a long train of unsettled consequences for the adoptee Sabrina Sidney, as I track in the final paragraphs of chapter 1.

Austen achieves two effects in this Box Hill moment, one thematic and one structural and narrative. Frank's antic behavior registers how British culture stigmatized adoption as suspiciously French, as the legacy of Rousseau and his English acolytes such as Thomas Day. Claudia Johnson supplies an important account of how the novel frames Frank as French, as un-English; for example, Knightley attacks Frank in these terms to Emma: "Your amiable young man can be amiable only in French, not in English" (160).[48] While Emma builds him a wife by adoption, Frank declares "I shall go abroad," which, post-Waterloo, is code for France. But Edgeworth had already performed a Francophobe dance on the heads of Rousseau and Day in *Belinda.* Austen

---

45. Moore, *Perfect Wife*; and Uglow, *Lunar Men,* 185–88.

46. On the day of publication of *Emma* in December 1815, Austen requested that her publisher John Murray send a presentation copy to Edgeworth; Le Faye, *Chronology,* 525.

47. Edgeworth, *Belinda,* 362. Clarence Hervey cares for a "deserted child," Virginia, as a guardian; her birth father is discovered as a gentleman listening to the "singing at the Asylum for children, in St. George's Fields." "It occurred to Clarence, that the gentleman might probably visit the Foundling Hospital" (392–93). Virginia feels herself a "deserted child" (409); but her hope is in "the belief in what the French call *la force du sang*" (409). Virginia is reunited with her father, Mr. Hartley, who has made his fortune in the West Indies; Clarence Hervey is now free to marry Belinda.

48. Johnson, *Equivocal Beings,* 191–203.

NATURAL CHILDREN 101

goes Edgeworth one better and simultaneously works a more complex narrative game, in which she leverages the contingency and fictiveness of adoption (which are otherwise bad French habits) to destabilize hegemonic marriage culture. Within the generic form of a marriage novel, Frank Churchill's antics at Box Hill erase the boundary between adoption and marriage. Austen twins marriage and adoption as isomorphic forms of contingent human action.[49]

Austen exploits this identity of form to tilt marriage culture off its throne in the famous final sentence of the novel. Those final words of the novel snap the generic marriage plot to an apparently happy close: "the perfect happiness of the union" (528). But there is a disruptive adoption plot lurking in that benediction. The celebrated union is, narrowly, the marriage of Emma Woodhouse and George Knightley. But the signifier "union" escapes this single reference. During the hurry of publication, Austen was anxiously persuaded to dedicate the novel to an interested reader, the prince regent—the head of state of the union of England, Wales, Scotland, and Ireland, since 1801 the United Kingdom.[50] The layers of Austen's style risk a curse that refuses the closure of that final blessing: hovering over the final phrase of the novel is the perfect unhappiness of the broken union between the prince regent and Princess Caroline, who when the novel was published was larking it about in Italy with her adulterous lover Count Pergami and her adopted child William Austin. At Box Hill, Mr. Weston launches a game, asking what two letters of the alphabet "express perfection." His own answer is "M" and "A" (Em-ma), to which, ironically, Knightley sourly objects: "*Perfection* should not have come quite so soon" (404). "Perfect," etymologically, signifies finished and closed—fully realized and complete. At the end of *Emma*, the marriage plot seems to snap to a perfected close, but the twinned adoption plot insists instead that marriages, like adoptive lives, are radically open-ended and contingent.[51]

Contingency and fictiveness are forms of Churchillian adoptive performativity that are most offensive to Mr. Knightley. Among its general condemnation in Highbury, the most high-handed verdict about Frank's secretive behavior comes from Mr. Knightley, as he annotates Frank's epistolary attempt to explain his secret engagement: "Mystery; Finesse—how they pervert the

---

49. Compare the opening verses of "Ode on a Grecian Urn" (1819), where John Keats pairs marriage and adoption as figural and grammatical appositives for an artifact: "Thou still unravished *bride* of quietness, / Thou *foster-child* of silence and slow time"; Keats, *Poetry and Prose*, 461.

50. For a useful map of Austen's take on the prince regent, see Murray, "Portraits," 132–44.

51. Austen performs the same ploy with "perfect" in the final sentence of *Mansfield Park*, which also undermines "patronage": the place "soon grew as dear to her heart, and as thoroughly perfect in her eyes, as every thing else, within the view and patronage of Mansfield Park" (432).

understanding! My Emma, does not every thing serve to prove more and more the beauty of truth and sincerity in all our dealings with each other?" (486). Emma then dutifully sings from this proper Highbury hymnal: "Oh! if you knew how much I love every thing that is decided and open!" (502).[52] As a different Austen narrator remarks of Anne Elliot on a beneficent mission in Austen's next novel, *Persuasion,* these late-breaking maxims in *Emma* are "almost enough to spread purification and perfume all the way."[53]

The manifest irony is that, as praiseworthy as they may be, these high standards of truth, sincerity, decidedness, openness, and transparency would slam the brakes on the production of the very text in which they emerge, belatedly, as ideals. Emma Woodhouse loves nothing more than a good undecided opportunity for open-ended fiction-making, for concocting stories, for making stuff up: perhaps Harriet Smith (perhaps a gentleman's daughter?) is a good match for Mr. Elton? or perhaps for Frank Churchill? perhaps Jane Fairfax nurses a flame for Mr. Dixon, who has just married Jane's adoptive sibling, the daughter of Colonel and Mrs. Campbell? perhaps that pianoforte that mysteriously appears comes from Mr. Dixon? The many concocted secrets of the many puzzles, charades, conundrums, and games in *Emma* all have final solutions, ultimately, but the spark of their energy and life, in spite of Mr. Knightley's dictum, dwells in the undecided mystery and finesse that suspend the closure of solutions.[54]

Which returns us at close to the puzzle of the "half-dozen natural children" conceived in Emma's fancy late in the novel. Again, the moment follows the Box Hill episode and the subsequent news that Mrs. Churchill, Frank Churchill's adoptive mother, has suddenly died, the consequences of which (not unhappy) event Emma immediately tries to puzzle out. Mr. Weston appears at her door, summoning her to the Weston household to hear a mysterious piece of news, which Emma chews upon: "Her fancy was very active. Half a dozen natural children, perhaps—and poor Frank cut off!" (429). One of the jokes here is that this fanciful surplus is already at play in the novel, in its superabundance of adoption tales. But the question that gives pause is this: in Emma's fancy, who is the father of these six bastards?—and never mind the mother or mothers, who simply do not count in the world of Highbury. In her study of illegitimacy in the eighteenth-century novel, Lisa Zunshine

---

52. By "open," Emma means "transparent," not "open-ended."

53. Austen, *Persuasion,* 208.

54. One year after the publication of *Emma,* John Keats famously theorized the alternative to Mr. Knightley's proscriptions as a quality Keats calls "negative capability," when a human "is capable of being in uncertainties, mysteries, doubts, without any irritable reaching after fact and reason"; Keats, *Poetry and Prose,* 109.

NATURAL CHILDREN 103

adopts Mr. Knightley's take on Frank and assumes that these dream-children must be progeny of that coxcomb puppy Frank Churchill; this sentence offers "the tragicomic vision of Frank Churchill's fending off the demands of his former mistresses and their bastard children."[55] Perhaps, as Emma says. But might not these abundant fantasy bastards instead be tallied in Emma's fancy not to young Frank but to the elder Mr. Churchill, who after the death of Mrs. Churchill would now be free from her formidable yoke to spend his fortune (it's his family fortune, not hers) on his secret progeny, at the inheritance expense (in Emma's fearful fantasy) of the adopted child ("poor Frank cut off!")? Apart from Zunshine, I can find no edition of this endlessly annotated novel that comments on this sentence. Those six "natural children" are shelved in narrative storage like a set of unclaimed frozen embryos.

The temptation to adjudicate this question of biological origins invites the reader to take a spin in Emma's lively narrative machine. Emma's fancy breeds fancy, and a perfect solution to the puzzle is precisely beside the point. However, the content of Emma's fanciful question ("Half a dozen natural children, perhaps?") points precisely to the ways in which figures of abandoned, orphaned, illegitimate, and surrogate children sponsor the cultural work of narrative itself. *Emma* offers a remarkable oversupply of primary adoption narratives, the cases of Harriet Smith, Jane Fairfax, and Frank Churchill—and even Emma herself, maternal orphan, as the O'Hanlon film reminds us. This redundancy has a generalizing force which suggests that all the narratives in the book begin to look like adoption tales. At the level of form, surrogacy operates in the novel as a figure for the novel's own fiction-making procedures. In *Emma* especially, surrogacy bids to be a groundwork figure for the profligate artifice and contingency—the narrativity and the inventedness— of human social action, including marriage, the care and charge of children, and the making of novels. To adopt yet another argument from narratological models in disability studies, I borrow one more sentence from Mitchell and Snyder's *Narrative Prosthesis*: "Disability's representational 'fate' is tethered to inciting the act of meaning-making itself" (6). Adoption incites just such meaning-making in *Emma*.

In 1801, in Maria Edgeworth's "Advertisement" to *Belinda,* her book that gave birth to a fictional account of Thomas Day's scheme to create a wife by adopting an orphan (or two), Edgeworth drew a boundary between "novels" and "moral tales" in figurative terms of legitimacy, illegitimacy, and adoption. Edgeworth wishes she could "adopt the name of novel" for her book, but

---

55. Zunshine, *Bastards and Foundlings,* 153.

104 CHAPTER 3

too many novels offer only illegitimate trash.[56] Thus, "the following work is offered to the public as a Moral Tale—the author not wishing to acknowledge a Novel." In Edgeworth's account, the novel as form is profligately illegitimate, an unacknowledged bastard, a "natural child" like those many unleashed in the superabundant adoption fictions of *Emma*.

---

56. Austen's famous defense of the novel as form in *Northanger Abbey* occurs in a passage that cites *Belinda*: "If a rainy morning deprived them of other enjoyments, they were still resolute in meeting in defiance of wet and dirt, and shut themselves up, to read novels together. Yes, novels;—for I will not adopt that ungenerous and impolitic custom so common with novel-writers, of degrading by their contemptuous censure the very performances, to the number of which they are themselves adding. . . . 'Oh! it is only a novel!' replies the young lady; while she lays down her book with affected indifference, or momentary shame.—'It is only Cecilia, or Camilla, or Belinda;' or, in short, only some work in which the greatest powers of the mind are displayed, in which the most thorough knowledge of human nature, the happiest delineation of its varieties, the liveliest effusions of wit and humour, are conveyed to the world in the best-chosen language"; Austen, *Northanger Abbey*, 30–31.

CHAPTER 4

Abandoned Children
Mary Shelley, Rousseau, and *Frankenstein*

When the Queen Caroline affair heated up in London in the summer of 1820, Mary Shelley kept a keen eye on English turmoil from Italy, the scene of Caroline's most recent troubles. When Shelley faced the prospect of returning to England in 1823 as a widow with her only surviving biological child and her own history of scandal, she compared herself pointedly to Caroline. Repatriated, both would be either shunned or embraced by rival segments of English society. Writing from Genoa to Thomas Jefferson Hogg in February 1823, Shelley feared that she might be forced to relinquish her child, to give up "the charge of my infant": "If I go to England will they not try to force him from me?" These villains "of rank," who dwell in the "mansions of the rich," included most perilously her late husband's father, Sir Timothy Shelley, who refused to meet her for the rest of his life:

> They will of course be much more prejudiced against me than they are, if I, unprotected, young & tireless, reside abroad—out of their English pale—the sanctuary of virtue & propriety—They will look on me indeed as a black-black sheep if I do not hasten to place myself beneath all the benefits of their clouded atmosphere & foggy virtue—I shall be *da paragonare* with the Queen alone.[1]

---

1. Shelley, *Letters*, I.318. Subsequent references are by volume and page number in the text.

• 105 •

Two years after the 1821 death of Queen Caroline, Shelley envisioned herself attacked in exactly the way dominant English culture ruled that Caroline's haphazard family ways rebelled far beyond its bionormative pale.

Shelley returned to England in September 1823, accompanied by her two-year-old son Percy and two published novels, and she lived and wrote there for the remainder of her life. In this chapter, I focus on several stages of Shelley's post-1823 life in England. The first takes up the early days of her return from the Continent, when for a year she and her toddler child lived only a few streets north of the London Foundling Hospital, where mothers and babies were cast apart institutionally, while Shelley navigated a custody struggle over her son with her late husband's father. In the second, I turn to Shelley's 1831 edition of *Frankenstein* and her most extensive alteration to the 1818 text, in which Elizabeth Lavenza, who is an adopted blood relative of Victor Franken-stein in 1818, becomes in 1831 a twice-abandoned and twice-adopted stranger taken into the Frankenstein family. In the new introduction to the 1831 edition, Shelley also draws attention to her own experience of abandonment by her London family during her youth. In 1838 Shelley published a biography of Rousseau among a set of French lives she wrote for Dionysius Lardner's *Cabinet Cyclopedia,* and in the next section I take up her blistering attack on Rousseau and his abandonment of his five children. The final section previews in Shelley's post-1823 English life the last two chapters in this book, where Shelley was shunned by one adoptive family but welcomed by another. Back in England, Shelley was ostracized by the socially climbing third wife of Basil Montagu, the bastard father of the maternal orphan Basil Caroline Montagu, the child of multiple adoptive caregivers who in the next chapter flails haplessly in the laboratory of the Romantic child. But in the same years Shelley was welcomed by old friends from her Godwinian childhood, Charles and Mary Lamb, siblings who when she returned to England had undertaken the adoptive care of a Cambridge orphan, Emma Isola, whose adopted life detailed in the final chapter became an instrumental part of Shelley's own untimely life back in England. The chapter closes with a genealogical glimpse of Shelley's only grandchild, who was the adopted daughter of her only surviving child, a child whom Shelley refused to abandon to surrogate care.

SPELDHURST STREET, BRUNSWICK SQUARE, 1823–1824

Mary Shelley and her toddler Percy ("Persino"), who as yet spoke no English, arrived in London from Paris on August 25, 1823, met by her father William Godwin and her half brother William Godwin—who, like his contemporary

William Austin, had been enrolled at Dr. Burney's school in Greenwich.[2] For two weeks, they lodged with Godwin's family in the Strand, before moving on September 8 to where Shelley "secured neat cheap lodgings" at "14 Speldhurst Street, Brunswick Square," which is the address she used to head all of her surviving letters for the next ten months. Brunswick Square was a signature feature of the London Foundling Hospital's land development scheme in the 1790s, immediately adjacent to the west of the hospital grounds; it was named to celebrate the new Princess of Wales, Caroline of Brunswick, at her 1795 marriage. Speldhurst Street (now Hastings Street) ran just a few blocks north of this landscaped signpost of royal bloodlines that defined the neighborhood, now two years after the burial in Brunswick of Queen Caroline, whose only surviving legatee, the biological child of London laborers, passed as her adopted son.

In the shadow of an institution filled with children separated from their mothers, Shelley, a widowed single mother, now battled for the custody of her sole surviving child. A fictional resident of Brunswick Square in Austen's *Emma*, Isabella Knightley pronounced this verdict about child abandonment in 1815: "There is something so shocking in a child's being taken away from his parents and natural home! . . . To give up one's child! I really never could think well of any body who proposed such a thing to any body else."[3] In the wake of his son's drowning in 1822, Sir Timothy Shelley proposed just such a thing to Mary Shelley in Italy, as a condition of miserly financial support for both child and mother. In the early months of 1823 in Italy, Shelley consulted with Lord Byron and other friends about Sir Timothy's conditions, which she summarized in a letter to Thomas Jefferson Hogg on February 28: "As for my boy, if I bring him to England, and will place him under the care of such a person as he will approve, he will afford him a suitable, tho' limited maintenance" (I.31). What Shelley omitted in this account is that her own precarious financial future also depended on these hard terms, since her own father was on the brink of bankruptcy. Two features of Sir Timothy's demands were

---

2. The younger Godwin, born in 1803, was a year younger than Austin, and Shelley saw much of her half brother after her return to London. His time at Greenwich just missed overlapping with Austin; in his 1835 memoir of his son, Godwin notes that he removed William from Charterhouse and enrolled him at Dr. Burney's school in "September 1814," which is when Princess Caroline began her self-exile on the Continent, with William Austin in tow. The younger Godwin remained at Dr. Burney's school through 1817 (where he likely heard tales of the odd royal); soon after his death in 1832, his father published his son's novel *Transfusion; or the Orphans of Uberwalden, by the Late William Godwin Jun with a Memoir of his Life and Writings by his Father* (1835). For a reading of this novel as endorsing genetic determinism, see Turner, *Romantic Childhood*.

3. Austen, *Emma*, 104.

108   CHAPTER 4

especially offensive. First was the condition that Percy Florence be returned to England, a prospect that deeply distressed Shelley in her Italian exile. But far worse was the condition that her son would not be taken into the charge and care of Sir Timothy and Lady Shelley (his paternal grandparents) but would be farmed out to surrogate care. In the words of Sir Timothy's offer, which Shelley recorded in her journal, "As to the child, I am inclined to afford the means of a suitable protection and care of him in this country, if he shall be placed with a person I shall approve."[4] As Shelley wrote to Byron, Sir Timothy's language revealed "by what mean principles he would be actuated—he does not offer him an asylum in his own house, but a beggarly provision under the care of a stranger" (I.314).

Shelley was adamant that she would not relinquish Percy to any form of surrogate care: "I would not part with him . . . I should not live ten days separated from him . . . he is my all. My other children I have lost . . . I could not live a day without my boy" (I.315–17). But in addition to this fierce maternal attachment, Shelley was alarmed by the price her own reputation might pay. Already stigmatized by the English "sanctuary of virtue and propriety" on the basis of improprieties attributed to her circle during the past decade, Shelley feared that if she were to yield to Sir Timothy's demands, she would confess herself unfit to be a mother: "I lose all—all honourable station & name when I admit that I am not a fitting person to take care of my infant." Her defiance was absolute: "What! Shall I proclaim myself unworthy to have the care of my boy? Never" (I.318). By the summer of 1823, she concluded that her only way forward was to return to England with Percy to continue to struggle with Sir Timothy for financial support. Her motive took the form of the modern adoption standard of "best interests" of the child, as she noted in her journal: "The idea of our Child's advantage alone enables me to keep fixed in my resolution to return. It is best for him—& I go" (462).

Shelley's long grief for four deceased children and her drowned husband found no relief in an alien London in October: "All is so desolate—Streets, mud—cockneyism—ballad singers—cries—hackney coaches—lodgeings— cheerless solitude—what a compound! Let me turn from it." Writing to Hogg, she confessed "the extreme melancholy that oppresses me—What can I do? Nothing that I wish—all is against the grain with me—hopeless—spiritless—I cannot write—I can hardly read—I feel degraded" (I.395). While she negotiated with Sir Timothy's agent for funds simply to survive, she refused to yield to the pressure to surrender the care and charge of Percy to the "beggarly provision" of a stranger chosen by the stranger who was his grandfather. When she passed by the walls of the Foundling Hospital on her daily walks to and

---

4. Shelley, *Journals,* 453–54. Subsequent references are by page number in the text.

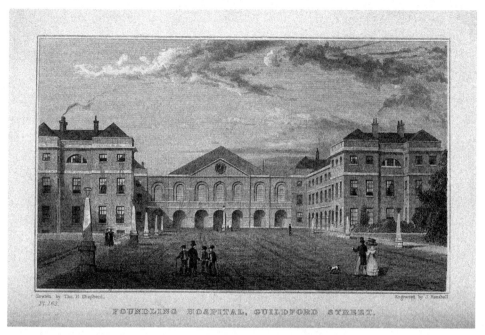

FIGURE 3. London Foundling Hospital, 1816. Used with permission of Wellcome Trust.

from the Strand and Holborn (figure 3), she could recall from her 1817 reading of Rousseau's *Confessions* how the Hôpital des Enfants-Trouvés in Paris spared the author of a child-raising guide the troublesome burden of his own children.

In the words of her bitter attack on Rousseau's "criminal example" in 1838: "Five of his children were thus sent to a receptacle where few survive; and those who do go through life brutified by their situation, or depressed by the burden, ever weighing at the heart, that they have not inherited the commonest right of humanity, a parent's care."[5] As she clung to her resolve to supply a mother's care for her sole remaining biological child, the misery of broken and dispersed families supplied the bass note of her daily life, as recorded in her journal: "I do not remember ever having been so completely miserable as I am tonight" (477). Spatially and institutionally, her dominant metaphor for her repatriated life was a prison: "Imprisoned in my centinel's box . . . I cannot—cannot live here. Of what use am I? confined in my prison-room—friendless" (473–76). Beyond her Speldhurst Street rooms, "I am imprisoned in a dreary town" (471). The entire country and its vile weather supplied shackles and

---

5. Shelley, "Rousseau," II.131. See note 20 for a modern critical edition.

manacles: "I detest England more & more—its fogs rains & wind are bolts bars and high walls" (397).

Yet Shelley's life in the ten months she cared for Percy near the institutional walls of the Foundling Hospital was by no measure solitary, as she tested the waters of old and new friendships and connections: "In this prison it is only in human intercourse that I can pretend to find consolation" (471). Like Frankenstein's creature longing for social life, "sometimes I get among friends & almost forget" (403). Only a few days back in London, Shelley met Charles Lamb again at her father's house, and Lamb and his sister Mary in their new digs in Islington became a welcome port of call. As she launched plans to publish a volume of her husband's posthumous poems, she met a new friend, the poet Bryan Waller Procter, who helped organize funds to publish the new book, much to the displeasure of Sir Timothy, who had the book suppressed. Evenings at the opera and theater offered relished relief, as did musical evenings at the home of a reacquainted friend, the Italian musician Vincent Novello. A special connection with her Italian past was her widowed friend Jane Williams, who after the deaths of their spouses had earlier returned to London and now lived in Kentish Town, where Shelley and Percy moved in the summer of 1824. But for much of the time she found relief from her life as a widowed single mother in simple motion: "In the mean time I enjoy (when it does not rain) all I can of the country, by help of prodigious walks—Ye Gods—how I walk!" (473)

During her first year back in England, Shelley quickly discovered to her pleasure how well *Frankenstein* had fared since publication in 1818, an offspring that in less than a decade she would describe as her "hideous progeny." In her first surviving letter from Speldhurst Street, giving an account to Leigh Hunt in Italy of "my 16 days in London," she echoed Byron: "But lo & behold! I found myself famous! Frankenstein had prodigious success as a drama. . . . On Friday Aug. 29th Jane My father William & I went to the theatre to see it" (I.378).[6] To capitalize on this stage success, her father published a new two-volume edition of the 1818 three-volume *Frankenstein*. In the spring of 1824, Shelley learned that George Canning, a prominent government minister, had praised *Frankenstein* in a debate on slavery in the House of Commons. As Shelley wrote to Edward Trelawny, "During the debate on that subject Canning paid a compliment to Frankenstein in a manner sufficiently pleasing to me" (I.417). In the published account of the debate, Canning praised "the

---

6. Byron famously remarked about the publication of *Childe Harold's Pilgrimage* in 1812: "I awoke one morning and found myself famous." Thomas Moore first attributed the phrase to Byron in 1830 (seven years after Shelley's epistolary phrase) as from Byron's "memoranda," which had been destroyed, but Doris Langley Moore, in *The Late Lord Byron*, p. 46, lists Mary Shelley as one of the readers of Byron's memoirs before they were destroyed.

splendid fiction of a recent romance, the hero of which constructs a human form." But Canning's salute to the creative powers of both author and hero quickly pivoted to the book's haunting image of child abandonment; the hero "recoils from the monster which he has made."[7] Canning trailed a long personal history with Caroline of Brunswick, including a romantic attachment in the early days when the princess at Blackheath wrestled with her forced separation from her daughter Charlotte, a separation of mother and child that led to her taking under her adoptive charge and care the waif Willy Austin. Two years after the death of Queen Caroline, Mary Shelley in London remained fierce in her refusal to abandon to some unknown surrogate the charge and care of her sole surviving child.

FRANKENSTEIN IN 1831

In *Thoughts on the Education of Daughters,* published ten years before the 1797 birth of her daughter with William Godwin, Mary Wollstonecraft posited that "it is possible, I am convinced, to acquire the affection of a parent for an adopted child."[8] Published thirty years later, her daughter's debut novel remains the most widely witnessed story from Romanticism about the abject failure of this possibility, a failure that launches the book and immediately turns the narrative away from adoptive possibility to the nightmares of the wildly improbable.[9] In Marilyn Butler's terms, "the plot of *Frankenstein* boils down to a scientist who fosters, or fails to foster, a monster. When it comes to parenting, Frankenstein is himself a monster."[10] In this section, I foreground

---

7. Hansard, *Parliamentary Debates,* March 16, 1824. Shelley recalls this tribute in August 1827, in a letter to Teresa Guiccioli, on the sudden death of Canning: "Did you know that he praised my Frankenstein in honorable terms in the House of Commons—extremely pleasing to me" (I.566).

8. Wollstonecraft, *Education of Daughters,* 4–5.

9. For human possibility in probabilistic fiction—the realist novel—as opposed to the impossibility of the improbable in romance and the gothic (the genres of *Frankenstein*), see Galperin, *Historical Austen,* 82–105. A serious handicap of the improbable for adoption narrative is suggested by Stanley Cavell's proposition that "science fiction cannot house tragedy because in it human limitations can from the beginning be by-passed"; *Claim of Reason,* 457.

10. Butler, "Introduction," xlii, xliv. Margaret Homans also reads the novel as an ethical critique of parenting, which she terms the "circumvention of the maternal": "Most succinctly put, the novel is about the collision between androcentric and gynocentric theories of creation, a collision that results in the denigration of maternal childbearing through its circumvention by male creation"; *Bearing the Word,* 113. For readings of *Frankenstein* and adoption that foreground the improbable Creature, see Peel, "Adoption," 244–53; Nelson and Hipchen, "Victorian Childhood," 20–23; and Diver, "Monstrous Othering," 247–75. For a reading of "Rousseau's overdetermined absence from *Frankenstein*" (8), see Dart, *Rousseau.*

Frankenstein as a tale of child abandonment in the context of Mary Shelley's repatriated return to England and refusal to relinquish Percy Florence to surrogate care. My focus is the most extensive set of alterations Shelley made to the 1818 three-volume novel for its one-volume 1831 third edition, which is the form of the text known by almost all readers for the next 150 years. The bulk of these changes features the "domestic circle" of the Frankenstein family in the book's early pages. Elizabeth Lavenza, Victor Frankenstein's bride-to-be later murdered by the creature, joins the Frankenstein family as a child in a kinship adoption in 1818, but in 1831 Elizabeth the child is not a blood relative but a stranger who is twice abandoned and twice adopted. This new excess also shapes hyperbolic claims from Victor Frankenstein about his own childhood in language redolent of the Romantic child. The heightened tension between this impossible ideal of childhood and the new abundance of broken childhoods inflects Mary Shelley's new glimpse of her own childhood experience of abandonment in the famous introduction added to the novel in 1831.

In the 1818 text, Elizabeth Lavenza, a Frankenstein family blood relation, is taken under kinship adoptive care by her Frankenstein uncle after the death of her mother and her abandonment by her biological father, which is the initial prolepsis in the novel of Victor's own fatal "recoil" from his creature. Victor supplies his family history to Robert Walton in this manner in the first chapter in 1818:

> My father had a sister, whom he tenderly loved, and who had married early in life an Italian gentleman. Soon after her marriage, she had accompanied her husband into his native country, and for some years my father had very little communication with her. About the time I mentioned she died; and a few months afterwards he received a letter from her husband, acquainting him with his intention of marrying an Italian lady, and requesting my father to take charge of the infant Elizabeth, the only child of his deceased sister.[11]

Most readings of these details simply register that, in 1818, Elizabeth is Victor's cousin and skate past the fact that, after the death of her mother and her abandonment by her father, her charge and care is a de facto kinship adoption in which she grows up, adoptively, as Victor's sibling. Because of underhistoricized confusions about the shifting social constructions of incest and mar-

---

11. Shelley, *Frankenstein*, 21. Susan Wolfson's base text in this "Longman Cultural Edition" is the 1818 version, but for the purposes of this chapter she also supplies key selections from the 1831 edition, including the new introduction and selections from volume 1, chapter 1, editorially headed "the adoption of Elizabeth" (186–95). Subsequent references to this edition are by page number in the text.

Abandoned Children

riage law, many textbook annotations imply that the 1831 alteration, in which Elizabeth is a stranger instead of a blood relative, is designed to back away from the specter of cousin marriage, as if Jane Austen had revived and altered Fanny Price's bloodline in *Mansfield Park*. What such accounts fail to register is that in both the 1818 and 1831 texts, regardless of her birth history, Elizabeth becomes Victor's adoptive sibling before she nearly becomes his wife.[12]

The difference between Elizabeth Lavenza in 1818 and 1831 is less a difference of birth kind (first a cousin, then a stranger) than a significant difference of adoptive degree, an alteration that underscores the perils and costs of abandonment. In 1818, Elizabeth's birth father abandons her; in 1831, Elizabeth Lavenza is abandoned not once but twice and adopted by strangers not once but twice. I read this excess as marks of the biogenealogical pressure Shelley fought against during her repatriated London life to abandon her sole surviving child to surrogate patrimonial care.

The 1831 alterations to the inset tale of Elizabeth Lavenza are remarkable for their length and detail.[13] Victor's account to Walton now includes a new primary scene of rural poverty and abjection, inflecting the tale like an episode in Shakespearean romance:

> For a long time I was their only care. My mother had much desire to have a daughter but I continued their single offspring. When I was about five years old, while making an excursion beyond the frontiers of Italy, they passed a week on the shores of the Lake of Como. Their benevolent disposition often made them enter the cottages of the poor. . . . During one of their walks a poor cot in the foldings of a vale attracted their notice, as being singularly disconsolate, while the number of half-clothed children gathered about it, spoke of penury in its worst shape. (193)

---

12. See, for example, Marilyn Butler's note: "The family and their blood-ties are carefully revised. Elizabeth is no longer F's first cousin, but a stranger. A lesser theme hinting at incest is thus removed" (200). Instead of the red herring of cousin marriage, classroom discussions might tackle the tangled legal and social history of incest and adoptive siblinghood; see Latchford, *Steeped in Blood*.

13. What modern scholarship calls "revisions" Romantic-period writers habitually called "alterations." Here is Mary Shelley opening the final paragraph of the introduction to the 1831 edition: "I will add but one word as to the alterations I have made." Instead of "revisions," throughout this book I use the Romantic-period term "alterations"; for the different action Romantic writers called a "revision" and the object they called a "revise," see Walker, "Rewriting Romantic Revision," 20–24. There is an economic backstory to Shelley's 1831 alterations; Shelley sold the copyright to Richard Bentley for inclusion in his new series of *Bentley's Standard Novels*, and "Bentley insisted that the author should correct errors and supply new material either in the text or as a paratextual preface or notes. Even if the changes were minimal, the revisions allowed him to claim a new copyright"; St Clair, *Reading Nation*, 361.

114   CHAPTER 4

To introduce Elizabeth, Shelley moves the Frankenstein patriarch offstage. In 1818, Elizabeth's kinship adoption—her abandonment by her biological father—is an economic arrangement between gentlemen. In 1831, what will become Elizabeth's second adoption is affective commerce between a sequence of adoptive mothers:

> One day, when my father had gone by himself to Milan, my mother, accompanied by me, visited this abode. She found a peasant and his wife, hard working, bent down by care and labour, distributing a scanty meal to five hungry babes. Among these was one which attracted my mother far above all the rest. She appeared of a different stock. The four others were dark-eyed, hardy little vagrants; this child was thin, and very fair. Her hair was the brightest living gold, and, despite the poverty of her clothing, seemed to set a crown of distinction on her head. (193–94)

Adoption enters the new story under the heading of difference: "She appeared of a different stock." James O'Rourke argues that, in this alteration, Shelley deploys the romance form to heighten the novel's liberal social critique.[14] While the story rescues Elizabeth and returns her to the social status of her birth, the new narrative also tags an ethical price readers must pay: the novel simultaneously creates and abandons, narratively, those four other children, the "half-clothed," "hungry," "dark-eyed, hardy little vagrants," the "victims of penury in its worst shape," who are differentiated and separated out, abjectly, by social codes of class and physical appearance. This narrative abandonment prepares the way for the book's central event: just so, the creature will be shunned and abandoned by all who lay eyes on him, a doomed pattern of abandoning recoil performed at its adoptive birth by Victor and first imaged in the book in this 1831 alteration.

Elizabeth Lavenza abandoned in the near-wild of romance first comes under the adoptive charge and care of what Shelley later refers to as "foster parents." She is placed with these "good people" to nurse in exactly the way that infants abandoned at the Foundling Hospital were first placed out to rural nurses until they were weaned and returned to the hospital:

> The peasant woman, perceiving that my mother fixed eyes of wonder and admiration on this lovely girl, eagerly communicated her history. She was not her child, but the daughter of a Milanese nobleman. Her mother was a German, and had died on giving her birth. The infant had been placed

---

14. O'Rourke, "1831 Introduction," 365–85.

with those good people to nurse; they were better off then. They had not
been long married, and their eldest child was but just born. The father of
their charge was one of those Italians nursed in the memory of the antique
glory of Italy,—one among the *schiavi ognor frementi,* who exerted himself
to obtain the liberty of his country. He became the victim of its weakness.
Whether he had died, or still lingered in the dungeons of Austria, was not
known. His property was confiscated, his child became an orphan and a
beggar. (194)

Orphaned and abandoned on the authority of the state, Elizabeth is still
defined by the biology of the absent father; her first adoptive mother explains
that "she was not her child." Presented as "fond" adoptive caregivers, the
hardscrabble peasant couple require only a priest's institutional blessing to
abandon their charge to a set of strangers who offer better material prospects.
Although an exchange initiated by mothers, adoption happens only with the
approval of the Frankenstein patriarch, returned from backstage in Milan:

With his permission my mother prevailed on her rustic guardians to yield
their charge to her. They were fond of the sweet orphan. Her presence had
seemed a blessing to them; but it would be unfair to her to keep her in
poverty and want, when Providence afforded her such powerful protection.
They consulted their village priest, and the result was, that Elizabeth Lavenza
became the inmate of my parents' house—my more than sister—the beautiful and adored companion of all my occupations and my pleasures. (194–95)

The parents of Victor Frankenstein are Elizabeth Lavenza's third set of parents,
after she, a maternal orphan, is abandoned first by her birth father on authority of the state and then by the sturdy peasant couple, her first set of adoptive
parents, with the backing of the church. Although a genealogical stranger,
Elizabeth in her second adoption shares a childhood with an adoptive sibling
who later, before he tries to marry her, tries to produce offspring all by himself
and abandons the result.

This surplus of abandonment and adoption in 1831 collides with Victor's
altered account of his own childhood. As abandonments increase in the book,
the stakes rise sharply for the sacralized figure of the Romantic child. Immediately before the Elizabeth Lavenza narrative, Victor's picture of his childhood
expands remarkably in Shelley's alterations. The 1818 version is cursory and
brief: "No creature could have more tender parents than mine. My improvement and health were their constant care, especially as I remained for several
years their only child" (21). That's the sum of it in 1818; when Victor's caregiv-

ers chalk goals and qualities on the board, "improvement and health" mark the figure of the useful child. In 1831, Victor instead parades on stage as the Romantic child, sanctified as an "idol":

> I remained for several years their only child. Much as they were attached to each other, they seemed to draw inexhaustible stores of affection from a very mine of love to bestow them upon me. My mother's tender caresses, and my father's smile of benevolent pleasure while regarding me, are my first recollections. I was their plaything and their idol, and something better— their child, the innocent and helpless creature bestowed on them by Heaven, whom to bring up to good, and whose future lot it was in their hands to direct to happiness or misery, according as they fulfilled their duties towards me. With this deep consciousness of what they owed towards the being to which they had given life, added to the active spirit of tenderness that animated both, it may be imagined that while during every hour of my infant life I received a lesson of patience, of charity, and of self-control, I was so guided by a silken cord, that all seemed but one train of enjoyment to me. (193)

"Mighty Prophet! Seer blest!," as William Wordsworth might exclaim, from the vantage of the Intimations Ode. Of her adoptive care with her brother William of the young Basil Caroline Montagu, Dorothy Wordsworth in 1796 declared that "our grand study has been to make him happy."[15] In 1831 Shelley spotlights this same mark of success, shadowed by its possible failure: as a child, Victor's "future lot was in their hands to direct to happiness or misery." Having escaped the miserable fate of his own creature at his own hands, Victor is absolute about his own past: "No human being could have passed a happier childhood than myself." In adoption discourse, such a sacralized goal of happy being still beckons Romantically, generated historically between the fading figure of the instrumentalized child and the emergent spreadsheet child of "best interests" calculations, the prevailing modern figure who also now trails, when off the institutionalized grid, the burden of the Romantic child.

In her reading of the backstory narrative of the two seduced and abandoned Elizas in Jane Austen's *Sense and Sensibility*, Claudia Johnson casts light on the "generalizing effect" of the doubled abandonment narratives of Elizabeth Lavenza in Shelley's 1831 alteration:

---

15. Wordsworth, *Letters*, I.180.

The most striking thing about the tales of the two Elizas is their insistent redundancy. One Eliza would have sufficed as far as the immediate narrative purpose, which is to discredit Willoughby with a prior attachment. But the presence of two unfortunate heroines points to crimes beyond Willoughby's doing, and their common name opens the sinister possibility that plights such as theirs proliferate throughout the kingdom. This redundancy has a generalizing effect, for it invites us to consider how much male behavior in *Sense and Sensibility* redoubles with what is depicted in their tales.[16]

In the same manner, Elizabeth Lavenza's doubled abandonments limn the terror of a widespread world in which parents abandon children. This doubling effect gained force from an additional change Shelley engineered for the novel in 1831, a new introduction. Well-known for its creation of the 1816 "ghost story" contest on the shores of Lake Geneva, the 1831 introduction also points to what Anne Mellor calls Shelley's "own experiences of childhood abandonment."[17] In the new introduction, Shelley refers to her separation as a maternal orphan from the unhappily reshuffled form of her birth family, but what she does not reveal is that abandonment happened to her twice, once in Scotland, as noticed in the new introduction, and once, earlier, at the Ramsgate seaside, where she was left alone to try to resolve her own physical disfigurement.

Shelley claims to offer the new introduction to answer a question posed by her new publisher and her readers: how did she come to write such a book? Before putting into circulation the ghost story tale, Shelley recalls a time in her adolescence when she was sent to live apart from her London family:

> I lived principally in the country as a girl, and passed a considerable time in Scotland. I made occasional visits to the more picturesque parts; but my habitual residence was on the blank and dreary northern shores of the Tay, near Dundee. Blank and dreary on retrospection I call them; they were not so to me then. (187)

Shelley's "considerable time" was a two-year stretch from 1812 to 1814 when, at age fifteen, her father shipped her off to Dundee in two intervals to live with a family of casual acquaintances. In Scotland, Shelley did manage to build close friendships with the daughters of the Dundee family, but in 1831 she underscores the shape of these years with the repeated phrase "blank and

---

16. Johnson, *Jane Austen: Women, Politics, and the Novel*, 57.
17. Mellor, *Shelley*, 216.

dreary." What she does not mention in 1831 is that the Scottish exile came on the immediate heels of a six-month interval in 1811 when she was sent away from the family to the seaside at Ramsgate to heal a disfiguring and disabling skin condition afflicting her right hand and arm. As Shelley's most recent biographer summarizes, Godwin, her surviving birth parent, "decided to send Mary away not once but twice" with the consequence that Shelley "spent the majority of her adolescence away from her family."[18] Emily Sunstein observes that these two episodes established a pattern of "self-exile and banishment" that would haunt Shelley's life.[19] Four months after she returned to London from Dundee in the spring of 1814, she escaped her London family for Europe with a young poet who was abandoning a wife and child. Four years later, she would publish Romanticism's most famous tale of abandonment.

THE ROUSSEAU BIOGRAPHY

Romanticism's most infamous history of abandonment belongs to Jean-Jacques Rousseau. In 1838 Shelley torched him at length for what she repeatedly calls this "crime": Rousseau "neglected the first duty of man by abandoning his children."[20] During her three decades repatriated in England while caring for her unrelinquished son, Shelley earned much-needed income as a prolific professional writer, including four more novels, short fiction, poetry, and reviews, many of which appeared in popular literary "annuals." From 1835 to 1839, she published dozens of short-form biographies of European writers and intellectuals in a multivolume series for a rising middle-class readership, the *Cabinet Cyclopedia,* published by Dionysius Lardner. In addition to multiple lives she wrote for volumes on Italy, Spain, and Portugal, her biography of Rousseau appeared in volume 2 of *Lives of the Most Eminent Literary and Scientific Men of France,* where her work ranged from opening lives of Montaigne and Rabelais to Madame de Stael at its end. Bookended by her lives of Voltaire and Condorcet, the Rousseau biography ("Rousseau. 1712–1778") extends to twenty-three thousand words over sixty-four pages.[21]

---

18. Sampson, *Shelley,* 59.

19. Sunstein, *Shelley,* 55.

20. Shelley, "Rousseau," II.172. Subsequent references are by page number in the text. For the modern critical edition, see Shelley, *"Literary Lives,"* ed. Orr, 320–66. Orr comments that "the essay's indignation concerning Rousseau's abandonment of his children marks it as one of the most personal of all her *Lives*" (xx).

21. For pathbreaking work on this text, see O'Rourke, "'Nothing More Unnatural.'"

Rousseau's own account of what Shelley terms his crime of abandonment had been in wide circulation in Europe since the posthumous publication of the first volume of his *Confessions* in 1782. Evidence in her notebooks indicates that Shelley had read the *Confessions* in the years immediately before writing *Frankenstein*; her most detailed record of (re)reading those volumes belongs to November 1817, while in England in final preparation of *Frankenstein* for publication at the turn of the year: "Nov. 3 read Tacitus & Rousseau's confessions . . . Nov. 4 read Rousseau's confessions . . . Nov. 5 read Rousseau's confessions . . . Nov. 6 read Rousseau's letters."[22] The 1838 biography confirms her rich familiarity with the text, which supplies the chronological framework and most of the information Shelley reshapes into a life narrative. But Shelley's retelling of Rousseau's story is not a jobwork summary. Engaged in a critical reading, Shelley sits in judgment of both the person and the book whose details she reports. A typical sentence steps back to frame the writer and his book while it relies on the book for information: "Even in his Confessions, where Rousseau discloses his secret errors, he by no means appreciates the real extent of his misconduct" (130). Rousseau is on trial not only as a father who abandoned five children but as a writer who later put that abandonment to work in books: "He at first acted, he says, without serious examination of the morality of his conduct; but when he commenced author, he gave attentive consideration to the point, and satisfied himself that he did right, and continued his course of conduct" (131). In Shelley's code, writing about one's own crime is not exculpatory.

Shelley's pages narrating Rousseau's acts of child abandonment appear midway through her text. But the opening paragraph of the biography announces the theme of criminality: "He was too alive to the sense of his own actions and feelings; and as he had committed many faults, not to say crimes, the recollection of these, joined to his sincere love of virtue, produced a struggle in his mind full of misery and remorse" (111). The language of crime reappears when Shelley turns to the moment in Rousseau's young life when he pondered what to do about a pregnant mistress: "He had heard young men of rank and fortune allude vauntingly to the recourse they had had on such occasions to the Foundling Hospital. He followed their criminal example" (131). Shelley's condemnation includes not just individual actors but the institutions like the Hôpital des Enfants-Trouvés that to her mind enabled such conduct, which she tags, unsparingly, as criminal: "The whole system takes a revolting and criminal aspect from which we turn with loathing" (133). After the

---

22. *Journals*, 182–83. The *Confessions* appears twice earlier in the *Journals* in lists of books read, once in 1815 (89) and once earlier in 1817 (101).

abandonment episode, Shelley sounds the criminal theme one last time at the conclusion of the biography: "We cannot help thinking that even while Rousseau defends himself by many baseless sophisms, that this crime, rankling at his heart, engendered much of the misery that he charged upon his fellow-creatures" (172–73).

When Shelley turns midway to the abandonments themselves, Rousseau's crime is also a "fatal act" that shapes his subsequent life: "He had been accustomed to domestic society, and in addition he felt that he needed the kind attentions of a woman, and this want led to the fatal act from which sprung so many of his misfortunes" (129–30). Shelley names and condemns with prejudice Rousseau's boarding-house mistress, "Thérèse le Vasseur," the mother of all five abandoned babies, who to Shelley plays a culpable role in the "evil" system. Shelley renders Rousseau's self-exculpation with a frosty euphemism turned back upon him and trailed by a monosyllabic punch: "When inconveniences arose from the connection, he was disposed to get rid of them on the easiest possible terms" (130–31). Once more, Shelley doubles up individual malfeasance and systemic evil: "This kindly-seeming society was a Moloch whom to pacify, little children were ruthlessly sacrificed" (133), an image of Old Testament brutality from which she and her readers "turn with loathing." In this middle section, Shelley tries and fails three times to stop staring at the inhuman spectacle. Before (not) turning away with loathing, she had proposed that "it is insulting to the reader to dwell on the flagrancy of this act" (131), before promptly dwelling on the flagrancy of this act. She tries to turn away a third time: "We now dismiss this subject. It was necessary to bring it so far forward as to show the evil effects of so bad a cause; it is too painful to dwell further upon" (134). But she cannot stop.

The middle narrative demonstrates Shelley's painful knowledge of the survival rate of infants abandoned to foundling hospitals: "Five of his children were thus sent to a receptacle where few survive; and those who do go through life are brutified by their situation, or depressed by the burden, ever weighing at the heart, that they have not inherited the commonest right of humanity, a parent's care" (131). When Shelley thus bundles infant mortality with the denial of a basic human right, she turns to dismiss Rousseau's self-defense in the *Confessions*—his argument invoking Plato that children belonged not to parents but to the state:

> We say little of Rousseau's vain excuses as to the probable destiny of his children. They were better, he says, brought up by the public, than rendered rogues by madame le Vasseur. . . . This futile reasoning does not need elaborate refutation. Rousseau talks of public care, as if that were, in such a place

as a Parisian foundling hospital, aught else but public desertion. The poor children in all probability died in their infancy. (131–32)

In mid-eighteenth-century Paris, the death rate of the children at the hospital was extraordinarily high. The London Foundling Hospital, which Shelley passed daily in 1823 and 1824, was charged with the care of four hundred children—but those were the children who had survived.

Shelley's summary condemnation of Rousseau in the middle narrative is that, as a parent, Rousseau "failed in the plainest dictates of nature and conscience" (131). His multiple acts of abandonment were crimes and fatal acts with consequences: "Our first duty is to render those to whom we give birth, wise, virtuous, and happy, as far as in us lies. Rousseau failed in this,—can we wonder that his after course was replete with sorrow?" (132). Pages later, the final paragraphs of the biography close the case:

Rousseau neglected the first duty of man by abandoning his children. He often dilates on simple pleasures—the charms of unsophisticated affections, and the ecstasy to be derived from virtuous sympathy—he who never felt the noblest and most devoted passion of the human soul—the love of a parent for his child! We cannot help thinking that even while Rousseau defends himself by many baseless sophisms, that this crime, rankling at his heart, engendered much of the misery that he charged upon his fellow-creatures. (172–73)

Like a prosecuting attorney who claims that she must turn away from the crimes she continues to narrate for a jury, Shelley does not allow her readers to stop staring at the spectacle of child abandonment.

ADOPTION AND REPATRIATED LIFE

Refusing to abandon her son to surrogate care by strangers, Shelley feared that her 1823 return to London would mirror the polarized reception of Queen Caroline on her raucous return to the kingdom in 1820. In the history of her repatriated life, Shelley's fierce condemnation of child abandonment and excoriation of Rousseau may seem signs that she was drifting away from the progressive heritage of her birth culture into the very precincts of "foggy virtue" she feared would entrap her in England, a nation where adoptions dwelled off the books. Shelley's polarized reception by two adoptive families from her past supplies a more complex map of how she negotiated in pragmatically progressive ways the fraught politics of adoptive families upon her return to England.[23] One adoptive family, Charles and Mary Lamb and their adopted daughter Emma Isola, welcomed her. But the Basil Montagu family, which Thomas Carlyle counted with "four genealogical species," instead shunned her. The full stories of these two adoptive families feature in the following two chapters. Here, in preview, I track these polar reactions to gain a better picture of the repatriated politics of a woman dogged by scandal who was determined to refute by action Rousseau's parental failure before taking him down in print.

Shelley grew up well acquainted with the siblings Charles and Mary Lamb as a familiar part of her father's circle in London. In August 1823, on her reluctant way back to England with Percy, she paused in Paris for ten days and spent three of them with English acquaintances at Versailles, catching up on London gossip. Writing to Leigh Hunt in Italy, she reported the latest, starting with news that the Lamb siblings had "made an excursion to France" during Charles's vacation the previous summer. When "Miss L. was taken ill in her usual way," Charles had arranged for her care and then stayed with these same friends at Versailles, "going on very well, if the French wine had not been too good for him." When Shelley left London in 1818, the Lambs had been living on the edge of Covent Garden; she now heard that "they have been moving, renouncing town & country house to take one which was neither or either—at Islington, I think they said" (I.373).

What Shelley does not report to Italy is that this atypical excursion to France in the summer of 1822 was the only time Charles and Mary Lamb ever traveled abroad, chiefly because of adoption. Their main motive was to improve their French to help school a fourteen-year-old orphan, Emma Isola, whom they had met two summers earlier in Cambridge during the height of the Queen Caroline affair and whose care they had begun to take on adoptively. Five days after Shelley arrived in London in late August 1823, she saw Charles at her temporary quarters with her Godwin family: "This same evening on my return to the Strand I saw Lamb who was very entertaining & amiable though a little deaf . . . he was very gracious to me, and invited me to see him when Miss L. should be well" (I.378–79). As set forth in chapter 6, this family who welcomed Shelley performed untimely adoption well outside biocentric norms. As a lifelong sibling pair now acting as surrogate parents to a Cambridge orphan, Charles and Mary upended normative marriage in the first degree (Charles called this their "double singleness"), and an adopted

---

23. For an influential reading of later Shelley as increasingly yielding to the masks of feminine propriety demanded by bourgeois patriarchy, see Poovey, *Proper Lady*.

child pushed the family ectopically beyond easy explanation. In her many visits with the Lambs over the next decade, Shelley was welcomed back not to a conforming center of familial propriety but to an adoptive periphery where the Lamb family behaved against the grain of an English nation where adoption occurred beyond the legal pale.

While Charles Lamb was remaining faithful to Queen Caroline's oppositional cause in the decade following her death, in 1827 the Lambs enlisted Shelley's aid as they tried to locate a tutor to jump-start Emma Isola's Latin, to increase her profile in the governess market. After Emma Isola married the young publisher Edward Moxon in 1833, Shelley's publishing life intersected with the Moxon firm and family at the end of that decade. Under Shelley's editorial supervision, Moxon published a four-volume edition of her husband's poetry in 1838, in which Shelley outmaneuvered Sir Timothy Shelley's ban on any form of biography of his radical son by embedding such information in notes to the poems. A year later, Shelley and Moxon published a one-volume edition of the poetry, which landed Emma Isola Moxon's husband in court on a charge of blasphemous libel. Unlike the four-volume edition, the one-volume edition contained an unexpurgated version of the radical poem *Queen Mab,* which had been cited in evidence in the 1818 trial denying Shelley's husband the custody of his two children by his first wife, who had drowned herself in the Serpentine in Hyde Park. At this 1839 moment in her repatriated writing and publishing life, Shelley in the *Cabinet Cyclopedia* separated herself sharply from the Rousseau who had appealed to her father's radical circle in the 1790s even as her friendship and partnership with the Moxon family of the Lambs' adopted daughter accomplished a newly inflected circulation of ideas and forms of radical opposition.

At the London custody trial for Shelley's husband's children in 1818, the lawyer Basil Montagu supplied legal advice for the losing side. Montagu was the acknowledged bastard child of the Earl of Sandwich, the corrupt Lord of the Admiralty during the American revolution. Cut off by his father at his 1791 marriage, Montagu became a disciple of Shelley's father in oppositional London in the 1790s and was one of Godwin's friends present at the death of Shelley's mother, Mary Wollstonecraft, a week after Mary's birth in 1797. Two years earlier, Montagu had handed off his own maternally orphaned son Basil Caroline Montagu to the adoptive care of William and Dorothy Wordsworth, who took the three-year-old to the remote west country where new poems helped breed the Romantic child.

In 1823 Basil Montagu the lawyer father was on his third marriage, with a London household of eight children from three mothers and two fathers, a

124   CHAPTER 4

"most difficult miscellany," in Thomas Carlyle's 1881 recollection.[24] After the death of his second wife in 1806, Montagu, the father of four sons by his first two wives, married in 1808 a Yorkshire widow, Anna Benson Skepper, who brought a nine-year-old daughter, Anne Skepper, to the new family, which was soon extended by two more sons and a daughter. This third wife, Anna Skepper Montagu, who appears as "Noble Lady" in Carlyle's correspondence, was an ambitious social climber to whom old Montagu friends such as the Wordsworth family took quick dislike. The latest Mrs. Montagu was the biological mother of four of the eight children in the Montagu household on Russell Square in Bloomsbury, and she distinguished between the two sets of offspring across a border of biology versus adoption: in a letter to Carlyle, she tells him how she needs to negotiate between "my Sons, real, and adopted."[25] In 1823 and 1824, Shelley came close to being pulled back into the orbit of this family shaped by adoption with deep roots in her past, but according to Shelley "Mrs. M" made certain that this did not happen, skirting any risky association with Shelley and whatever was rumored to be her unseemly baggage. As with Shelley's later alliance with the Moxon family, this breach opened up during plans to publish her husband's poetry.

As soon as she arrived in London in the late summer of 1823, Shelley began plans with friends in London and abroad to publish her husband's poetry left in manuscript at his death. In a letter to Leigh Hunt in Italy on September 18, 1823, Shelley wrote: "I spoke to your brother when I saw him concerning the publication of such MSS as I had of our S—and he agreed to it. Since then Procter called on my father to say that two gentlemen great admirers of S—were willing to undertake the risk of such a publication if I would agree to it" (I.384). The obstacle to such a publication was money; Hunt's publisher brother in London, John Hunt, was broke. The "Procter" whom Shelley reports called on Godwin with a financial solution was Bryan Waller Procter, a poet who had been at school with Byron at Harrow. As the project gained momentum, Shelley reported that Procter "called upon me, shewing a zeal in the affair, which considering that he is an author & a poet pleased me mightily" (I.384).

In Shelley biography, a standard topic in the narrative of her repatriated years as a widow is a roster of possible new partners, who would also serve as an adoptive parent to Percy Florence. Procter is the earliest in this list, and Shelley's attraction to him is remarkable: "Procter pleased me by his errand and also by his manners and appearance. He is evidently vain, yet not pretend-

---

24. Carlyle, *Reminiscences*, I.225–26.

25. Quoted from manuscript source in footnote to letter from Thomas Carlyle to Jane Baillie Welsh, January 14, 1826, *Carlyle Letters Online*.

ing, and his ill health is for me an interesting circumstance; since I have been so accustomed to Poets whose frame has been shattered by the mind, that a stout healthy person would rather seem to me a waggoner than a versifier" (I.384). In a letter to Leigh Hunt on October 20, 1823, Shelley continued this theme: "He is not well & that interests me also—as I told you before I have always a sneaking kindness for these delicately healthed Poets.—Poor Keats I often think of him now" (I.400).

But nothing came of Shelley's "sneaking kindness" toward Procter and his ilk. In a letter to Marianne Hunt eight months later, on June 13, 1824, Shelley remarks that "it is very, very long since I have seen Procter." Shelley's disappointment and sadness are clear in a journal entry in September:

> I have only seen two persons from whom I have hoped or wished for friendly feeling. One a Poet—who sought me first—Whose voice laden with sentiment, paused as Shelley's—& who read with the same deep feeling as he—Whose gentle manners were pleasing & who seemed to a degree pleased—who once or twice listened to my sad plaints & bent his dark blue eyes upon me—association, gratitude esteem made me take interest in his long tho' rare visits—they have ceased—It is four months since I have seen him—So much for my powers of attraction. (482–83)

On October 7, Procter married Anne Skepper, the daughter of Anna Skepper Montagu by her first husband and the adoptive stepdaughter of Basil Montagu. Shelley learned the news from the papers and wrote to Marianne Hunt in Italy on October 10:

> Procter is married he married A. Skepper last Thursday—of course I shall never see him again. When you spoke of him & H. offered me an introduction to him I declined it knowing that since he was connected with Mrs. M, all would happen—as it has happened; since introducing himself to me I have seen him i.e. that his gentleness, poetical taste & conversation would interest & please me, & then that he wd disappear from my horizon leaving regret behind. He called on me several times last winter and sat several hours, I was very much pleased with him—& I shall never see him again, which pains me. (I.452)

"Mrs. M." had clearly engineered a wall between her adoptive family and Shelley, a reproach that Shelley had anticipated on her return to London: "knowing that . . . all would happen—as it has happened." More burdened than even the Bennet parents in *Pride and Prejudice*, Basil and Anna Skepper Montagu had eight unmarried young adults on their hands in 1823 and 1824, including a bundle of unmarried sons such as the deeply unpromising adoptee Basil Caroline, who was five years older than Shelley, and Mrs. Montagu's adopted son Algernon Montagu, who married in 1828 on the eve of emigrating to Australia. Her own two "real" sons were yet in their teens; the first Montagu offspring to marry was her daughter by her first marriage, whose pairing with Bryan Waller Procter signified the Montagu family's absolute breach with Shelley, as she laments twice: "I shall never see him again."

Just as English society divided sharply about Queen Caroline in the summer and fall of 1820, so Shelley at her return in 1823 met both warm welcome and cold rejection from adoptive families, both with deep roots in her history. Although other serious prospects followed Procter, Shelly never married again. Tagging her most famous book in 1831 as her "hideous progeny," Shelley's own offspring tracked at last to an adoption, and only to adoption. In 1848, three years before his mother's death, Percy Florence Shelley married the widow Jane Gibson St John, an illegitimate child of a Newcastle banker. In the modern account supplied by William St Clair in his family biography *The Godwins and the Shelleys,* Percy Florence "was married to a widow rather older than himself who outstripped him in energy, ability, and ambition, and there were no children."[26] The final statement misses the mark, because in 1855 Percy and Jane Gibson St John Shelley took on the adoptive charge and care of a three-year-old girl, Bessie Florence Gibson, known as "Flossie," who was the daughter of Jane's widowed brother Edward Gibson. In Betty Bennett's notes to her edition of Shelley's letters, Flossie Shelley's adoptive trail, which includes a failed repatriation, unfolds in these terms: "Several years later her father remarried and brought Bessie Florence home. She, however, was unhappy without her 'mother,' as she referred to Jane Shelley, who equally desired her return. From this point on, Bessie Florence lived permanently with the Shelleys, and she was legally adopted by Percy Florence Shelley" (III.374). Although it corrects St Clair, this final statement is also off target, since "legal adoption" did not exist in England until 1926, and both of Bessie Florence Gibson Shelley's adoptive parents were dead by 1899. As in many matters in Mary Shelley biography, Emily Sunstein offers the most succinctly careful account of the marriage and children of Percy Florence Shelley and Jane Gibson St John Shelley: "Being unable to have children, they adopted Jane's niece Bessie Florence Gibson."[27] Describing a kinship adoption characteristic of the period, Sunstein's verb "adopted" func-

---

26. St Clair, *Biography of a Family,* 492.

27. Sunstein, 388.

tions in the instrumental and pragmatic extralegal register faithful to period history. From outside the period, modifiers such as "formal," "official," or "legal" distort through a modern lens the adoptive history of Mary Shelley's only grandchild, an adopted offspring born a year after her adoptive grandmother's death in 1851, nearly three decades after her return to England with her sole surviving child, determined not to abandon him.

CHAPTER 5

Unexplained Children

Basil Caroline Montagu and the
Wordsworth Circle

In the spring of 1813, from the village of Brampton to the northwest of Cambridge, Basil Caroline Montagu, a twenty-year-old unhappily discharged from the navy, addressed a letter to "My dear mother" in London: "I have today been visiting the tomb of my Mother and my second Mother who, side by side, are waiting in peace for that day on which we hope to meet again free from the cares & anxieties of this transitory existence." Such a tangle of mothers invites unspooling. Basil Caroline's biological mother, born Caroline Want in London in 1768, died in early January after his birth near Brampton in late December 1792. His "second mother" buried by her side in Brampton is her maiden sister, Charlotte Want, who during several stretches assumed the adoptive charge and care for the maternally orphaned Basil Caroline in Brampton before her own death in 1802. His third mother who is alive in London, receiving his letters, is Anna Skepper Montagu, since 1808 the third wife of Basil Caroline's biological father, also Basil Montagu. At this juncture, an introductory map of this signally haphazard family unfolds a sheet of tabloid history. Basil the father, born in 1770, was the bastard son of the fourth Earl of Sandwich, the corrupt First Lord of the Admiralty during the American Revolution, and his society mistress, the singer Martha Ray, who was murdered by a spurned lover—soon hanged—after an evening of London theater in 1779, a tale that filled the London papers for months. When Basil the bastard son of Martha Ray, orphaned at age nine, married

• 128 •

the orphaned Caroline Want of Brampton in 1791, his father the earl cut off all support.

Shuffled back and forth among multiple adoptive caregivers during his own orphaned childhood and young adulthood, Basil Caroline Montagu suffered the whiplash of ever-shifting homes at an alarming rate. Especially because three years of that history—from the time when he was nearly three until he was nearly six—weave in and out with the lives of writers who were busy fostering the infancy of the Romantic child, the life of Basil Caroline Montagu as an adoptee speaks tellingly of the ambitions, shaky foundations, and subsequent costs of that hegemonic construct. This chapter tracks the unhappy life story of the adoptee Basil Caroline in three stages. After grounding his birth culture and early infancy in the Rousseau-inflected Godwinian circles of oppositional London in the mid-1790s, I turn to the defining years of his adoptive care by Dorothy Wordsworth and William Wordsworth in the west country of Dorset and Somerset from 1795 to 1798, the years that generated the earliest of Dorothy's journals and the poems published, anonymously, by William and Samuel Taylor Coleridge in 1798 in the volume titled *Lyrical Ballads,* a literary cradle for Romantic childhood. The last stage tracks a less familiar portion of Basil Caroline's story, including his efforts as a repatriated adoptee to navigate the family chaos of his birth father's many married lives and children; failed navy service under the sponsoring eye of a vice-admiral uncle, who was also a bastard son of the Earl of Sandwich; a bitter falling-out and uneasy reconciliation with his adoptive Wordsworth family in Cumbria in his early twenties; and his retreat into illness and aimless London and Cambridgeshire life before his unheralded death in 1830. In the British book of the Romantic child, the historical child who most closely shadows the emergence of that illusory figure is this forlorn adoptee, who bore the names of both his bastard father and the mother who died at his birth.

One last preliminary. A primary document shaping this chapter is an adoption memoir, a remarkably early instance in the history of that genre that now dominates adoption writing.[1] Sometime in the late teens, father Basil, heartbroken in the aftermath of Basil Caroline's rough visit to his adoptive caregivers in Cumbria in 1813–14, felt moved to compose a long account of the life of Basil Caroline, to try to explain his son's shattered life to himself and to the man he most admired, as he declares on an early page: "I consider my having met Wm Wordsworth the most fortunate event of my life." Quoted throughout this chapter, the unpublished, unfinished, and untitled

---

1. See Novy, "Memoirs," 308–24, in which she reports patterns from nearly four dozen contemporary adoption memoirs, from the late 1960s through 2021.

manuscript—in 8,300 words in 115 handwritten pages—is a lawyer's attempt at an adoption memoir by a birth father, filling about half its pages with copies in a clerk's hand of Basil Caroline's letters, submitted to a very private court as documentary evidence.[2] What seems at its first sentence to promise an autobiography of Basil Montagu the father—"I was twenty one in 1791"—immediately becomes instead an adoption memoir focused relentlessly on the melancholy adoptive life of his son, Basil Caroline Montagu.

BRAMPTON AND LONDON, 1792–1795

When the lawyer Robert Want died in London in 1777, his widow and their seven daughters removed to Brampton, a village on the outskirts of Huntingdon, a town near Cambridge that boasted Hinchingbrooke, the estate of the Fourth Earl of Sandwich. When the youngest of these Want daughters, Caroline, died soon after December childbirth in early January 1793, her newborn son Basil Caroline was taken under the charge and care of her several unmarried sisters, who lived together in a Brampton home supplied by their mother's will at her death in 1781.[3] Basil Caroline's now-widowed birth father, Basil Montagu, one of the several acknowledged "natural children" of the earl, suffered his bereavement twenty miles down the road in Cambridge, where he had been scrambling to fund life day by day after his father cut him off when he married Caroline Want in 1791.[4] These Huntingdonshire and Cambridgeshire anchors would later often pull the orphaned Basil Caroline Montagu back to the clouded grounds of his birth and bereavement after the

---

2. The manuscript is held by the Wordsworth Trust at the Wordsworth Library, Jerwood Centre, Grasmere, UK: WLMS A / Montagu, Basil / 26. Bound in boards with a spine label "Basil's Letters," the paper is watermarked 1811. The 115 ms. pages are not numbered; subsequent references in this text are to "WLMS" (Wordsworth Library Manuscript). Used by permission of the Wordsworth Trust.

3. Among the thickets of web-based genealogy, the most detailed and reliable set of facts about "the Want family of London and Huntingdonshire" is presented in web pages devoted to Hughan family history. See Sherro46, "The Continuation of the Story of Ruth Hughan & Francis Holworthy," *Hughan Genealogy* (blog), May 10, 2010, http://hughanhistory.blogspot. com/2010/05/continuation-of-story-of-ruth-hughan.html.

4. There is no full biography of Basil Montagu to date; in addition to the 2004 entry by V. Markham Lester in the *Oxford Dictionary of National Biography,* secondary biographical sources include two substantial articles: Wardle, "Basil and Anna Montagu"; Graham and Tribe, "Basil Montagu QC." The Wordsworth Library holds a typescript copy of Margaret Crum's 255-page 1950 Oxford B.Litt. thesis (unpublished), *Literary Work and Literary Friends of Basil Montagu Q.C.:* WLMS 22/2.

UNEXPLAINED CHILDREN

estrangements he subsequently suffered in the alien settings of London, the west country of Dorset and Somerset, the British navy, and Cumbria.

Until his father took Basil Caroline with him to London in 1795, this new-born child of the youngest sister was cared for during his first two years by the three unmarried sisters remaining in the Want home in Brampton—Catherine, Arabella, and especially Charlotte, the closest of the three in age to Caroline. Years later, when his disappointed father attempted to diagnose what he termed Basil Caroline's "diseased affection," he attributed his son's chronic ill temper in part to a spoiling excess of surrogate maternal care: "He had lived much with excellent old ladies to whom the dear Basil was all in all" (WLMS). When Basil Caroline became the adopted infant-in-residence in the Want home of "excellent old ladies" from 1793 to 1795, in addition to five aunts at immediate hand or nearby, there were multiple Want cousins in the village, a logjam of six kindred children from ages ten to one. Basil Caroline's intense solitude in the nursery of Romantic childhood during his Dorset and Somerset years stands in sharp contrast to these earliest Brampton months, crowded with Want kin in the wake of his mother's death and with that death imprinted deep in somatic sediments of memory.

Basil Caroline's biological father was meanwhile in Cambridge, spending his breath to make ends meet, chiefly by taking pupils. Raised at Hinchingbrooke, where in his own phrase he was "cradled in aristocracy,"[5] the acknowledged bastard Basil Montagu was schooled at Charterhouse in London from 1780 (a year after the murder of his mother) and then at Cambridge from 1786, where he received his BA in 1790, at age twenty. A year later, his marriage to an orphaned Brampton girl cost him the financial and familial support of his father the earl; as he later put the breach, "From that moment my father never spoke to me" (WLMS). Suddenly widowed, he offloaded the care of his newborn son to the Want sisters and tapped a makeshift revenue plan to tutor sons of wealthy merchants with his Cambridge contemporary Francis Wrangham.

Basil Caroline's adoptive infancy soon shifted from a village loaded with kin to teeming London with a single parent in student digs. One of father Basil's tutors at Cambridge, the Reverend John Lane, supplied funds to enable him to scrape together a plan to study law. In early 1795, he moved from Cambridge into London legal chambers in Lincoln's Inn, not alone but with a two-year-old son. In the father's own words, several decades later: "My child was with me: he was entrusted to my protection when I was little able to protect myself" (WLMS). Unlike "care," which was the culture's prevailing

---

5. Mackintosh, *Memoirs*, I.149–50.

term for a surrogate charge, "protection" assumes and foregrounds threat.[6] In such terms, the precariousness of the two reunited lives invites a question of agency. Who made the decision to risk moving Basil Caroline from the kinship adoptive care of village aunts to the uncertain "protection" of his widowed and impecunious birth father in metropolitan London? Again and again in Basil Caroline's later young adult life, temporary hosts or caregivers were more than happy to see him vacate the premises, including in one instance the benevolent John Lane himself. Early on, precarious uprootedness marks this adoptee's life pattern as an often-unwanted child.

Basil father and Basil son did not remain a solitary London pair for long. In February another young Cambridge graduate, William Wordsworth, arrived from the north and bunked for a time with the two Basils in their Lincoln's Inn chambers. Although the two graduates were the same age and had overlapped as students at Cambridge, this was a new friendship with a remarkable mirror effect. Shortly before the birth of Basil Caroline in late December 1792, Caroline Wordsworth, William's first child, an illegitimate daughter, was born on December 15 in Orléans, only days after her absent father had decamped from Paris to England. The two-year-old Basil Caroline thus shared a name with a two-year-old daughter Wordsworth had never seen and would not meet for another seven years. In the early months of 1795, Basil Caroline's caregivers in a law student's London digs were now his widowed bastard birth father and a new adoptive stranger, a father who had left behind his French lover, Annette Vallon, and, unseen, his firstborn illegitimate child.

Two decades later, Basil senior framed his new friendship in these terms: "By an accident I became acquainted with Wm Wordsworth. We spent some months together. He saw me, with great industry, perplexed and misled by passions wild & strong. In the wreck of my happiness he saw the probable ruin of my infant" (WLMS). Radical metropolitan politics were the primary fuel stoking Basil the father's "passions wild & strong," which threatened with catastrophe—"wreck" and "ruin"—the well-being of Basil Caroline. Through the first half of 1795, both Montagu and Wordsworth circulated in the oppositional intellectual orbits around William Godwin, whose righteous two-volume *An Enquiry Concerning Political Justice* had appeared two years earlier. Wordsworth first appears in Godwin's meticulous diary at a dinner of fellow travelers on February 27, and the modern editors of the diary describe Montagu as "one of Godwin's earliest 'pupils'—abandoning his law training

---

6. "Care" survives as governing term at the national level in the modern UK, in the umbrella national office of "Cared-for Children," which in the US is the corresponding national umbrella office for "Child Welfare."

(temporarily) after reading *Political Justice*."[7] More than three decades later, long after the fever had passed, Montagu wrote of this period to the son of Sir James Mackintosh: "At this time the wild opinions which prevailed at the commencement of the French revolution misled most of us. . . . It is scarcely possible to conceive the extensive influence which these visions had upon society. . . . I had till this period studied law with great intensity, but these doctrines paralysed me; I closed my books, and almost relinquished my professional pursuits."[8]

A more conforming diarist of the period left this telling account of a typical dinner in these circles, where oppositional politics and ideas struck sparks:

> Mr Montagu is a natural Son of the late Lord Sandwich; and seems to have imbibed in a violent degree the speculative principles of the New Philosophers. He pleaded against the existence of *Instinct,* and said that Poets are made by *education.*—That a Parent should not love his Child better than the Child of another, but in proportion as the Child might possess better qualities and endowments.[9]

In the wake of Locke and Rousseau, the education of children had become a primary proving ground of revolutionary activism. Godwin's *Enquiry* is forthright about its debt to Rousseau, dutifully footnoting early pages on education: "The arguments of this chapter respecting education are for the most part an abstract from the Emile of J. J. Rousseau."[10] Godwin's notoriously cool rationalism and Rousseau's multiple abandonments lurk in Montagu's reported dinner remark about the duty of a parent to weigh with indifference the claims of a biological child and the claims of any other kind of child. The "qualities and endowments" of a child are to be measured not by genealogical status but by simple observation and experiment, which shade into alarming procedures in the *Enquiry*:

> The child at the moment of his birth is totally unprovided with ideas, except such as his mode of existence in the womb may have supplied. His first impressions are those of pleasure and pain. But he has no foresight of the tendency of any action to obtain either the one or the other, previously to experience. A certain irritation of the palm of the hand will produce that contraction of the fingers, which accompanies the action of grasping. . . .

---

7. Godwin, *Diary.*
8. Mackintosh, *Memoirs,* I.149–50.
9. Farington, *Diary,* III.700.
10. Godwin, *Enquiry,* I.18.

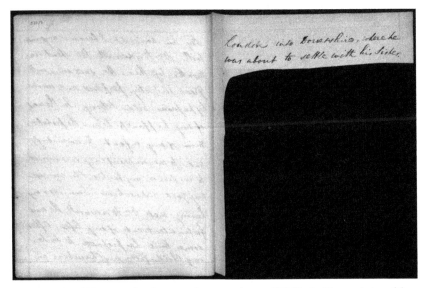

FIGURE 4. Basil Montagu adoption memoir manuscript, ca. 1817. Used with permission of the Wordsworth Trust.

> Present to the child, thus far instructed, a lighted candle. The sight of it will produce a pleasurable state of the organs of perception. He will stretch out his hand to the flame, and will have no apprehension of the pain of burning till he has felt the sensation.[11]

Basil Caroline, uprooted from the adoptive care of maternal aunts in Brampton, was now the likely subject of cutting-edge and radically inflected experimental child care in a rowdy metropolis, where the inherited value of genealogical inheritance was a foundational standard suddenly subject to intense scrutiny and debate.

At the end of the summer of 1795, Basil Caroline's young life suddenly shifted again. After eight months under the London "protection" of a birth parent, the two-and-a-half-year-old child was exported westward, to undergo the remotely rural adoptive care and charge of a young sister and brother, Dorothy Wordsworth and her older sibling William.[12] Basil the father closed

---

11. Godwin, I.14–15.

12. The term "adopted" appears only late in the record of Basil Caroline's life, when father Basil's third wife refers in an 1826 letter to "my Sons, real, and adopted" (see note 43). In the absence of a settled lexicon for de facto adoptive care in the period, modern critics supply substitutes in their narratives of Basil Caroline's early west-country years; for example, Nicholas Roe offers that the Wordsworth siblings "acted as guardians" (in Gill, *Cambridge Companion*, 210–11) and Adam Sisman describes the Wordsworth siblings as Basil's "surrogate parents" (*Friendship*, 124).

his later account of the London interval of 1795 with this tribute to his new friend: "I consider my having met Wm Wordsworth the most fortunate event of my life. He unremittingly, and to me imperceptibly, endeavoured to eradicate my faults, & to encourage my good dispositions. After some time he proposed to take my child from my Chambers in London into Dorsetshire, where he was about to settle with his sister" (WLMS). This adoption scheme in planning and execution played out in less than fully settled fashion. In the manuscript of the elder Basil's account, the bulk of the page following that last sentence is cut away, like a piece of redacted adoption paperwork (figure 4).

DORSET AND SOMERSET, 1795–1798

Chronically short of funds, Basil Montagu drew survival income in these years from tutoring John and Azariah Pinney, two sons of Bristol mercantile wealth and its foundations in the Atlantic slave trade. The Pinney boys were so taken with their introduction to Wordsworth that in July 1795, they offered the twenty-five-year-old poet rent-free their Bristol father's rural retreat, Racedown, in secluded Dorset about a dozen miles inland from Lyme Regis on the southern coast. William's sister Dorothy, a year younger and now twenty-four, had been shuffling among relatives for much of her life since the death of their mother when she was seven and their father's death when she was twelve. For several months in 1794, these orphaned siblings had shared time together near Keswick and at Whitehaven in their native Cumbria, and by the summer of 1795, they were eager to light upon a plan to find another shared dwelling, while William led a vagabond life in London with the two Basils and Dorothy lived in Halifax with Rawson kin, under a looming call to extended-family childcare duty with Cookson kin near Norwich.

After a flurry of correspondence and planning, in early September Dorothy wrote to a close friend, Jane Pollard Marshall, from Halifax:

Know then that I am going to live in Dorsetshire. Let me . . . methodically state the whole plan. . . . I think I told you that Mr Montague [*sic*] had a little boy, who as you will perceive could not be very well taken care of either in his father's chambers or under the uncertain management of various friends of Mr M with whom he has frequently stayed. He was lamenting this circumstance, and proposed to William to allow him 50 £ a year for his board provided I should approve of the plan.[13]

---

13. Wordsworth, *Letters Early Years,* 146–47. Subsequent references are by page number in the text.

In Montagu's much later account, Wordsworth, an adoptive parent, pitched the childcare proposal, whereas in Dorothy's secondhand contemporary account, Basil the birth parent launched the adoption idea. Dorothy's account also spotlights finances, which are always at stake in adoption—of necessity, or predatorily. From 1795 to the years after Waterloo, the financial transactions between Montagu and Wordsworth fill a spectacularly messy account book of legacies, loans, interest payments, and insurance policies. For the adoption history of Basil Caroline, it is enough to note that the west-country adoption agreement included a primary annual payment of £50 from a surviving impecunious birth parent to the impecunious adoptive sibling parents. The irony is that Montagu's shaky capital underwriting these payments was chiefly a loan from Wordsworth himself from a recent legacy, for which Montagu also owed Wordsworth 10 percent annual interest—and which, like the childcare payments, only sporadically appeared. Only apprentice lawyers and apprentice poets flush with Godwinianism could have cooked up such a circular scheme to shift the expenses of a motherless child from London to Dorset.

Dorothy's September letter reveals that the Dorsetshire adoption plan was an even larger-scale moneymaking venture for the Wordsworth siblings. In prospect, there was to be another child with them at Racedown, the illegitimate daughter of a cousin in India:

> A natural daughter of Mr Tom Myers (a cousin of mine whom I daresay you have heard me mention) is coming over to England by the first ships which are expected in about a month, to be educated, she is about 3 or 4 years old, and T. Myers's Brother who has the charge of her has requested that I will take her under my care. (148)

Other letters indicate that the Wordsworths also hoped to attract the third and youngest Pinney brother as a student, who at the going Pinney tutorial rate of £100 a year would put the Wordsworth sibling accounts nicely in the black. In the event, the Myers natural daughter and the Pinney son never materialized. Such a speculative Racedown academy became instead a family of sibling adoptive parents with a single adopted child, living rent-free in rural seclusion on uncertain funds from a London birth father. As Dorothy imagines the two young children under her care in prospect, it is telling that she thinks in explicit terms of motherhood, not of Basil, but of the natural daughter from India, who was a blood relative: "Basil Montagu is yet by no means a spoiled child notwithstanding the disadvantages under which he has laboured. As for the little girl I shall feel myself quite as a mother to her. I hope she will be healthy, that will be of great importance to my comfort and happiness" (150).

Dorothy Wordsworth had never met Basil the father or Basil the son, but the September letter indicates that she had attempted a degree of due diligence before committing herself to becoming an adoptive parent. William and Dorothy's younger brother Christopher, known to them as Kit, was then a Cambridge undergraduate, and Dorothy relied on him for a firsthand report of the lives she was about to encounter: "Kitt has seen the little boy, he says he is a very fine healthy looking child. It will be a very great charge for me I am sensible, but is of a nature well suited to my inclinations. You know I am active, not averse to household employments, and fond of children" (148). Over the next three years, Dorothy's letters offer a host of details about the practical daily care of Basil Caroline. The many women in service who cared for Basil as an infant at Brampton and as a toddler at Lincoln's Inn never left marks in the record. At Racedown, Dorothy and William hired a single servant, Peggy Marsh, with whom she shared quotidian childcare chores, but Dorothy from the start never planned to offload her charge: "I am determined to take the whole care of the children such as washing, dressing them &c upon myself. . . . I am quite equal to the charge. I expect to have some trouble with the children at first, but I am determined to act with resolution and steadiness, I hope I shall succeed" (149).

Basil Caroline and his new adoptive caregivers arrived at Racedown in late September 1795, via Bristol; Basil was three months short of his third birthday. It is not clear who transported Basil Caroline from London to Bristol. William was in Bristol from late August, but there is no indication that Basil Caroline accompanied him westward. Dorothy did not meet Basil the father for the first time for another eighteen months, so if she received Basil Caroline before she arrived in Bristol on September 22, Basil Caroline's father was not part of the handoff. In a letter six months later, Dorothy recalls Basil Caroline at arrival as "a shivering half starved plant" (166), the product of the "uncertain management" in London she had diplomatically danced around before meeting him, instead relying hopefully on young Kit Wordsworth's inexperienced report of a "very fine healthy looking child."

In this ad hoc Romantic-period version of an open adoption, the shared-custody plan originally promised visits to Dorset from the London birth father. But two months after arriving at Racedown, Dorothy wrote to Jane Marshall: "Mr. Montague [sic] had intended being with us a month ago but we have not seen him yet; we hope however that he will be with us before Christmas. I have the satisfaction of thinking that he will see great improvements in Basil" (161). In the same November, William wrote to their mutual friend Francis Wrangham, near London in Cobham: "We expect Montagu at Christmas and should be very glad if you could make it convenient to come along with him" (159). But Basil the father never showed up. Dorothy wrote again to Marshall in early March 1796: "We have not seen Mr. Montague [*sic*] which has disappointed us a good deal; he was at first prevented by a dangerous illness from coming at the appointed time, and afterwards by business; perhaps we may not see him now before the end of the summer" (165).

In the event, Basil-from-London never appeared in Dorset for another year, eighteen months after he had last seen his son.[14] In March 1797, he arrived unannounced, as Dorothy again reported to Jane Marshall: "Mr M. came upon us unexpectedly before we were risen on Wednesday morning. Wm has accompanied him to Bristol where they will spend about a fortnight and then William will return to Racedown" (181). At this first meeting with the birth father of the child in her adoptive care, Dorothy was suitably impressed: "I am excessively pleased with Mr M. He is one of the pleasantest men I ever saw, and so amiable, and so good that every body who knows him must love him" (181). But instead of spending overdue parenting time with Basil Caroline in remote seclusion, Basil the widower immediately headed for Bristol on the courtship prowl. Two potential marriage prospects at Racedown itself—Dorothy and the visiting Mary Hutchinson, later William's wife—did not long detain the young widower because the money was in Bristol. John Wedgwood, a son and heir of the wealthy Wedgwood pottery family, had settled near Bristol as a banker and country gentleman. In March 1797, John Wedgwood was hosting his several sisters, the youngest the unmarried Sarah Wedgwood, and Basil on the hunt and Wordsworth dined with the family on March 27. During that summer, instead of a return visit to Dorset, Basil and William Godwin left London (and a pregnant Mary Wollstonecraft) for a tour of the midlands to pay calls on the Wedgwood family, in the wake of which tour an engagement between Basil and Sarah Wedgwood failed. Basil had previously filed a suit in Chancery to gain a piece of a legacy from his father the earl, who had died in 1792, a year after cutting off his bastard son. The recent failure of that suit seems to have scuttled Basil's hopes for marital prosperity with the wealthy Wedgwood clan, a marriage that would have hugely altered the material course of Basil Caroline's life.[15] Instead of an anticipated marriage of their friend, in early September the Godwin household suffered the wrenching death of Mary Wollstonecraft after the birth of her daughter

---

14. Because of the elder Basil's absence and the pages cut from the document, there is almost no information about Basil Caroline's west-country period in his father's manuscript memoir. The record dwells chiefly in the Wordsworth correspondence.

15. Crum (see note 4) affirms the engagement and connects its failure to the failed legacy suit in Chancery. Graham and Tribe (see note 4) also confirm the failed engagement and refer readers to "Montagu/Wedgewood correspondence, University of Keele" (5).

Mary. Basil the apprentice lawyer was among the Godwin household over the fraught final week and summoned the doctor to attend her final agony, which replayed before his eyes the death of Caroline Want five years earlier. Mary Wollstonecraft Godwin in 1797 and Basil Caroline Montagu in 1792 both began their lives suddenly severed from a living mother.

During the two years at Racedown in which Basil the birth father made only one drive-by visit, William and Dorothy were, in the words of a recent biographer, "learning what it meant to be parents"—and Basil Caroline was learning what it meant to be an adopted child.[16] After arrival, Dorothy immediately got to work: "I have been making Basil colored frocks, shirts, slips, &c, and have had a good deal of employment in repairing his clothes" (161). Initially there was much mending required for the "shivering half starved plant": "At first when he came he was extremely petted from indulgence and weakness of body; and perpetually disposed to cry" (180). But her reports of her experience of the "perpetual" duties of charge and care soon turned almost uniformly positive. In November 1795, "Basil is a charming boy, he affords us perpetual entertainment" (160), and in March 1796 "he is my perpetual pleasure" (166). The "pleasure" she registers as adoptive parent dwelled especially in a monitory role, which expresses her investment in a systematic approach to childhood education: "But I do not think there is any Pleasure more delightful than that of marking the development of a child's faculties, and observing his little occupations" (160).

Eighteen months with Basil equipped Dorothy to enlarge on method, which shows her consciousness of how her daily labor in a remote English setting occurred in a wider context of education theory unleashed by Locke and Rousseau. In March 1797, she replied to a query from Jane Marshall: "You ask to be informed of our system respecting Basil; it is a very simple one, so simple that in this age of systems you will hardly be likely to follow it." Dorothy boiled down the Wordsworth method at Racedown to this Godwinian template:

> We teach him nothing at present but what he learns from the evidence of his senses. He has an insatiable curiosity which we are always careful to satisfy to the best of our ability. It is directed to everything he sees, the sky, the fields, trees, shrubs, corn, the making of tools, carts &c &c &c. He knows his letters, but we have not attempted any further step in the path of *book learning*. Our grand study has been to make him *happy*. (180)

---

16. Gill, *Wordsworth*, 103.

140 CHAPTER 5

Happiness as a goal of adoptive childcare occupies historical middle ground between tribal, baseline survival (Basil the father's residual assumption of a parental duty of "protection") and, emergingly, "best interests," the modern human rights standard enshrined in the UN Convention on the Rights of the Child. Whether or not it yields happiness (he would later complain bitterly that it did not), Basil Caroline's free-range curiosity at Racedown operated within the superstructure of a programmatic system of experimental childhood education, Dorothy's "grand study," which marks this scene of adoption, in the wake of Rousseau and Godwin, as a proving ground for the Romantic child.

In the early spring of 1796, Dorothy proudly reported first-term results. The petted, weak, crying, shivering, half-starved plant from September 1795 had become "a lusty, blooming fearless boy" (166). What emerges is not only an older, healthier Basil Caroline Montagu, the historical child, but the abstracted specter of the Romantic child, marked by solitude and a spontaneous, unmediated relationship to benign nature. In Dorothy's generalizing terms in a letter to her aunt, Mrs. William Rawson, "As to his activity I believe that the solitude of Racedown tended considerably to increase it. Till a child is four years old he needs no other companions, than the flowers, the grass, the cattle, the sheep that scamper away from him when he makes a vain unexpecting chase after them, the pebbles upon the road, &c &c" (222). Shared in letters by young women learning to be caregivers, recipes for brewing the Romantic child morphed into verse in the workshops of male companions, apprentice poets intent at least as much on publishing as on childcare. Here are lines from "The Foster-Mother's Tale: A Fragment" by the Wordsworth siblings' new west-country friend, Samuel Taylor Coleridge, which appeared in *Lyrical Ballads* in 1798, immediately following the lead poem, "The Rime of the Ancient Mariner." The foundling featured in the poem follows the script prescribed for Basil Caroline, who in his solitude, according to Dorothy, kept happy company with "pebbles upon the road":

The babe grew up a pretty boy,
A pretty boy, but most unteachable—
And never learnt a prayer, nor told a bead,
But knew the names of birds, and mocked their notes,
And whistled, as he were a bird himself:
And all the autumn 'twas his only play
To get the seeds of wild flowers, and to plant them
With earth and water, on the stumps of trees.[17]

_____

17. Wordsworth, *Lyrical Ballads*, 792–94. Subsequent references in the text to Wordsworth poems are by page number to this volume.

UNEXPLAINED CHILDREN   141

A manifest irony of this literary breeding ground of the Romantic child is how it regularly lowballs the print culture in which it lives and moves and has its being. In Dorothy's account of their "system," Basil Caroline "knows his letters, but we have not attempted any further step in the path of *book learning*" (180), like the "most unteachable" foundling in Coleridge's verse.

Coleridge and his own young family appeared in Basil Caroline's adopted life in the third and final year of his west-country chapter. After two years for the new Wordsworth family at Racedown, the Pinney brothers' Bristol merchant father discovered the rent-free deal and cut it off. In the summer of 1797, the two Wordsworths, one young Montagu, and the servant Peggy Marsh shifted north to Somerset, to a new house, Alfoxden, attracted by the nearby Coleridge home in Nether Stowey. The west-country locals were puzzled by the Wordsworth trio; in the words of a later nineteenth-century account: "The profound seclusion in which they lived, the incomprehensible nature of their occupations, their strange habit of frequenting out-of-the-way and untrodden spots, *the very presence of an unexplained child that was no relation to either of them,* all combined to produce an impression of awe and mistrust."[18] The enigma of an adopted child shares signifying force with solitude, nature, and idle wandering in this sketch of early Romanticism living light on the land.

During the following year, Wordsworth and Coleridge produced much of the poetry that appeared in *Lyrical Ballads* in 1798, where Basil Caroline, the unexplained child, makes several cameo appearances as "Edward." Wordsworth's lyric titled "Lines, Written at a Small Distance from my House, and Sent by my Little Boy to the Person to whom they are Addressed" strikes a characteristic note of principled indifference to intellectual culture belied by the poem itself as a scripted invitation to privilege nature over books:

> My Sister! ('tis a wish of mine)
> Now that our morning meal is done,
> Make haste, your morning task resign;
> Come forth and feel the sun.
>
> Edward will come with you, and pray,
> Put on with speed your woodland dress,
> And bring no book, for this one day
> We'll give to idleness. (63–64)

---

18. Sandford, *Thomas Poole*, 1.240; emphasis added. Similarly confused, the current entry for Basil Montagu *père* in the *Oxford Dictionary of National Biography* testifies that "Wordsworth and his wife undertook the care of Montagu's young son."

142   CHAPTER 5

Wordsworth later replaced the original long title with the brief title "To My Sister," which is how the poem circulates in most modern reprints. The family of three encircled in the original title shrinks to the two adult principals, symptomatic of the fading role of the historical Basil Caroline in the emerging literary scene of Romantic childhood.[19]

"Edward's" most notable role in *Lyrical Ballads* is the poem known by its short title, "Anecdote for Fathers." Like "We Are Seven," the poem rehearses an odd conversation between an adult and a child who are packaged as father and son on a rural morning stroll:

> I have a boy of five years old,
> His face is fair and fresh to see;
> His limbs are cast in beauty's mould,
> And dearly he loves me.
>
> One morn we stroll'd on our dry walk,
> Our quiet house all full in view,
> And held such intermitted talk
> As we are wont to do. (71–73)

The conversation turns on a whimsical contest between two homes, their current home at "Liswyn farm" and their former home at "Kilve." In the register where "Edward" signifies Basil Caroline, these place-names function as placeholders for Alfoxden and Racedown. The father asks "my little boy" not only "which like you more?" but also, raising the stakes, where "had you rather be?" In "careless mood," the child answers that "At Kilve I'd rather be / Than here at Liswyn farm." A coin toss to the boy, this response proves unsatisfactory to the adult mind, and the father now addresses Edward by name: "'Now, little Edward, say why so; / My little Edward, tell me why;' / 'I cannot tell, I do not know.' / 'Why this is strange,' said I." Like the persistently skeptical adult interlocutor in "We Are Seven," Edward's father is relentless: "And five times did I say to him, / 'Why? Edward, tell me why?'" So put to the test, Edward catches random sight of a weather vane there at Liswyn farm "Upon the house-top, glittering bright," leading to the final two stanzas:

> Then did the boy his tongue unlock,
> And thus to me he made reply;

---

19. Forty-five years later, when Wordsworth dictated a set of notes to his poems that often point to their historical circumstances, he left Basil Caroline unnamed: "My little boy messenger on this occasion was the son of Basil Montagu"; Wordsworth, *Fenwick Notes*, 37.

"At Kilve there was no weather-cock,
"And that's the reason why."

Oh dearest boy! my heart
For better lore would seldom yearn,
Could I but teach the hundredth part
Of what from thee I learn.

The extensive commentary on the poem foregrounds the father's consciousness, for whom the temporal contest between past and present bears adult weight: the father's "thoughts on former pleasures ran," pleasures that are associated with Kilve "a long, long year before," whereas now at Liswyn farm "with so much happiness to spare / I could not feel a pain," an adult negotiation of human temporality that anticipates the far more intricate temporal layers in the final poem in the book, "Tintern Abbey."

But instead of an existential puzzle about how grown-up people experience time, the poem locates the child Edward's lottery choice in favor of Kilve in a curious ethical register in the poem's subtitle: "Anecdote for Fathers: Shewing How the Art of Lying May Be Taught." This title language sets up the scene of instruction in the final stanza, the "lore" that is "learned" by the father from Edward's arbitrary response, precategorized by the subtitle as a lie—or, to use the language of Swift's Houyhnhnms, *the thing which was not* (for they have no Word in their Language to express Lying or Falshood)."[20] As a speech act, saying "the thing which was not" was apparently the historical Basil Caroline's habit; in a letter to Francis Wrangham in spring 1796, William notes that "Basil is quite well quant au physique mais pour le moral il-y-a bien à craindre. Among other things he lies like a little devil" (168), a behavior borne out by many reported incidents in Basil Caroline's later life. But instead of an ethical rebuke, the 1798 poem inflects Edward's choice honorifically as an "*art* of lying," an action that in the poem's drama instructs the adult powerfully. Frances Ferguson points to Rousseau's "basic claim" in *Emile* "that children and adults speak different languages, and that most of their conversations are lies, in being differentially understood by parties to the exchange," by which means the Romantic child poses for emergent liberalism a "problem as fundamental as it is insoluble."[21] To shift the focus on the poem from adult consciousness to the "careless mood" of the child is to glimpse how the poem measures the imperative power—the artifice—of contingency,

20. Swift, *Writings*, 203.
21. Ferguson, "Rousseau," 196.

accident, and arbitrariness in the haphazard life of this particular adopted child. At the time of the poem, the five-year-old Basil Caroline had known the conditional provisionality of four homes, not just the two shared in the poem with his avatar Edward: first Brampton, then London, then Racedown (Kilve), and then Alfoxden (Liswyn Farm). Asked where he would rather be among such an ever-shifting range of choices, the adopted child has early learned the art of flipping a coin, an arbitrary choice between saying one thing and saying another thing that is not.

Framed as contingent adoptee, Edward lines up with the other children in *Lyrical Ballads* who form a company of mad suspects: the little girl who cannot count how many of her siblings are still alive in "We Are Seven" and the Idiot Boy who looks at the moon and calls it the sun, both of whom steal a win by saying the things that are not. This set of offbeat children becomes sequestered in the abstract figure of the "Child" celebrated as "Thou best Philosopher . . . Mighty Prophet! Seer blest!" in Wordsworth's "Ode" published in 1807, the poem rightly known, in Ann Wierda Rowland's phrase, as "the period's manifesto of childhood."[22] In that poem, Wordsworth hijacks surrogate care as a governing figure for the relationship between nature and humanity at large, her "Foster-child." Among that fostered set, the poem singles out children as a special and privileged subset: "Behold the Child among his newborn blisses, / A four year's Darling of a pigmy size!" In 1815 Wordsworth changed the age of this poster Child from four to six, and this particularized attention invites speculation about a particular historical child sequestered in the abstract figure. The best modern scholarship records a prevailing consensus that Wordsworth "is thinking in particular of Hartley Coleridge," Coleridge's oldest child, born in September 1796, whom William, Dorothy, and Basil Caroline had known as a neighboring toddler during their year at Alfoxden when Basil was four and five.[23] No doubt Hartley Coleridge is a proximate historical child veiled in the figure of the Romantic child in the "Ode," but his solo recovery in scholarship comes at the cost of an adopted child who also shadows the Child of the "Ode," Basil Caroline Montagu, whom William as apprentice parent watched daily when Basil was three, four, and five. To recover Basil Caroline the historical child in the "Ode" is to hear in the key of adoption a particular form of mourning in a poem fundamentally elegiac, a simultaneous celebration of and lament for the loss of a primary figure denominated The Child. The figure of the adopted child, differentiated, folds diminishment into this cornerstone figuration of the differ-

---

22. Rowland, *Romanticism and Childhood*, 3.
23. Wordsworth, *Poems, in Two Volumes*, 271–77 (text) and 428–30 (notes).

entiated Romantic child; one form of the burden bequeathed to the adopted child is the impossible charge to represent the lost origins of all others.

The weather attending the Romantic child in the "Ode" is unremittingly benign: "Thou Child of Joy" shouts with pleasure "This sweet May-morning . . . while the sun shines warm." It is no surprise that it was not uniformly so for the historical child. On March 19, 1798, Dorothy recorded in her new journal at Alfoxden, "Wm and Basil and I walked to the hill-tops, a very cold bleak day. We were met on our return by a severe hailstorm. William wrote some lines describing a stunted thorn," a stormy outing soon followed by William's lyrical ballad "The Thorn," a scene of severe abjection (77–85).[24] In the poem, William appropriates the name of Basil Caroline's murdered grandmother, Martha Ray, for a mad mother drawn repeatedly to her "infant's grave," where in her solitary grief she suffers nothing but hard weather "when the whirlwind's on the hill / Or frosty air is keen and still." In the Wordsworth "system," Basil Caroline experienced similar conditions of solitude, which Dorothy reads as plucky rather than abject scenes of grief: "He dreads neither cold nor rain. He has played frequently an hour or two without appearing sensible that the rain was pouring down upon him or the wind blowing about him" (166). Basil Caroline may have thought otherwise, of course. Fifteen years later, his father was called to intervene as his son shuffled among family friends between London and Cumbria, who had forwarded alarmed reports of outbursts of what his father terms his "morbid feeling." In his father's account:

> Basil had, day after day, vilified Wordsworth: he had stated, that when living with his Sister, they had treated him with such cruelty that he was constantly employed in the most menial occupations: and, but for the pity of the poor Villagers, who privately supplied him with such pittance as they could ill share, he should have been starved. I had reason to suspect other calumnies. (WLMS)

To heal this distemper before taking the twenty-year-old Basil to visit his former adoptive parents, Basil the father prescribed a hasty course of Wordsworth's poetry, which the son gamely attempted. Reading Wordsworth, Basil Caroline encountered the gulf between the Romantic child and the pulse of his own adoptive history.

In the late summer of 1798, Basil Caroline suffered yet another separation from his latest temporary home. While arranging the publication of *Lyri-*

---

24. Dorothy Wordsworth, *Journals*, I.13.

cal Ballads, Dorothy, William, and Coleridge decided to set off for Germany, without Coleridge's family and without young Basil. In Dorothy's account:

> Poor Basil! We are obliged to leave him behind as his father, on account of having altered the course of his pursuits in the law, will not be able to pay the additional expenses which we should incur on his account. This, however, might be got over as he has friends who would do it for him, but as the experiment of taking a child of his age into a foreign country is at any rate hazardous, and might be prejudicial if we were not so placed that he might see much of other children, we think upon the whole that it is better that he should not go, taking into the calculation the certain expense. (221)

When William, Dorothy, and Basil Caroline arrived in London from the west country on August 27, 1798, William reported the next day that "Montagu is not in town" (227). William and Dorothy sailed for Germany on September 16. Absent these absent caregivers, the adoptive charge of Basil Caroline defaulted to his birth mother's sisters in Brampton, the first home he had known at his birth and her death. He was now a few months shy of his sixth birthday.

BRAMPTON, CAMBRIDGE, AND LONDON, 1798–1806

The elder Basil's account of Basil Caroline's adoptive repatriation to Brampton omits the Wordsworth siblings' interval in Germany: "After having resided two or three years in Dorsetshire, Wm Wordsworth resolved to settle at Grasmere and my Child was received by his Aunt, the Sister of his Mother, who lived upon a small income at Brampton in Huntingdonshire. With this excellent Woman he remained for some years" (WLMS). The solitary child from the west now reexperienced a crowded network of village kin—aunts, uncles, and cousins. Meanwhile, his widowed birth father continued his hunt for a new wife, which again shifted the course of Basil Caroline's life. In the late summer of 1801, the widowed Basil headed for Scotland with an eighteen-year-old, Laura Rush of Wimbledon, accompanied by her parents, Sir William and Lady Rush, and her five older sisters. The wedding party picked up William Wordsworth to stand with the groom on their way north to a wedding in Glasgow on September 6.[25] Outmatched by the six Rush sisters, the nine-year-old Basil Caroline did not make the wedding journey and was not present at this creation of a new family structure he now needed to learn, repatriated.

25. Reed, *Chronology Middle Years.*

UNEXPLAINED CHILDREN   147

After her year in Germany, Dorothy Wordsworth in Cumbria with William kept Basil Caroline fondly in mind. In her Grasmere journal in February 1802, she records a "poor woman" who had come to beg with "her little Boy, a pretty little fellow, and whom I have loved for the sake of Basil, [and who] looks thin and pale."[26] A year earlier, Dorothy had been left alone in Grasmere by William and their brother John, away on an excursion, as she wrote in a September 1800 letter to Jane Pollard Marshall:

> During their absence, I felt myself very lonely while I was within doors, I wanted my little companion Basil, and poor old Molly did but ill supply to me the place of our good and dear Peggy who was quite as a friend to us. Basil is with an Uncle in Huntingdonshire—we wish his father to send him to some school, if possible in the North of England that he may be near us. (298)

After his 1801 marriage, the elder Basil and the new Mrs. Montagu removed from London to Cambridge for an interval, where the young lawyer produced a work on bankruptcy law that helped establish his career. For Basil Caroline, the possibility of school in the north near his adoptive Wordsworth family did not come to pass; he instead removed from Brampton to boarding school in East Anglia. In his father's account, "Basil was at School at Bury St. Edmunds, & spent his holidays either at Mr. Lane's or with us in Cambridge" (WLMS). This Mr. Lane is the Cambridge tutor who had supplied the elder Basil with the money to undertake his legal apprenticeship in London in 1795. John Lane became the latest in the series of surrogate caregivers for Basil Caroline: "Mr. Lane has not any children. He is one of the most affectionate of living beings. With the remembrance of his Mother, and the consciousness of the happiness which he had bestowed upon both of us, he soon became attached to Basil. I can confidently say with more than a parent's love" (WLMS). The measure of parental love in the last sentence aims at a high compliment when understood superlatively (Lane's love exceeds even the love of a parent), but when understood comparatively (the love of this nonparent exceeds the love of this parent) it cannot escape a shadow of parental neglect.

There was a good reason that Basil Caroline might have preferred holiday time with Mr. Lane ("who has not any children") to his father's temporary home in Cambridge, which rapidly filled with new children. After father Basil's marriage, a son, Algernon, was born in 1802, followed by a second son, Alfred, in 1804. Basil Caroline was a decade older than these new half sib-

---

26. Dorothy Wordsworth, *Journals*, I.111.

148   CHAPTER 5

lings, whom he met in a home with a birth father he had rarely known at first hand and a new stepmother devoted to her own small children. The inevitable unhappiness took recorded form not in a Montagu family quarrel but in abuse of the benevolent John Lane. In father Basil's account:

> Having completed my work upon the bankrupt laws I took a small house in London to commence my professional pursuits. Basil who had been very unwell was with Mr. Lane in the Country. I had not been settled many weeks when Mr. Lane requested that he might never see Basil again: that he had been obliged to dismiss him from his house as his kindness had been returned by ["ingratitude" crossed out; "calumny" overwritten] which he could never forget. I was silent. We received Basil under our roof and endeavoured as far as was in our power to add to his comfort. (WLMS)

This second temporary home for Basil Caroline in London soon crumbled in tragedy. After the birth of a third son, William, in May 1806, Laura Rush Montagu died suddenly in June, which replayed for Basil Caroline the events of his own birth and mother's death a dozen years earlier. There was no comfort for anyone in this new temporary home.

Before the sudden death of his birth father's second wife, Basil Caroline unloaded his unhappiness on her as well as on Mr. Lane, according to his father, who reported "Basil's reproaches, who while an inmate under our roof, went from house to house representing that my wife treated him with the unkindness of a Step Mother" (WLMS). In the late spring of 1806, the Wordsworth family in Grasmere followed the London pregnancy and subsequent afflictions closely. Dorothy wrote to a friend in London with news about "our anxiety for poor Mrs. Montagu":

> About three weeks ago she was delivered of a Boy, and Montagu wrote in great spirits for she seemed to be going on very well, but yesterday we received a letter from him to tell us that we must not be surprised if we saw him any day, for that his wife was very ill, and that if she *should* fall a victim he feared he should lose his senses if he did not see William. Therefore if he did not come down hither he begged William to go to him.[27]

After the news of Laura Rush Montagu's death reached Grasmere, letters filled with hurried plans for the Wordsworths to host for care not only the griev-

---

27. Wordsworth, *Letters Middle Years, Part I*, 37. Subsequent references are by page number in the text.

UNEXPLAINED CHILDREN 149

ing husband but also Basil Caroline, who was sharpening his habit for saying "the thing which was not." Dorothy wrote, "Montagu does not say on what day he shall set off, but he says, 'I, and probably Basil shall be with you most likely before the end of next week'" (49). But repeating the pattern of the ever-delayed visits to Dorset a decade before, the Wordsworths were still waiting a month later, still eager to help. In Dorothy's words, "Montagu and Basil are coming down very soon. Poor Man, he stayed in the hope of being able to attend to business in the Bankruptcy Courts at the end of last month, but he could not do it. He seems to be terribly depressed. . . . We shall contrive to have a bed for him and Basil" (61). William joined in keeping the invitation open: "I am very sorry to find that you continue to be so disturbed in mind. . . . Come as soon as you can and with Basil; I think it would certainly be of great service to you" (62).

The therapeutic visit never happened. His own well-being never fore-grounded in these exchanges, Basil Caroline seems an afterthought to these plans, filling the familiar role of the surplus relative who can't be accommo-dated anywhere else. Had the two Basils journeyed in the wake of the father's grief to Grasmere, they would have been leaving to someone else's care in London three small children: a four-year-old Algernon, a two-year-old Alfred, and a month-old William. A custody battle broke out with Laura Rush's par-ents, which is the most likely reason that Basil the father remained in London:

> Broken hearted by my loss I was little able to attend to the various conflicting duties which I was then called upon to perform.—Sir Wm and Lady Rush were desirous to take my three infant Children under their care. Convinced that I ought, if possible, to insure to them happiness, which no wealth can procure, I declined to comply with their Grandfather's wishes. The conse-quence was such misrepresentation to the children of my conduct [multi-ple words heavily overscored] that I was reluctantly compelled to terminate [word overscored] all intercourse between them and the Parents of their Mother. I resolved that for a few years they should never meet. (WLMS)

In the wake of Laura Rush Montagu's death, Basil Caroline witnessed his father's determination to keep under his own care his three new sons "to insure to them happiness," a duty of care he had regularly offloaded for his first son. The Montagu family in London was now a twice-widowed father, three small children, and their older half sibling, an alienated, repatriated, and seriously disaffected teen. For Basil Caroline, a tempting escape soon opened: "In the depth of my sorrow Basil was received by my brother Admiral Mon-tagu, where he formed the injudicious determination to be a Midshipman"

(WLMS). In the father's language, Basil Caroline after his adopted years in the west country was first "received by his Aunt," then "received by us," and then "received by my brother." Basil Caroline circulated passively like a piece of lost luggage.

THE ROYAL NAVY, 1806–1812

Seven years older than his lawyer brother Basil, Robert Montagu was the oldest "natural child" of the Earl of Sandwich, First Lord of the Admiralty, by their mother, the Earl's mistress Martha Ray. Robert Montagu began service as a naval lieutenant in 1779, age sixteen; he was soon a captain and commander in the East Indies and saw action in the American Revolution and the war with revolutionary France. From 1799 to 1805, he quickly moved up through the ranks of rear-admiral appointments, including a stint as commander of the Jamaica Station. When he became the next surrogate caregiver for Basil Caroline in 1806, he was a vice admiral, reaching the top of the rigging as admiral in 1810.[28]

When onshore in 1806, Vice Admiral Montagu kept a house in Tooting near the Rush family home in Wimbledon, which is where his brother Basil sought refuge during his second wife's illness and death. As reported by Dorothy Wordsworth, "Poor man, he was at his Brother's house two miles from Wimbledon when his dear wife died, and he said that by walking a little way he could see the house" (49). Basil Caroline, now fourteen, was more interested in his uncle's tales than his stepmother's last affliction: "I am not astonished that in conversing with my brother upon the battles in which he had been engaged and the accidents from which he had escaped and the countries which he had seen the boy set his heart upon going to Sea. He imparted his resolution to me at a time when beat to the earth I had not strength to destroy these illusions" (WLMS). The grieving widower attempted to dissuade Basil Caroline, ending his plea with a startling image of abjection, grounded in the prospect of his own death: "I explained as well as I was able the miseries in which he would involve himself. That he had not health or strength to encounter the difficulties of such an arduous occupation . . . and that after the sacrifice of some of the most important years of his life he might return an uneducated orphan Cripple" (WLMS). The argument between father and son turned on the question of who would fill the role of father; according to Basil senior, his entreaties "were treated with contempt. My fears for his welfare,

---

28. Marshall, *Royal Naval Biography,* I.1.135–36.

Unexplained Children

he assured me, were groundless as Admiral Montagu had said that, in the event of my death, he would be his father. My brother with great kindness confirmed to me the assurances which he had made to Basil" (WLMS). The irony of these exchanges in 1806 is that the role of father had been at risk for the entire course of Basil Caroline's life.

Seafaring life did not go well. By 1808 Basil Caroline had turned on Admiral Montagu, blaming him for his own illusions and for sibling disrespect: "Basil, after he had been 2 years at sea, importuned me to obtain his discharge, into which, as he said, he never should have entered but for the misrepresentations of Admiral Montagu & the disrespectful manner in which he had spoken of me" (WLMS). The lawyer father attempted vocational counseling, suggesting the unlikely prospect of a church living, a style of life long overpopulated with idle sons of the gentry, but "the church he spurned" (WLMS). Basil Caroline decided to take a second shot at naval life, but with a noteworthy qualification: "After various deliberations he returned to Sea, but not with my brother's friendship" (WLMS). In 1808 Vice Admiral Montagu was in the course of promotion from the penultimate vice-admiral rung to the ultimate perch, and his flourishing career did not need the ungrateful aspersions of a disaffected midshipman whom he had, like John Lane in Cambridge, taken under his surrogate paternal wing.

The last four years of navy service, from 1808 when he was sixteen to 1812 when he was twenty, nearly broke Basil Caroline's heath, always at risk. In his father's words, "In the Autumn of 1812 he was sent home with an excellent character from his officers, but with scarcely any hope of life" (WLMS). Two years after the 1806 death of Laura Rush, the twice-widowed Basil Montagu had married a third time, a widow, Mrs. Anna Benson Skepper, who was helping him care for the three young boys and whose own daughter Anne, born in 1799, joined the London household. Two new Montagu children quickly followed, Charles in 1810 and Emily in 1812. The London home into which the broken Basil Caroline returned in 1812 counted three half-sibling brothers (the three sons of Laura Rush, two of whom were now at school), a new stepsister, a second stepmother, and two new half-sibling toddlers. While recovering in such a haphazard nest, Basil Caroline broke with the navy as a career: "During his sufferings he expressed a desire to be emancipated from his profession.—Without saying a word to him I wrote to Sir Richard Middlestone who has known me from a boy and obtained his discharge which I enclosed in a letter to Basil" (WLMS). It is clear that Basil Caroline was nursed in the family home during his recovery; the formality of epistolary communication between father and son registers not only a lawyer's cautious habit but also seriously compromised affection on both sides.

The discharge was accomplished in May 1813. By the end of that year, Basil Caroline was living in Ambleside in Cumbria, dining with his former adoptive Wordsworth family almost daily. His arrival there was shaded by a series of events that further tangled the Montagu and Wordsworth families while Basil Caroline was away at sea. Basil the lawyer and Mrs. Anna Skepper Montagu shipped the oldest son of the Laura Rush marriage, Algernon, to school in Ambleside in the spring of 1810 when he was eight, and Basil Caroline's younger half sibling was already well established ahead of him in the Wordsworth circle by 1813, forming school friendships with the Coleridge boys Hartley and Derwent and William and Mary's oldest son Johnny. On an autumn visit to see the newly enrolled Algernon in 1810, the London Montagus precipitated one of the most famous cock-ups in British literary Romanticism, the breach between Coleridge and Wordsworth. Coleridge was then in a sad state, lodging with his Southey relatives in Keswick after a spell with the Wordsworth family in Grasmere, all the while battling his fondness for drink and an opium habit. The Montagus offered him a home with them in London, where he could be treated by Anna Skepper Montagu's physician. On their journey south, Montagu repeated to Coleridge very blunt warnings about Coleridge's behavior that Wordsworth had shared with him privately, and the next two years were filled with recriminations and counter claims until a frosty détente was negotiated by Charles Lamb and Henry Crabb Robinson in 1812.[29] The Wordsworth family had taken a dislike to the third Mrs. Montagu even before this episode played out, William dismissing her to his wife Mary as an "odious Creature" in a letter dreading the autumn 1810 visit, and her eagerness to draw Coleridge into her London social circle only compounded their distaste.[30] After the 1810 contretemps, Basil the father did not show up in Cumbria again until the fall of 1813, when he was accompanied only by Basil Caroline, who was meeting his west-country adoptive caregivers for the first time since 1798.

CUMBRIA, 1813–1814

In the late spring of 1813, on the recommendation of a physician for a "change of air and cheerfulness," Basil the lawyer put Basil Caroline on the road: "After some deliberation I resolved that no expense should be spared. I instantly suggested he should travel in different parts of England," the itinerary to finish its northern run with a visit to the Wordsworths in Cumbria. On his return

---

29. For a reliable history of the quarrel, see Barker, *Wordsworth*, 408–29.
30. Wordsworth, *Love Letters*, 85.

south, Basil Caroline might be offloaded in Devonshire: "Mr [Teed?], one of my Pupils, had kindly offered that his Mother should receive him at her house" (WLMS). To solve the lifetime puzzle of who might receive him, Basil Caroline now rated only a thirdhand invitation, from the mother of a pupil of his father.

The first stop on the journey was the old Want family home in Brampton, where Basil visited the "tomb of my Mother and my second Mother," as he wrote to his "dear Mother" in London. In May 1813, Anna Skepper Montagu had just given birth to her third child with lawyer Basil, adding an eighth child to a family that Thomas Carlyle would later describe as "a most difficult miscellany" as he tallied the "fourth genealogic species among the children."[31] Unlike his animosity toward his father's second wife, Basil Caroline tumbled all over himself with compliments for the new Mrs. Montagu. Reporting his visits to the maternal tombs in Brampton, he was also glad to be "telling you once again how happy I am and how much more that happiness would be increased if you were but here and able to participate in it" (WLMS). In late April, having moved on to Warwick, he addressed her as "my more than Mother, who by the practice of every virtue has contributed so largely to my salvation from little better than a state of brutality," her "love and esteem being what I most prize upon earth" (WLMS).

Although Basil Caroline remained on uncharacteristically good terms with Anna Skepper Montagu, he maintained his habitually sour attitude toward almost everyone else. At Brampton, in addition to visiting the tomb of his adoptive caregiver Aunt Charlotte, he complained in a letter to his father that she had stiffed him in her will when she died in 1802: "Basil discovered that his Aunt had acted very unjustly in having left to him so small a legacy as £200" (WLMS). As Basil traveled north from one family acquaintance to another, reports made it back to his father in London: "To my great astonishment, I heard that, at the house of my friend into which I had thus introduced him, he was constantly speaking disrespectfully of me his father and, that these censures might appear with the advantage of contrast, in the constant praise of the tender affection of my Wife" (WLMS). In addition to Basil Caroline's aspersions cast on Mr. Lane, Laura Rush Montagu, and Admiral Robert Montagu, new targets began to pile up: "I learnt that the calumnies with which he had vilified me at Warwick were extended to many of my different friends to whom I had introduced him in different parts of England: in Staffordshire in Shropshire and in London" (WLMS). During his annual holiday in September 1813, father Basil joined Basil Caroline on the journey north to Cumbria.

---

31. Carlyle, *Reminiscences*, I.225–26.

154 CHAPTER 5

As he prepared for the visit to the Wordsworth family, the lawyer experienced firsthand the effects of Basil's bile:

> In September we proceeded towards the north. We stopped at Warwick at the house of my friend Mr. Parkes. One of Mr. Parkes' sons was to accompany us. I accidentally expressed the happiness I should experience in introducing him to William Wordsworth. To my great astonishment I observed a strange silence [four or five words heavily overscored] through the whole family. I hate mystery. I soon learnt the cause. Basil had, day after day, vilified Wordsworth. (WLMS)

The account continues with the sentences on the "cruelty" Basil Caroline alleged he experienced at the hands of his Wordsworth adoptive caregivers in Dorset and Somerset nearly twenty years earlier, when, "but for the pity of the poor Villagers, who privately supplied him with such pittance as they could ill share, he should have been starved" (WLMS).

Alarmed by Basil Caroline's deep-seated "asperity" toward nearly everyone, father Basil in Godwinian gear attempted an analysis of the "causes, effects, and remedies" of what he termed Basil Caroline's "diseased affection" and "morbid feeling" (WLMS). For causation, the lawyer emphasized Basil Caroline's lifetime of physical infirmity, stretching back from the health crisis at the end of his navy career to his west-country time, when in the spring of 1797 Dorothy grimly reported to her brother Richard in London that "poor Basil was very, very ill. I was afraid we should have lost him" (186). Father Basil's one stab at psychological analysis fixed on Basil Caroline's return from the navy. At sea, Basil felt superior to his shipmates, but back at home in the crowds of London, his insignificance didn't sit well with him and he lashed out. What his father did not venture in explanation is an account of Basil Caroline's lifetime of adoptive contingency, except his remark that at Brampton "he had lived much with excellent old ladies to whom the dear Basil was all in all" (WLMS).

Basil Caroline's "morbid feeling" was an open topic of concern shared among Basil Caroline, his father, and Anna Skepper Montagu. In his letters to his father's third wife, Basil Caroline confessed his "repugnance to saying civil things" and his instinctive "spirit of opposition," which he promised to try to remedy (WLMS). Before arriving in Cumbria, his father prescribed a dose of poetry:

> I availed myself of every opportunity, by reading Wordsworth's works to eradicate his opinion of Wordsworth.—After having passed some weeks in

this delightful country: Basil voluntarily said to me that he was sensible of his injustice & unkindness to her and to Mr Wordsworth & begged that I would permit him to proceed to Grasmere & atone to Wordsworth for the misrepresentations which had been said to him & which he had, under the impression of their truth, repeated. (WLMS)

When the two Basils arrived in Cumbria on this mission of reconciliation, they met a Wordsworth family still deeply marred by the sudden deaths of two of the five children of William and Mary during the previous year. Basil the lawyer returned to London, leaving Basil Caroline under the watchful care of the nearby Wordsworth household. A doubled-back repatriation, the autumn of 1813 in remote Cumbria now replayed the adoptive circumstances of the autumn of 1795 in Dorset.

In October 1813, Mary Wordsworth wrote to her sister Sara that "young Basil Montagu is a constant dish with us every evening."[32] The Wordsworth family had only recently moved into their new home at Rydal Mount; Basil Caroline boarded with Mrs. Ross in nearby Ambleside with other boys at school with Mr. Dawes, including his half sibling Algernon, who was half his age. Basil Caroline busied himself as big brother, reporting the success of Algernon's acne treatments to their stepmother Mrs. Montagu and vetting coach schedules for Algernon's Christmas journey to London. As Basil Caroline was folded into the social round of Ambleside and the Wordsworth circle, William wrote to his father that Basil "has much interested all who have known him in this country."[33] Burdened by the need for a scheme to make his way in the world, Basil Caroline made desultory efforts at his own self-managed schooling toward some kind of life in the church, which he had earlier scorned. In a letter to Mrs. Montagu, he made pious reference to "the plan I have adopted . . . while viewing with wonder and awe the stupendous works of the Almighty," and on his way north he asked her to "have the kindness to let my bible be sent with the parcel which is coming, and some flannel drawers" (WLMS). At Ambleside, he sorted his curriculum with Mrs. Montagu rather than with his father directly: "With respect to my Father's question about arrangements if he means with Mr Dawes I have made none as I can learn the rudiments of Latin & Greek quite as well myself" (WLMS). In a December letter, in addition to a request for "any hair or clothes brushes I have left behind as I much want them," he sharpened pencils to prepare for New Testament studies: "Will you be so kind enough to let somebody go to

---

32. Mary Wordsworth, *Letters*, 12.

33. Wordsworth, *Letters Middle Years, Part II*, 130. Subsequent references are by page number in the text.

Mr Wilson's printing office Duke Street Lincolns Inn fields & get his 8vo Edition of the Greek Testament unbound & let it be sent to Satchell's to be bound up with two sheets of blank paper between each leaf & if the volume will be too large, he may bind the epistles & acts by themselves & so make 2 Vols" (WLMS).

In spite of his resolve to curb his asperity, in correspondence Basil Caroline freely indulged his sour temper. Dorothy Wordsworth especially got on his nerves: "The young Wordsworths were there & slept at our house as the night was wet & I contrived to be very gracious all the time tho' Miss Wordsworth (that is old Dorothy) contrived to fidget most amazingly" (WLMS). The woman who most inflamed his misogynistic itch was a new acquaintance, Mary Barker, a friend of Robert Southey. He initially chafed at Mrs. Montagu's efforts from London to recommend her: "I wish you had said nothing to me about Miss Barker. . . . There is something so very unpleasant in her manners that I cannot like her do what I will and I attribute much of it to the spirit of opposition which makes me above doing what I am told" (WLMS). After a second social gathering, Basil Caroline reported that he "did not like Miss B—any better if any thing less. I like women to be women and she looks like anything but one you have drawn these remarks upon yourself by putting me on my guard so do not write and tell me I am as uncharitable and fanciful as ever" (WLMS). Although Miss Barker "is not a woman that I can ever admire," Basil Caroline felt obliged to accept an invitation to visit her in Keswick in the new year: she "begged I would go and spend a week with her at Keswick which I must do if not unwell as she made a point of it & I think would be hurt if I refused" (WLMS).

In January 1814, Basil Caroline nearly died during the visit to Miss Barker's home in Keswick. He lay dangerously ill there through April, nursed for sixteen weeks by the very targets of his epistolary spleen, Mary Barker and Dorothy Wordsworth. The most vivid account of his crisis is a letter from Coleridge's estranged wife, Sara Fricker Coleridge, who lived in the Southey household next to Miss Barker. She wrote to Tom Poole, one of the old Somerset friends, in February:

> You must remember Basil Montagu a little boy at Alfoxden, he lies dangerously ill at the house of our friend Miss Barker next door to us—to whose house he came from Ambleside 5 weeks ago—for a visit of a few days; he has been at sea for the last 7 years, & being in ill health his father sent him to Ambleside to a lodging there for a little recreation:—the day after his arrival at Keswick he was sitting in Southey's study, he began violently to vomit blood. . . . Southey & the surgeon supported him across the garden to his

UNEXPLAINED CHILDREN 157

bed at Miss B's, where he has lain almost ever since, bleeding 2 or 3 times in the 24 hours, until the last week, when he sat up a little—but *now* he has a violent pain in his side—is *blistered* and *again bled* in the Arm, and cannot get out of bed but for a few minutes with the help of Miss B's boy and the Surgeon—and Miss Wordsworth tells us to-day that she sees no prospect whatever of his removal—Miss B—& Miss W take [it] by turns to watch his bed side, & sometimes they are assisted by an old servant of Miss B's.[34]

Miss Barker broke the news to London, in lawyer Basil's account: "Early in January we received a letter from Miss Barker informing us that Basil had been suddenly attacked, the day after his arrival at Keswick by the rupture of a blood vessel and that his life was in danger. . . . My wife was desirous to go to Keswick :—but from the delicacy of her health and of my own I would not permit her during that inclement season to undertake such an arduous journey" (WLMS). On January 20, William wrote to Basil in London: "My sister went over to Keswick yesterday to see Basil and to assist Miss Barker. . . . He is deplorably reduced" (129). Three days later, Dorothy was grim in a letter to the Wordsworths' brother Richard in London: "I fear there is little chance of his final recovery. We apprehend that a Consumption will come on" (130). In early February, she was more hopeful: "I am still [at] Keswick—Basil Montagu continues in a state of great weakness; but the discharge of Blood has ceased, and we hope he will be enabled to move from this place in the course of a few weeks, if the Frost should go away; but this extreme cold is much against him" (131). Two months later, in late March, Dorothy was still there, writing to another old friend from the Bristol days: "His disorder was a violent Haemorrage, which brought him to the last state of weakness; but he is now recovering, though I fear that his Life will not be long. There is great cause to apprehend a Consumption" (134). In mid-March, Basil Caroline was able to write to London himself: "My health is much the same, for great agitation of mind but ill accords with great bodily weakness. I have left my room today for the first time; for the Sun having tempted some flowers to make their appearance Miss Barker thought I might venture" (WLMS).

A month later, in late April, Dorothy wrote to her friend Catherine Clarkson, "You will be surprised at the date of this letter 'still at Keswick'" (137). Basil Caroline at last departed Keswick for Ambleside on May 13 "without any dangerous symptom remaining upon him," according to Robert Southey.[35]

---

34. Coleridge, *Minnow among Tritons*, 25.
35. Southey, *Letters*, May 1814.

158 CHAPTER 5

Dorothy was charged with getting him resettled in Ambleside, but in spite of her caregiving instincts she was ready to be done with him:

> I am to take Lodgings at Ambleside for Basil M, who, I am sorry to say, has shewn very little delicacy, being loth to remove from good quarters where he lives *Scot Free*. This I much suspect to be the case, or some expression of uneasiness would long since have broken from him, from the reflection that he had for four months kept Miss Barker and her house and servants constantly devoted to him, and he would have proposed to move as soon as there was any possibility of it. He rides out daily and is now to all appearance nearly as well as before he had the first attack of haemorrhage; but he must spend the next winter in a warmer Climate. (139)

The patient was back in London by the early summer, at odds with the world in general and his birth father in particular. Basil Caroline continued to unload upon Mary Barker, according to his father: "Upon Basil's return to London he told me that, of all persons Miss Barker was to him the most odious. She was drunk half the day by asafatido and the other half by opium. Such was the state of this poor boys mind" (WLMS).[36] Suspicious that his father never spoke well of him now, Basil Caroline attempted to enlist his father's good friend, the liberal reformer Sir Samuel Romilly, to intervene with his father on his behalf. Basil the lawyer did not yield, breaking off his unfinished adoption memoir by now claiming "happiness" instead of "protection" as the standard of care that governed his behavior toward all his children: "I told my friend Sir Samuel, and I dare say he well knew, that, loving and respecting him as one of the best of men, he [?] & would give me credit for acting in the best manner I [was?] [able?] to [preserve?] the happiness of my children" (WLMS).

In the wake of Dorothy's lengthy investment in his illness and recovery, the Wordsworth family kept up with the reports of Basil's health through the fall of 1814. In late October, Mary Wordsworth wrote to Dorothy, who was away on postponed visits: "Basil gains strength daily, he says, in answer to my asking why he did not go abroad: that all agree that his complaint is not pulmonary and that the climate of the I. of Wight is as good as any for him" (17). A week later, "I have had another letter from Basil, who, poor fellow, has had an influenza—but was better; he said he was about as well as before the complaint came upon him" (23–24). But after these last 1814 letters, Basil Caroline disappears from the Wordsworth correspondence. At the same post-Waterloo moment, William expressed a desire to settle accounts with father Basil, writ-

---

36. Asafoetida was an exotic and pungent cooking herb with medicinal qualities.

UNEXPLAINED CHILDREN 159

ing in May 1816 that "I also wish that you would conclude your little affairs with me; for I am heartily sick of all long-pending accounts, whether small or great" (311). On a visit to London in November 1817, William and lawyer Basil, who had been assisting—unsuccessfully—Percy Bysshe Shelley in the trial for custody of his first set of children, brewed up a final sharp disagreement about the many knots of their finances, stretching back to the adoption deal in 1795. The last issue was a dispute over who owned an old life insurance policy; Basil threatened to go to chancery to stake a claim in equity. Before the matter was settled in late December, their mutual friend, the lawyer and diarist Henry Crabb Robinson, noted that "I could gladly interfere in this business, but I fear to attempt it. The parties are too much irritated against each [other]."[37] For the rest of their long lives, the correspondence between William and lawyer Basil was cordial but perfunctory, typically thank-you notes from Rydal Mount for a copy of Basil's latest edited volume of the works of Francis Bacon. Basil Caroline is never again mentioned.

LONDON AND CAMBRIDGE, 1815-1830

In December 1814, the Montagu family moved into new London quarters at 25 Bedford Square, which became a social and intellectual center over the next several decades, what Thomas Carlyle later described as "a most singular social and spiritual menagerie."[38] After he established his initial London perches in the 1820s, Carlyle was a frequent visitor, cultivated assiduously by Anna Skepper Montagu, who appears as "Noble Lady" in his correspondence and memoirs. A rare image of Basil Caroline after 1815 appears in Carlyle's 1881 account of his first visit to London in 1824: "That first afternoon, with its curious phenomena, is still very lively in me. Basil Montague's eldest son, Mr. Montague junior, accidental guest at our neat little early dinner, my first specimen of the London dandy—broken dandy; very mild of manner, who went all to shivers, and died miserable soon after."[39] Instead of a glimpse of an older Basil Caroline as a failed curate, Carlyle recalls a failed dandy. In 1813, on his way north to Cumbria, in the letter in which he asked for his Bible and some flannel drawers, Basil Caroline shifted into higher sartorial gear as a clerical dandy ephebe: "I shall want a pair of black silk stockings, too, as I intend getting a compleat suit of black." As he made the holiday rounds in Cumbria

---

37. Robinson, *Books and Their Writers,* I:210–11.
38. Carlyle, *Reminiscences,* I.223.
39. Carlyle, I.213.

before his illness, he confessed his marked preference for ladies dressed in "black velvet gowns" (WLMS).

In the *Reminiscences* in 1881, Carlyle emphasized the remarkably haphazard character of the crowded Montagu household that the repatriated Basil Caroline confronted after his discharge from the navy in 1812: "Basil had been thrice married. Children of all his marriages, and one child of the now Mrs. Montagu's own by a previous marriage, were present in the home; a most difficult miscellany."[40] Anne Skepper, the daughter whom the third Mrs. Montagu brought to the family, was in Carlyle's tally "the fourth genealogic species among those children."[41] Following his reference to the "miserable end" of Basil Caroline, Carlyle warmed to his theme: "Still worse the three sons of the second marriage, dandy young fellows by this time, who went all and sundry to the bad, the youngest and luckiest soon to a *madhouse,* where he probably still is. Nor were the two boys of Mrs. Montagu Tertia a good kind; thoroughly vain or even proud, and with a spice of angry falsity discernible amid their showy talents."[42] In an 1826 letter to Carlyle from the third Mrs. Montagu, in which she laments the hardships of her oldest biological son, Charles Parr Montagu (who had been sent down from Cambridge), Anna Skepper Montagu closed with this telling sentence: "So much for my Sons, real, and adopted."[43] The term "adopted" performed cold work in the Montagu household to differentiate with a hard line manifold sets of offspring among four genealogic species. Mrs. Montagu's language defines the two closed categories Basil Caroline faced in the "sad miscellany" that passed for his London home after 1813: Basil Caroline was either a real Son or a not-real Son, otherwise known as adopted.

In a Christmas Day letter to London from Ambleside in 1813, a lonely Basil Caroline pitched a bid for sympathy: "I far distant from all those I love, an old batchelor at 20, have only a solitary fireside" (WLMS). Among the Montagu household miscellany in the 1820s, a march of marriages commenced. Mrs. Montagu's daughter Anne Skepper, born seven years after Basil Caroline in September 1799, married Bryan Waller Procter in 1824. When Algernon, born in 1802, sailed to begin a legal career in Australia in 1828, he was accompanied by his new wife. An old bachelor at twenty, Basil Caroline the broken dandy at thirty left no such record. Returning from the navy at twenty in the spring of 1813, he found a home filled with young brothers and a new stranger, a fourteen-year-old adoptive sister. Soon launched by his father on therapeutic

---

40. Carlyle, I.225.
41. Carlyle, I.226.
42. Carlyle, I.225–26.
43. *Carlyle Letters Online,* January 14, 1826.

travels, Basil Caroline awkwardly navigated the fraught boundaries of sex and adoptive kinship in an April letter to Mrs. Montagu, when he turned to sentences about his "sentiments" and a gift he had given her daughter "Annie": "I shall never have but one towards her, love for her while virtuous and intellectual. . . . When we meet again I hope and trust we shall be more aware of the real sentiments which we feel towards one another" (WLMS).

After a lifetime of precarious health, Basil Caroline died in Cambridgeshire in 1830. A death notice appeared in the *Gentleman's Magazine* for July 1830: "*Cambridge*—June. At Cambridge, Basil C., eldest son of Basil Montagu, esq. of Lincoln's Inn."[44] That's the sum of it. After a relentlessly busy and modestly distinguished legal career in bankruptcy law and on reformist issues such as capital punishment, Basil the father died in Boulogne in 1851, ironically evading debt liability from bad deals with publishers. William Wordsworth had died a year earlier, in 1850; Dorothy Wordsworth lasted in long decline until 1855; Admiral Robert Montagu died in November 1830, six months after Basil Caroline. Arabella Want, the last surviving sister who had helped care for the orphaned Basil Caroline, died in the family home in Brampton, twenty miles up the road from Cambridge, in 1838; her sister Henrietta, who had married the Reverend Charles Holworthy and lived in Brampton, died there in 1835. Basil Caroline's last days in 1830 perhaps passed near the adoptive watch of these two aged aunts near the place of his mother's marriage and death and his own birth, but there was no reunion in the grave—he is not buried in the Brampton churchyard where his birth mother's 1793 grave is still visible, which he visited in 1813. He was instead buried on June 3 twenty miles down the road in Cambridge in the Church of the Holy Sepulchre, better known as the Round Church, across from the entrance to St. John's College, near the time of Basil Caroline's birth the academic way station of one of his many later adoptive parents, William Wordsworth.[45]

POOR BASIL, POOR RICHARD

In the Wordsworth family correspondence about Basil Caroline in the years after Racedown and Alfoxden, the chronically ill and chronically troubled Basil Caroline most often appears as "poor Basil!" His fate calls to mind the comically cool postmortem fate of a minor character, Richard Musgrove—repeatedly "poor Richard!"—in Jane Austen's final novel, *Persuasion*, pub-

---

44. *Gentleman's Magazine*, July 1830, p. 92.

45. "England Deaths and Burials, 1538–1991," database, *Family Search* (https://familysearch.org/ark:/61903/1:1:JZGF-HPN: March 16, 2020), "Basel [*sic*] Cardene [*sic*] Montagu, 1830."

lished in 1818. Richard Musgrove is the unlamented younger son of a large gentry family who died early on at sea in undistinguished navy service. Engaged socially with naval officers on leave, his mother, the generously sized Mrs. Musgrove, suddenly affects maternal grief for "poor Richard!," whereupon Austen's narrator quickly deflates her "large fat sighings over the destiny of a son, whom alive nobody had cared for."[46] The narrator supplies a frosty obituary for poor Dick Musgrove:

> The real circumstances of this pathetic piece of family history were, that the Musgroves had had the ill fortune of a very troublesome, hopeless son; and the good fortune to lose him before his twentieth year; that he had been sent to sea, because he was stupid and unmanageable on shore; that he had been very little cared for at any time by his family, though quite as much as he deserved; seldom heard of, and scarcely at all regretted, when the intelligence of his death abroad had worked its way to Uppercross, two years before.[47]

Apart from the notice in the *Gentleman's Magazine,* the only references to the death of Basil Caroline Montagu waited upon Carlyle in the *Reminiscences* in 1881. Following his remark that Basil Caroline after their meeting in 1824 "went all to shivers, and died miserable soon after," Carlyle a few pages later cast a last cold eye on Basil Caroline, before passing by: "He soon ended by a bad road."[48] That road was the burdened path of a forlorn, diminished adoptee, a nonperson scarcely at all regretted, who was early swept up contingently into the impossibly clouded wake of Romantic childhood.

---

46. Austen, *Persuasion,* 73.

47. Austen, 54.

48. Carlyle, *Reminiscences,* I.225.

CHAPTER 6

Found Children

Emma Isola and Charles and Mary Lamb

In the *London Illustrated News* on February 14, 1891, an item headed "Charles Lamb's Adopted Daughter" led with this paragraph:

> One of the few remaining links that united the present with the literary past of the earlier years of our century has been severed by the death of the widow of the "poets' publisher," Edward Moxon, which occurred at Brighton on Feb. 2. Mrs. Moxon had attained the ripe age of eighty-two years, and was the Emma Isola, the "nut-brown maid," the "girl of gold," the adopted daughter of Charles and Mary Lamb.[1]

Approaching the turn of the century, metropolitan journalism smoothly skated past the disruptive fact that the phrase "adopted daughter" designated a deeply equivocal category in Britain. Just two years earlier, the House of Lords had slammed the door to an "Adoption of Children Bill," reaffirming a closed border: "Adoption is wholly unknown to the law of England."[2] Until 1926 de facto adoptions continued to slip across bionormative family borders, a history of ad hoc practice long familiar to the culture even if beyond the law.

---

1. *London Illustrated News*, February 14, 1891, x.
2. *Hansard*, House of Lords Debate, July 16, 1889.

164 CHAPTER 6

In this final chapter, I add to these untimely adoption histories an especially ectopic adoptive family, worthy of much note. In Cambridge in the summer of 1820, during the heat of Queen Caroline's trial in London, a twelve-year-old orphan, Emma Isola, met a vacationing Charles Lamb, an alcoholic essayist and clerk nearing fifty, and his intermittently mad coauthor and older sister Mary. Through her marriage in 1833 to Edward Moxon, Emma, Charles, and Mary performed a de facto adoption that stymied explanation. The remarkable feature of the Lamb siblings as surrogate parents is that their status as a couple was itself a surrogate performance of marriage, what Charles famously referred to as "a sort of double singleness."[3] A sibling couple unsettled normative marriage in the first degree.[4] A surrogate child then rendered this surrogate marriage a further invention, to a degree that balked interpretation, much like the confusion of west-country natives puzzled by the Wordsworth siblings with their mystery child, Basil Caroline Montagu. The manifold surrogate diversity of this Lamb family unit confounded the normative biologism that sustained dominant constructions of the family, tribe, and nation. A rich caricature, this trio both reproduced and parodied a bionormative family model: mother, father, child. Performatively, the trio queered the biogenetic props of both family and nation, in untimely alliance with the adoptee Willy Austin on the royal stage.

Almost all accounts of this decentered adoptive family foreground domestic affect, understood narrowly. Because the domestic history of the Lamb family is choppy water—it features mental illness, alcoholism, and matricide—it is unsurprising that mid-twentieth-century fiction and biography swerved off the road into tabloid ditches when the topic was Emma Isola: Charles Lamb is in one fictional account a closet pedophile, and in a biography, Mary Lamb's madness is exacerbated by incestuous jealousy.[5] In this chapter, I frame the story of Emma Isola outside the drawn shades of Lamb domesticity, focusing instead on the multifamilial and political spaces where adoption takes place. To track the history of the adoption, the first section sorts the mul-

---

3. Lamb, *Elia*, 86.

4. A sibling pair (a brother and sister) is the first human pair described in the first paragraph of Jane Austen's first published novel, *Sense and Sensibility*. The heteronormative married pair must wait its turn in line.

5. Bell, *Perish*; and Anthony, *Lambs*. In response, the Charles Lamb Society commissioned a study by Ernest Carson Ross, *Charles Lamb and Emma Isola: A Survey of the Evidence Relevant to Their Personal Relationship* (1950; rep. 1991). Ross builds the case that Charles and Mary were appropriately "parental"; he finesses the adoption question by referring to Emma Isola as the Lambs' "ward," a legal term that appears nowhere in the record. A major new biography of Lamb rehearses these claims and plays the matter equivocally: "The nature of Charles's relationship to Emma must remain a mystery"; Wilson, *Dream-Child*, 387.

FOUND CHILDREN 165

tiple forms of de facto adoptive care shared between the Lambs in London and Emma's Cambridge family, measuring the costs to Emma the adoptee, her adoptive caregivers, and members of her birth family. The second section turns to Emma's history as a governess, which tellingly tracks the gendered fate of an adopted orphan of the middling classes, the threat Jane Fairfax confronts in Austen's *Emma*. In the final section, I return as in chapter 2 to the politics of adoption in 1820, when the commencement of the Lamb adoption doubled up oppositionally with the adultery trial of Queen Caroline, whose misbehavior trailed in its wake the national discomfort of an adopted child.

DIVIDED CARE: CAMBRIDGE AND LONDON

When the orphan Emma Isola finished boarding school at age eighteen and was ready to test the governess market in 1827, her adoptive parent Charles Lamb put out employment feelers to his circle. Lamb opened such letters by emphasizing Emma's immigrant Cambridge identity, as in this August 1827 letter to Robert Jameson: "We have a *young person domesticated with us,* whom you have seen, in whose well-doing, we are much interested. She is daughter to the late Mr. Isola, Esquire Bedel to the University of Cambridge, and her Grandfather was Italian, and taught Italian there, and was a man, I have heard, very highly esteemed there."[6] Emma Isola's father, Charles Isola, a minor university official and the son of Agostino Isola, a venerated Italian tutor at Cambridge, died in 1814. Emma's mother, Mary Humphreys, died the following year, at the birth and death of her seventh child. Born in Cambridge in 1808, Emma became at her mother's death in 1815 a seven-year-old orphan with three surviving younger siblings. When not at school, Emma and her younger sister Harriet lodged in Cambridge with her mother's sister Miss Humphreys at Kenmare House, the Trumpington Street home opposite Pembroke College of Mrs. Elizabeth Paris, the sister of the Lambs' friend William Ayrton. In the summer of 1820, when Emma was twelve, she met Charles Lamb, then in his mid-forties, and his sister Mary Lamb, in her mid-fifties, who were taking an annual holiday in Cambridge from Charles's job in the accountancy offices of the East India Company. Over evenings of whist and spirits at Kenmare House, not far down the road from the Lambs' rented rooms opposite King's College, the three hit it off so well that Emma spent an extended Christmas holiday with the Lambs in London. While at boarding school in Dulwich over

---

6. Lamb, *Letters,* III.123. Subsequent references are by volume and page number in the text.

166   CHAPTER 6

the next several years, Emma spent her school holidays with the Lambs. When she left school in 1827, she lived with the Lambs year-round while they tutored and prepped her in the skills required of a governess, a position she took up in 1828 in Fornham in Suffolk, near Bury St. Edmunds.[7] In 1830 and again in 1831, she became dangerously ill and returned to the Lambs to recover. In 1833 she married Lamb's protégé the young publisher Edward Moxon; Charles Lamb died a year later, in 1834; Mary Lamb, his older sister, died in 1847.

The absence of adoption law in England yielded a host of hedged terms in later nineteenth-century accounts of the Lambs and Emma Isola. Emma is, variously, "practically adopted," "virtually adopted," and "unofficially adopted." Henry Crabb Robinson in 1852 recorded her as "a kind of adopted daughter of Charles Lamb"; Barry Cornwall in 1866 noted that "ultimately she was looked upon in the light of a child."[8] In his notes to the Lamb *Letters* in his 1935 edition, E. V. Lucas introduced Emma in 1820 as the girl whom the Lambs "later adopted," which nicely ducked the question.[9] Lamb himself floated various phrases to explain the puzzle of Emma, who is, variously, an "Orphan" (III.86), a "young person domesticated with us" (III.123), our "inmate" (a synonym for any indwelling resident, III.243), our "young friend" (III.199), our "very dear young friend" (III.255), and, at least once, "our adopted young

---

7. Wilson's new biography of Lamb gets these dates wrong: "By 1823, Emma lived with the Lambs year-round" (382), which repeats the error in Lucas's 1905 biography.

8. Robinson, *Diary*, II.127; and Cornwall, *Lamb*, 207. The writer of the *London Illustrated News* obituary in 1891 wobbled about Emma's identity category, after leading with the unequivocal status of "adopted daughter"; when the obituary narrates the meeting of the twelve-year-old orphan and Charles and Mary Lamb in Cambridge in 1820, Emma Isola "was afterwards domiciled in their house almost as a daughter." In his 2022 biography of Lamb, Wilson regularly refers to Emma as the Lambs' "adopted daughter" (182, 454), with this qualification: "Though they never legally adopted her [it was not an option], she became their de facto daughter" (382). In a 2022 book about Charles Lamb and book collectors, Denise Gigante inflects the adoption three ways: Emma is the Lambs' "adoptive daughter" (xiv), their "adopted daughter" (5), and, in quibble quotes, the "orphan . . . whom they 'adopted' as their own" (27).

9. In Lucas's phrase, Emma Isola in 1820 is the girl "whom later he and his sister adopted" (*Letters*, II.290). In his 1903 edition of Lamb's *Works*, Lucas in a note commented that "the exact date of her adoption by the Lambs cannot be ascertained now" (*Works*, 5.310). But in his 1905 biography of the Lambs (still a standard source for their later lives), Lucas pegged the "adoption" to the death of Emma's father Charles Isola, which he mistakenly dated as 1823 (Charles Isola died in 1814): "In 1823, when Charles Isola died, Charles and Mary Lamb seem definitely to have adopted Emma Isola as their daughter" (*Life*, II.42). That mistaken 1823 date both for the death of Charles Isola and for Emma's adoption regularly appears in subsequent Lamb scholarship; for example, by Ross in his 1950 monograph about Emma Isola (10, 13); by Jonathan Bate in his "Chronology" in the 1987 Oxford *Elia* edition; by Susan Tyler Hitchcock in her 2005 Mary Lamb biography; by Eric Wilson in his 2022 biography of Lamb (382); and by Denise Gigante in her 2022 book about Charles Lamb and book collectors (28).

friend" (III.224). In an 1830 letter to William Wordsworth, Lamb registered how Emma "grew natural to us" (III.245).

The fraught issues of naming and identity for a surrogate child come to sharp focus in another 1830 letter Charles wrote to his local apothecary, Dr. Asbury, during Emma's illness. In support of his adoptive child, Charles reported that Emma insisted upon her separate orphaned self, defined by her genealogical immigrant kin in Cambridge:

> Dear Sir, Some draughts and boluses have been brought here which we conjecture were meant for the young lady whom you saw this morning, though they are labeled for
>
> Miss ISOLA LAMB.
>
> No such person is known [here], and she is fearful of taking medicines which may have been made up for another patient. She begs me to say that she was born an *Isola* and christened *Emma*. Moreover that she is Italian by birth, and that her ancestors were from Isola Bella (Fair Island) in the kingdom of Naples. She has never changed her name and rather mournfully adds that she has no prospect at present of doing so. She is literally I. SOLA, or single, at present. Therefore she begs that the obnoxious monosyllable [Lamb] may be omitted on future Phials,—an innocent syllable enough, you'll say, but she has no claim to it. It is the bitterest pill of the seven you have sent her. (III.264–65)

The letter twins the perils of adoption and marriage for a twenty-two-year-old orphan governess. Just as she risks the erasure of her genealogical past in de facto adoption when she is addressed as Lamb rather than Isola, so she will face a sanctioned erasure of her birth name and selfhood under coverture when and if she marries. In such a wilderness, the linguistic trace of her genealogical heritage anchors her identity, which in her adoptive present is solitary and isolated. The complex irony of the letter is that her adoptive caregiver acts in parental solidarity to affirm her solitude and isolation.

Emma Isola's immigrant Cambridge past grounded her in complex fashion during her adopted life with the Lambs in London. During the popular wave of literary annuals and albums in the 1820s, Charles and Mary engineered from their wide literary circle an album of autograph verses addressed to Emma.[10] As Charles wrote to John Bates Dibdin in September 1827, "Emma Isola, who is with us, has opened an ALBUM: bring some verses with you for

---

10. The album is now in the Special Collections at Houghton Library, Harvard University: "Emma Isola Moxon Autograph Album," MS Eng 601.66, fol. 10.

it on Saty evening" (III.125). Easy to discount as a courtship tool to connect Emma with scribbling London bachelors, the album gave Charles and Mary the eager opportunity to solicit contributions about both her Cambridge birth culture and her immigrant ancestry. Charles's old friend George Dyer, who unlike Lamb had matriculated at Cambridge, responded with a tribute to her grandfather Agostino, the Italian tutor: "Worthy he was, as those who *knew* him say, / To be thy model, make him, Emma, such, / And let imagination picture him / As ever present, though invisible" (III.169). In thanks, Charles noted that "I know she will treasure up that among her choicest rarities, as from her *grandfather's* friend, whom not having seen, she loves to hear talked of" (III.160).[11] Introduced to the Lambs and Emma in 1832, Walter Savage Landor, just returned from more than a decade in Italy, contributed three quatrains on that country addressed "To Emma Isola" (III.343), and Matilda Betham added forty-nine lines in the month of Emma's marriage "In Memory of Mr. Agostino Isola, of Cambridge."

When Emma returned to her adopted home with Charles and Mary after her illness, the trio set themselves the task of learning Italian to add to her governess stock of languages and worked their way through the *Inferno,* with the help of the new blank-verse translation by their friend Henry Francis Carey. When Henry Crabb Robinson visited the Lamb household in July 1831, he noted in his diary that "after breakfast read some Italian with Miss Isola, whom Lamb is teaching Italian without knowing the language himself."[12] In accounts of the Dante project in Charles's correspondence, it is clear that Emma already knew more Italian than Charles and Mary.[13] As Charles wrote to Carey, "You will be amused to hear that my sister and I have, with the aid of Emma, scrambled through the 'Inferno' by the blessed furtherance of your polar-star translation" (III.384). Soon after Emma's marriage, Charles reported to Thomas Manning that "[Mary and I] were beginning the Purgatory, but got on less rapidly, our great authority of Grammar, Emma, being fled" (III.409). In Emma's post-Cambridge adoptive life, the native language of her immigrant past supplied a bridge to her paternal Cambridge birth culture.

Emma Isola was also not a physical stranger to her surviving Cambridge family. Emma's two Cambridge birth relatives who sporadically appear in

---

11. Henry Payne Stokes (Whitaker and Stokes, "Isola Papers") dates Agostino Isola's appointment at Cambridge in 1764 and adds more details about his subsequent Cambridge career and life. Thomas Noon Talfourd in 1837 commented that Agostino Isola "had been compelled to fly from Milan, because a friend took up an English book in his apartment, which he had carelessly left in view"; Talfourd, *Sketch,* II.141.

12. Robinson, *Diary,* II.131.

13. The Moxon family holds an 1826 letter in schoolgirl Italian from "E. Isola" on holiday in London to a Dulwich schoolfriend; my thanks to John Moxon for access to this manuscript.

Charles's correspondence (the primary record for Emma's life before her marriage) are her mother's sister Miss Humphreys and Emma's own younger sister Harriet. Before turning to these blood kin, there is another significant Isola relative who is absent from Lamb's record, Emma's younger brother Frederick. A piece of trace evidence about Frederick Isola suggests a powerful reason why Charles, Mary, and Emma hit it off so well in the summer of 1820 in Cambridge and launched their adoptive family experiment outside biocentric norms, which in Romantic-period Britain underwrote ideals of normative speech.

Like Charles Lamb, Frederick Isola stuttered. Born in 1813, Frederick was two and Emma seven when their mother died in 1815. Until she was twelve in 1820, Emma helped care for Frederick from his time as a toddler to his seventh year. Archived in the Cambridge University library manuscript collections, a set of early twentieth-century anecdotes about Frederick's daughter, a "washerwoman" employed by the writer, records this picture of her father, who as an adult was a baker in Chesterton on the north edge of Cambridge: "Those old people who remember him, describe him as a slightly built man, rather the butt for the witticisms of the village, willing to sing, gabble a little Latin, and spell words backwards; these accomplishments all being enhanced in the ears of his audience by an impediment of speech."[14] Described by his daughter as "a baker, and a thirsty soul, a good-natured, erratic, rather helpless man," Frederick always had "a ready retort on his lips, that gained in humour from the queerness of its expression." In the summer of 1820, Emma Isola had banked five years of experience with a sibling who stammered. In her 1983 biography of *Young Charles Lamb*, Winifred Courtney noted "Lamb's odd and hostile behaviour, particularly with strangers, who were coming upon his impediment for the first time."[15] For the twelve-year-old Emma Isola on Trumpington Street in Cambridge in 1820, Lamb's impediment was no impediment. Emma's early sibling experience with a stutterer and Lamb's lifetime experience of what Emily Stanback terms his many forms of "non-normative embodiment" mark the de facto adoption of Emma Isola as an alliance among outsiders.[16]

Frederick Isola appears to have been something of a Cambridge favorite of his older sister, on through her married life. The recollections of Frederick's

---

14. Whitaker and Stokes, "Isola Papers."

15. Courtney, *Young Charles Lamb*, 348.

16. Stanback, *Aesthetics of Disability*, 273–309. In Jared Richman's summary, "Stutterers in [Georgian] Britain existed as a marginalized group unable and often unwilling to participate in most social and political arenas where power was concentrated, notably in government service and the church"; "Other King's Speech," 279–304. Essaka Joshua, in her new *Physical Disability in British Romantic Literature*, does not discuss Lamb. See also Wilson, *Dream-Child*, 37–39.

daughter, who "seemed rather surprised that an aunt of hers was in a book," include this: "Of her Aunt Emma Isola (Mrs. Moxon) she remembered very little, though she remembered her coming to Cambridge and visiting her sister 'who was well to do' and lived, she thought, in Trumpington Street (a Mrs. Humphreys?). Mrs. Moxon frequently sent presents to her father; particularly she remembered a beautiful box of clothes." This "Mrs. Humphreys of Trumpington Street" was Emma's unmarried maternal aunt, who lived with the Lambs' friend Mrs. Paris in Kenmare House, where Emma's younger sister Harriet also boarded.[17] The adoptive care of Emma was, de facto, an ad hoc arrangement of shared charge and care between the Lambs and Miss Humphreys, the maternal blood relative in Cambridge who thereby always held the upper hand of genealogical kinship, even though after 1820 Emma nearly always lived with the Lambs when she was not at school or employed at Fornham. A decade of tension in these de facto adoption arrangements boiled over in the immediate aftermath of Emma's wedding in 1833.

The first experiment in shared care was the 1820 Christmas holiday, when the twelve-year-old Emma ventured from Cambridge to taste life in the fast-lane metropolis. In a letter from Emma and Charles to Miss Humphreys in Cambridge on January 9, 1821, Emma addressed "My Dear Aunt":

> I arrived quite safe and Miss Lamb was at the Inn waiting for me. The first night I came we went out to spend the evening. The second night Mr. Lamb took me to see the wild beasts at Exeter Change. Saturday night being twelfth night I went to a party and did not return till four in the morning. Yesterday Miss Lamb took me to the theatre at Covent Garden. I cannot tell you how much I liked it. I was so delighted. (II.290)

Shared delight prompted a request for additional holiday leave. Charles characteristically took up, unseriously, the serious task of asking permission:

> Here Emma ends and I begin. Emma is a very naughty girl, and has broken three cups, one plate and a slop-basin with mere giddiness. She is looking

---

17. Harriet Isola seems to move back and forth between life with her aunt in Cambridge and residence in London. In references in Charles's letters in 1828 (III.172) and 1830 (III.286), she is in London, but in the wedding year of 1833 she seems to be with Miss Humphreys in Cambridge (III.383 and III.388). In the 1841 census, Harriet is listed in Chesterton in north Cambridge, near her brother Frederick and his family; "Elizabeth Humphreys" is also in Chesterton (given her age, almost certainly Miss Humphreys). In the 1851 and 1861 census reports, Harriet Isola is listed in London in Kentish Town, St. Pancras. The Moxon family holds an 1852 letter from Elizabeth Humphreys to Emma Moxon, reporting events in Cambridgeshire and mentioning Harriet; my thanks to John Moxon for access to this manuscript.

FOUND CHILDREN

over me, which is impertinent. But if you can spare her longer than her holidays, we shall be happy to keep her, in hopes of her amendment. . . . Will you, dear Miss Humph. permit Emma to stay a week or so beyond her holidays. She is studying algebra & the languages. I teach her *dancing.* (II.290)

Nearly three weeks later, the Lambs and Emma were still dragging their feet about Emma's return to Cambridge, now using the excuse of academic ceremonies, as Charles wrote to Miss Humphreys on January 27. Because few letters from the Lambs to Miss Humphreys survive, I quote this last January 1821 letter in full:

Dear Madam, Carriages to Cambridge are in such request, owing to the Installation, that we have found it impossible to procure a conveyance for Emma before Wednesday, on which day between the hours of 3 and 4 in the afternoon you will see your little friend, with her bloom somewhat impaired by late hours and dissipation, but her gait, gesture, and general manners (I flatter myself) considerably improved by—*somebody that shall remain nameless.* My sister joins me in love to all true Trumpingtonians, not specifying any, to avoid *envy*; and begs me to assure you that Emma has been a very good girl, which, with certain limitations, I must subscribe to. I wish I could cure her of making dog's ears in books, and pinching them on poor Pompey, who, for one, I dare say, will heartily rejoyce at her departure. Dear Madam, Yours truly, foolish C.L. (II.291–92)

Charles's polished manner of foolishness traces his new habit to tease a teenage girl about "*somebody that shall remain nameless.*" In the January 9 letter to her aunt, Emma reported that on Twelfth Night "I went to a party and did not return till four in the morning," to which Charles added: "She came home at 5 o'clock in the morning with a strange gentleman on Twelfth Night" (III.290). Likely to be tallied by Miss Humphreys in the same deficit column with "late hours and dissipation," this teasing manner did not play well in Cambridge.

Through the 1820s, Miss Humphreys in Cambridge potentially threatened recall and repatriation. The most telling evidence is an 1827 letter from Charles to Edward Moxon, a young poet in the London publishing world who was becoming a regular suitor of the nineteen-year-old governess prospect: "Thanks for your attentions of every kind. Emma will not fail Mrs. Hood's kind invitation, but her Aunt is so queer a one, that we cannot let her go with a single gentleman singly to Vauxhall; she would withdraw her from us altogether in a fright; but if any of the Hood's family accompany you, then there can be small objection" (III.104–5). The threat to "withdraw her from us altogether" was a serious risk to the Lambs. When Emma left the Lambs to take up her governess job near Bury St. Edmunds in the spring of 1828, Charles wrote to Thomas Hood that "she has left an ugly gap in our society, which will not close hastily" (III.160).

Emma's illness while a governess exposed serious fault lines between her Cambridge birth kin and her London adoptive caregivers. In the spring of 1828, Emma became governess for the family of the rector of All Saints Fornham, on the north edge of Bury St. Edmunds, twenty-five miles to the east of Cambridge. After hearing news of Emma's serious illness in late February 1830 (a "brain fever," most likely meningitis), Charles wrote in a panic to Mrs. Williams, the rector's wife, thinking first of Emma's Cambridge kin: "Can I go to her aunt, or do anything? I do not know what to offer. We are in great distress. Pray relieve us, if you can, by somehow letting us know. I will fetch her here, or anything" (III.248). When in early March there was news of Emma's improvement, Charles wrote in relief and asked Mrs. Williams to extend his "very kindest congratulations to Miss Humphreys" (III.250), which suggests that Emma's aunt had at least visited Fornham from nearby Cambridge soon after Emma had taken ill. But after this early cameo, Miss Humphreys disappeared from the record of Emma's recovery. When, weeks later, Emma was able to travel, it is clear that, to recover, Emma would not go to Cambridge but back to the Lamb home in Enfield on the northern outskirts of London. During those weeks, Lamb's correspondence unfolded the plans for Charles to come to Fornham to "fetch" Emma, with no more word of Miss Humphreys. Even though the coach from Bury to London ran through Cambridge, none of Emma's birth kin appeared in Charles's detailed account of the journey he immediately sent to Mrs. Williams in Fornham.

After her recovery, Charles accompanied Emma back to her governess family in Fornham in the late spring of 1830, where she was happily employed for the next year, spending holidays with Charles and Mary. In March 1831, she again fell ill at Fornham; while Emma was recovering with the Lambs a second time, Mrs. Williams wrote from Fornham to release Emma from her job. In a letter from Charles to Emma's schoolfriend Maria Fryer about this unhappy chain of events, Emma's Cambridge life cast a dark and unclear shadow: "She left us at Christmas quite well and cheerful, but some untoward events at Cambridge, on her way home, quite unsettled her."[18] This letter confirms that

---

18. Princeton University holds an important set of Lamb letters about Emma Isola that are not included in the 1935 Lucas edition of the Lamb correspondence (a later scholarly edition of the letters remains halted and incomplete, short of the Emma decade); the Princeton set is printed in Finch, "Companionship," 179–99. Subsequent parenthetical references are by page number to "Princeton."

Emma's journeys between her London home and her Fornham governess home included stops in Cambridge, which on the evidence of Charles's letter did not always go well. The same letter indicates that the recovering Emma needed to steel herself to correspond with Miss Humphreys: "We have been walking this fine summer, warm, but *blowy* morning for an hour, & she is set down to answer a letter of her Aunt's quite composed and tranquil" (Princeton 187). A year later, after the unemployed Emma had been visiting Maria Fryer for half the year at her home in Chatteris, twenty miles to the north of Cambridge, Charles wrote to Maria about Emma's journey home to London, lamenting that she would have to pause her trip in Cambridge, that scene of untoward and unsettling events: "I wish she could save her Cambridge journey, but there is no altering the map." Emma in Cambridge also meant that Charles would have to negotiate with Miss Humphreys for Emma's time: "I will write to her Aunt while she is there, but I almost fear it will look ungracious to have been so patient in a halfyear's absence, and to stand upon an additional week or so with her Aunt" (Princeton 188).

For Emma Isola in a de facto adoption, the Cambridge of her birth was both anchor and trial. In July 1833, Emma and Edward Moxon prepared for a London marriage on July 30 at St. George's in Hanover Square. As weddings so often do, the ceremonial occasion stirred up divisions. One week before the wedding, Charles wrote to Moxon to confirm his own attendance in spite of his ill health and Mary's current incapacity; in the same letter, he indicated that he was attempting to manage what may have been frosty correspondence with Cambridge about the event: "I will be at the wedding, and keep the 30 July as long as my poor months last me, as a festival gloriously. We have not heard from Cambridge. I will write the moment we do" (III.378–79). On Sunday before the Tuesday wedding, Charles wrote to Moxon to "beg Emma's pardon for my keeping her so late, it was her goodness not to quit me till I was safe coached. I am nursing myself well to present myself to her aunt as one not unworthy of her acquaintce" (III.379). The phrase "nursing myself well" signified to Emma that he was trying to curb his drinking in order not to offend Miss Humphreys, who was long inclined to think him unworthy.[19]

Cambridge in the persons of Miss Humphreys and Harriet Isola did manage to arrive in time for the ceremony. The fraught contingency of this adoptive family network expressed itself in particular in the ad hoc manner in

---

19. Emma occasionally tried to keep Charles's drinking in check. Here is his account of her concern when he arrived in Fornham to take her back to London in 1830: "Poor Emma, the first moment we were alone, took me into a corner, and said, 'Now, pray, don't *drink*—do check yourself after dinner for my sake; and when we get home to Enfield, you shall drink as much as ever you please, and I won't say a word about it'" (III.279).

174 CHAPTER 6

which Charles assumed the ceremonial role of "father." As Charles wrote to an Enfield neighbor a few days after the ceremony, "Well, I was father at the wedding" (III.381), and to another: "I was at church, as the grave Father, and behaved tolerably well" (III.381). On August 2, Charles wrote to Emma's friend Maria Fryer with more details about the days before the wedding:

> On Saturday I accompanied E. to meet her Aunt's arrival. We took apartments in Southampton Buildings at very good old friends & Landladies long since of ours. There I staid Saturday night, and leaving town on Sunday, return'd Monday evening. I found Moxon & I had come to one conclusion, that our two parties,—Emma, Harriet, Aunt, & I, & M. and & his Brother & Sister should *quietly* breakfast separately, and he brought a coach for us at 9. Rogers excused himself, and I was father.[20] (Princeton 192)

Lamb's friend the poet and banker Samuel Rogers was Moxon's financial backer in his new publishing enterprise, the kind of establishment figure who might have pleased Miss Humphreys as a ceremonial surrogate parent for Emma, but Rogers "excused himself" and yielded place to Charles. The wedding day itself otherwise passed without apparent strife. Charles made it home to Mary "calm, sober, happy," as he later reported to the Moxons, and the absent Mary experienced a remarkable stroke of recovery on the day of the wedding, which she reported to the newlyweds. When her nurse proposed a toast to the health of Mr. and Mrs. Moxon, Mary writes that "it restored me, from that moment: as if by an electrical stroke: to the entire possession of my senses—I never felt so calm and quiet after a similar illness as I do now. I feel as if all tears were wiped from my eyes, and all care from my heart" (III.380). In a postscript, Charles added: "Never was such a calm, or such a recovery. 'Tis her own words, undictated" (III.381).

The major storm with Cambridge broke a month after the wedding, ignited by an offensive letter from Miss Humphreys to Edward Moxon's sister. The issue seems to have been the perennial puzzle faced by newly married couples: what are the new rules about family visits, now that families have rearranged? Charles got wind of trouble by the end of August, as he wrote

---

20. Charles sent a brief note to Maria Fryer from the postceremony celebrations in Moxon's nearby publishing house: "We have had a very happy wedding, and Mr & Mrs Moxon are gone off to Brighton & to Paris. Miss Moxon, Mr Wm Moxon, Miss Humphreys, Harriet, & me myself in especial, send loves to you" (Princeton, 191). Maria Fryer responded with a letter "full of good wishes, I am crying with good wishes"; MS. Pforzheimer Collection, New York Public Library.

to Charles Ryle on August 26: "We will not wait for the Moxons, for they are staying at Paris; & when they return, they will be encumber'd for a month or more longer with a troublesome Aunt and Sister of dear Emma's" (III.383). By September 13, Charles and Mary had been drawn into the dispute between Cambridge and London. An adoptive parent for more than a decade, Charles entered the fray with a long and remarkable letter to Emma and her husband about kinship, adoption, and marriage.

Until her marriage, the orphaned Emma Isola navigated an open border between her Cambridge birth family and her London adoptive family. But in Charles's estimation, marriage reconfigured the border crossing. The dual claims on Emma were now her Cambridge birth family and her London married family, and in Charles's judgment, marriage constituted a closed border of separation. This replacement of the claims of adoption with the claims of marriage enabled Charles to write much more severely about Miss Humphreys, expressing a decade's worth of adoptive uncertainty and frustration with Emma's primary adult blood relative. As a closed legal structure, marriage for Charles in the letter substitutes for what was unavailable in his experience as a parent, a de jure adoption with set boundaries. In Charles's letter about how to navigate this new family landscape, his kinship terms shuffle around just on the edge of confusion, which measures the pressure of these changes on an ill and grieving adoptive parent in a de facto adoption.

Charles opened his letter, which is addressed to both Emma and Edward Moxon, in full sympathy with the newlyweds: "Mary, who has more sense, and worse spirits, than *all three of us,* says, it *must* be a quarrel. After that letter to your Sister, which is absurd to the brink of insanity, I see no hope. I see no middle way—I wish to God I did—between poor Emma's breaking off with her, and her riding triumphant over you. Tis a sad alternative" (III.384). Charles then shifted to a summary of the fraught obligations Emma has owed her Cambridge kin, in the wake of which Miss Humphreys has now been acting not as an "aunt" but as "a mother," a status that he immediately discounts in light of what she is not, "a real mother":

> But let me witness, and to the whole world I am ready to do it, that in point of gratitude & obligation Emma has never, never failed in one instance. I have been scolded again & again by her, when I have whispered against the other. She has repaid, on my conscience I believe, more (tho' that is much) than she is indebted. Why, a mother, a real mother, had no right to write such a letter. What I possibly can do in it, I see not. I have no communication with her, even by Letter. (III.385)

The letter then shifted to address Emma even more directly. Charles navigated a maze of kinship categories that pressed upon the orphaned Emma's relationships with her Cambridge birth family: aunt, niece, adopted daughter, adoptive mother, real mother, daughter. All those relationships were now superseded by her new status as a spouse, which trumped all claims of blood:

> I fear, Dearest Emma, that you cannot keep the love of your Aunt with your love of our dear M[oxon]. Tis a terrible conflict. You have been a good Neice, I would tell any body. But she had no right, whatever her feelings were, to write such a damnable letter to Miss M_____. She must be too insane (I will call it) to make it necessary for you to consult her feelings at all. I will answer that you have had for her every feeling that a Neice, or adopted Daughter, ought to have. But when She, or when a real Mother even, intrudes upon the sacredness of married life, the bonds of daughtership are snapped asunder. (III.385)

Framing Emma's choice as divided between marriage and blood kin, the letter elides Charles and Mary as adoptive parents even as Charles dispensed parental advice.[21] The category "Parent" belongs not to Miss Humphreys genealogically or to Charles and Mary adoptively, but to Emma's birth parents, both dead by the time she was seven:

> And, Emma, think not I set light by the obligations you acknowledge to your ancient friend, all that you can remember of a Parent. But divided Duties cannot stand. I see, as plain as prophecy, that unless She can get a perfect ascendancy over you, there is no peace for your dear mind. I do not believe that if you invited her one, two, or three months, to your house, she would be satisfy'd. I think, Emma, you understand me. I mean, that she would plant herself in your way, & be a thorn endlesslye—. (III.385)

The severity of Charles's sentiments about Miss Humphreys in this new skirmish are a residue of a dozen years of the uncertainties and anxieties of open and divided adoptive care.

A month later, the quarrel resolved with a plan for Emma to pay a visit to Cambridge. As Charles wrote to Edward Moxon on October 17, 1833: "Tell Emma I grieve for the poor self-punishing self-baffling Lady; with all our hearts we grieve for the pain and vexation she has encountered; but we do not

---

21. Frequently ill in these later years, Mary was especially at risk of exclusion by Charles himself, as when Charles describes Miss Humphreys's letter as "absurd to the brink of insanity" and her actions as "too insane (I will call it)."

FOUND CHILDREN 177

swerve a pin's-thought from the propriety of your measures. God comfort her, and there's an end of a painful necessity. But I am glad she goes to see her. Let her keep up all the kindness she can between them" (III.388). This postscript to the wedding hostilities offers a glimpse of Charles as an adoptive parent momentarily sympathizing with Emma's surviving Cambridge blood kin, even though Miss Humphreys remains a "poor self-punishing self-baffling Lady." In November, Lamb wrote to Edward Moxon to invite the Moxons to a celebration of Mary's birthday: "Love to the whole Moxonry, and tell E. I every day love her more, and miss her less. Tell her so from her loving uncle, as she has let me call her" (III.392). The wheel of kinship terms in the history of Emma Isola's adoption now sorted Charles and Miss Humphreys into the same familial bin, sharing the parental care of an orphan as a Cambridge aunt by blood and a London "uncle" by adoption. Regardless, the 1870 Moxon edition of *The Complete Correspondence and Works of Charles Lamb* announced on its title page that it included "The Recollections of The Author's Adopted Daughter."[22]

THE GOVERNESS GIG

Orphaned at an early age like Emma Isola and taken under the adoptive care of the Campbell family, who proposed "undertaking the whole charge of her education," Jane Fairfax in Austen's *Emma* grew up aimed at a "path of duty": "The plan was that she should be brought up for educating others; the very few hundred pounds which she inherited from her father making independence impossible."[23] In *Emma,* the governess system is a grim prospect: "With the fortitude of a devoted noviciate, [Jane] had resolved at one-and-twenty to complete the sacrifice, and retire from all pleasures of life, of rational intercourse, equal society, peace and hope, to penance and mortification for ever" (175). When the busybody Mrs. Elton later attempts to manage Jane's first "situation," the novel doubles down on the oppressiveness of the governess system with a comparison to slavery. Jane puts off Mrs. Elton's interference: "When I am quite determined as to the time, I am not at all afraid of being long unem-

---

22. The edition presents "An Essay on [Lamb's] Life and Genius" by Thomas Purnell, with a note about Emma's knowledge of Mary Lamb's matricide: "Mrs. Moxon tells me, that during the whole period of her residence with the Lambs she was completely ignorant of the terrible event. One night, Charles and Mary Lamb and herself were seated at table. The conversation turned on the elder Lamb, when Miss Isola asked why she never heard mention of the mother. Mary thereupon uttered a sharp, piercing cry, for which Charles playfully and laughingly rebuked her; but he made no allusion to the cause" (xxix). What this note confirms is that, at least by 1870, Emma Moxon was fully aware of the Lamb family tragedy.

23. Austen, *Emma,* 175–76.

ployed. There are places in town, offices, where inquiry would soon produce something—Offices for the sale—not quite of human flesh—but of human intellect" (325). When Mrs. Elton takes the reference to slavery too literally, Jane unpacks the comparison:

> "I did not mean, I was not thinking of the slave-trade," replied Jane; "governess-trade, I assure you, was all that I had in view; widely different certainly as to the guilt of those who carry it on; but as to the greater misery of the victims, I do not know where it lies. But I only mean to say that there are advertising offices, and that by applying to them I should have no doubt of very soon meeting with something that would do. . . . A gentleman's family is all that I should condition for." (325)

For both the fictional Jane Fairfax and the historical Emma Isola, adoption offered care while it simultaneously underscored their marginalized status as impoverished orphan women prepping in haphazard families for the governess-trade.

The advertising columns of the *London Times* in 1829 contained dozens of notices about the traffic in governesses:

> AS GOVERNESS.—A young Lady wishes to ENGAGE herself in a Gentleman's Family, to INSTRUCT two or three YOUNG LADIES, not exceeding 12 years of age. She would undertake English, writing and arithmetic, with the usual routine of education, drawing in all its branches; French, music and dancing in the absence of masters. Address, post paid, to X. Y. Darnhill's library, Richmond. Most respectable references will be given and required.[24]

To prepare for just such a life, until she was eighteen Emma Isola was boarded at "Mrs. Richardson's" school in Dulwich, south of the Thames in London, spending her holidays with the Lambs.[25] The main Dulwich school had been

24. *The Times Digital Archive*, January 19, 1829, 2.

25. The school is named in Charles and Mary's letter to Fanny Kelly on March 10, 1828 (III.155–56). The several Isola orphans, children of a university official, must have received some financial support from university sources; after the deaths of their parents, the males were "bluecoat boys" boarded at school in London and Emma was boarded at Dulwich. As Charles worked on Emma's prospects in 1827, in a letter to Robert Jameson he asked whether an appeal to the "Royal Duke" at Cambridge might help (III.124). Prince William Frederick, second Duke of Gloucester and Edinburgh, had become chancellor of the university in 1811, before the death of Charles Isola. Even though he was generally thought "priggish and extremely pompous," his politics would not have displeased Lamb: "During the regency he acted with the opposition, supporting the duke of Sussex against the prince of Wales, and later supported Queen Caroline during the parliamentary proceedings against her." *Oxford Dictionary of National Biography*, entry by A. W. Purdue, May 21, 2009.

established in 1619 by the actor Edward Alleyn for orphan boys from several London parishes; in 1741 the headmaster James Allen added a school for impoverished girls, with instruction in sewing and reading.[26] Unlike Jane Fairfax's more isolated experience, a primary benefit of the Dulwich years for the orphaned and adopted Emma was a network of female friends in shared circumstances, who appear in anonymous cameo roles in Lamb's letters. In September 1824, for example, a friend of the Lambs has supplied "orders" for theater seats, but Charles reports that Mary "is laid up with a most severe cold, which will prevent her going; but Emma, and some friends of hers, mean to avail themselves of them" (II.439). At the moment when Emma found her own "situation" in Fornham in 1828, she recommended a Dulwich school-friend for another opening: "Emma has taken the liberty to name the situation to a young friend who will wait upon you immediately, and whom Emma thinks equally qualified with herself in French, and very *superior to her in music,* being a most excellent singer also. Emma hopes you will pardon her recommendation—from her intimate knowledge of her young friend, whose disposition she describes as excellent, and her parents and connections as most excellent also" (III.155). In the wake of her illness and loss of her position in 1831, Emma spent six recuperative months in Cambridgeshire with the best of these Dulwich friends, Maria Fryer, who was the first person Charles wrote to after Emma's wedding.[27] For the orphaned Emma Isola, the dual claims on her of Cambridge birth and London adoption were crucially supplemented by her independent circle of Dulwich friends, whom the Lambs as adoptive caregivers welcomed and encouraged.

When Emma finished boarding school in 1827 and took up full-time residence with the Lambs, Charles put out queries to his circle about a governess position. From a letter to Charles Ollier in May 1827:

> We want a situation as Governess for her in a private family, where there are young Ladies, not older we will say than twelve. She is nineteen, her French (you know I am no critic there) is I believe very good; she can teach drawing & music to the extent requisite for children at or below the age I mention, & knows a little of Italian. . . . She has spent all her holydays with us these last six years, during which time she has been apprenticed to a very good school at Dulwich. (III.86)

---

26. Latter-day forms of the schools—Dulwich College and James Allen's Girls' School (JAGS)—thrive there today.

27. Maria Fryer proved to be a lifetime friend; the Moxon family holds a letter in 1849 from Edward Moxon to Emma, who is on holiday without the children in Malvern with "Miss Fryer"; my thanks to John Moxon for access to this manuscript.

To prepare an adopted daughter for life as a governess, Charles and Mary found themselves revisiting after two decades their curricular and pedagogical differences with one of the most influential figures in educational theory and practice at the turn of the century, Anna Letitia Barbauld, whose work was grounded in her own firsthand experience of a de facto kinship adoption.

As set forth in the opening to chapter 1, Barbauld and her husband Rochemont, who had no biological children, in 1777 adopted the two-year-old Charles Aiken, the third son of her brother John Aiken. Barbauld soon turned adoptive parenting to practical use, publishing *Lessons for Children,* which quickly became a beloved reading primer for generations. Lamb infamously deplored the enterprise and torched Barbauld in a letter to Samuel Taylor Coleridge in 1802:

> Mrs. Barbauld's stuff has banished all the old classics of the nursery; and the shopman at Newbery's hardly deigned to reach them off an old exploded corner of a shelf, when Mary asked for them. Mrs. B's and Mrs. Trimmer's nonsense lay in piles about. Knowledge insignificant and vapid as Mrs. B's books convey, it seems, must come to a child in the *shape of knowledge,* and his empty noddle must be turned with conceit of his own powers when he has learnt that a Horse is an animal, and Billy is better than a Horse, and such like; instead of that beautiful interest in wild tales. . . . Damn them!— I mean the cursed Barbauld Crew, those Blights and Blasts of all that is Human in man and child. (I.252–53)

Lamb's 1802 complaint about Barbauld brewed nostalgia with misogyny. More useful contributions were the works he and Mary published on competing principles for William Godwin's Juvenile Library in the same decade: *Tales from Shakespeare* (1807), Mary's *Mrs. Leicester's School* (1808), and their *Poems for Children* (1810). During the Emma decade, Henry Crabb Robinson recorded a cool meeting between Charles and Barbauld in June 1824: "After dinner Lamb and I took a walk to Newington. I sat an hour with Mrs. Barbauld. She was looking tolerably, but Lamb (not his habit) was disputatious with her, and not in his best way. He reasons from feelings, and those often idiosyncrasies; she from dry abstractions and verbal definitions. Such people can't agree, and infallibly dislike each other."[28] The next year, Charles stuck to his pedagogical guns in an *Elia* essay on "The Old and the New School-Master": "The modern schoolmaster is expected to know a little of every

---

28. Robinson, *Diary,* I.406.

FOUND CHILDREN

thing, because his pupil is required not to be entirely ignorant of any thing. He must be superficially, if I may so say, omniscient."[29]

In their care for Emma in the 1820s, the Lambs' recalcitrant traditionalism appears most tellingly in their last-minute strategies to prep Emma for a livelihood. The governess advertisements in the London papers all feature the same toolkit for "the usual branches of education," the gendered assumption of which phrase a few ads render explicitly as "female education": the ability to teach English, drawing, music, arithmetic, geography ("the globe"), and modern languages, especially French and, occasionally, Italian.[30] In this gendered market, no ad ever mentions the masculinist high road of classical languages, but Charles and Mary were determined, in spite of the market, to bring Emma up to speed as an apprentice Latinist, to ratchet up the status of her employment.[31] In a July 1827 letter to Mary Shelley, Charles hoped that skill with Latin might "qualify her for a superior governess-ship" (III.110). Charles wrote to a Mrs. Dillon in July 1827, "We are both very thankful to you for your thinking about Emma, whom for the last seven weeks I have been teaching Latin, & she is already qualified to impart the rudiments to a child" (III.108–9). In August, Mary wrote to Lady Stoddart: "Charles and I do little else here than teach her something or other all day long. We are striving to put enough Latin into her to enable her to begin to teach it to young learners" (III.114). But the crash course in Latin did not go well. Charles confessed that "tis like feeding a child with chopped hay from a spoon. Sisyphus his labours were as nothing to it."[32] By September, Charles shrugged off the Latin project in his nonsense manner, in a letter to John Bates Dibdin: "Emma has just died, choak'd with a Gerund in dum. On opening her we found a Participle in rus in the pericardium" (III.126).

Emma's employment prospects began to open in the fall of 1827. In a letter to Mary Shelley in October, Charles noted that "when your letter came I was gone to town with Emma after a situation in a greatest family, with a Mrs.

---

29. Lamb, *Elia*, 60.

30. Charles and Mary Lamb took their sole vacation trip abroad in the summer of 1822, to Paris; it is likely that they were giving their French a workout to help prepare Emma for her governess prospects; see Lucas, *Life*, II.122.

31. Charles's and Mary's hopes for a "superior" position generate Charles's appeal to royal connections at Cambridge, in an August 1827 letter to Robert Jameson about Emma's governess search: "I have heard you name Mr. Gunning who bears the same office at Cambridge, which her father did formerly. Would there be any impropriety in naming the circumstances to him, and begging his interest, whatever he may have, as holding that office, in the Royal Duke?" (III.124). For the Royal Duke, see note 25.

32. Two years later, Mary published a poem in *Blackwood's Magazine*: "To Emma, Learning Latin, and Desponding": "Droop not, dear Emma, dry those falling tears, / And call up smiles into thy pallid face" (III.109).

Compton that hath her town and country family and twenty servants—and they seem to approve of her, £25 a year salary. We shall have a definite answer in a few days & if it break off, I will let you know. But I fear it is only for a few months, still that is a beginning, and will be a recommendation" (III.142). An actual job did not appear until the spring of 1828, when Emma took a position with the family of a clergyman and his wife with two daughters in Fornham, near Bury St. Edmunds.[33] When Emma departed at the end of April, she had been with the Lambs daily for nearly a year, and her planned and anticipated leave-taking was nevertheless painful to her adoptive family. As Charles informed Thomas Hood, Emma "departed for Cambridge on Thursday, and will be at Bury to day. She has left an ugly gap in our society, which will not close hastily" (III.160). In a letter to George Dyer, Charles attempted to bandage the pain with a pun; Emma is now in Suffolk, "where she is, to us, alas, dead and Bury'd; we sorely miss her" (III.160).

Emma's governess tenure with the Williams family near Bury was a success until cut short by her illnesses. After a year, Charles reported to Bernard Barton in June 1829: "You will be glad to hear that Emma, tho' unknown to you, has given the highest satisfaction in her little place of Governante in a Clergyman's family, which you may believe by the Parson and his Lady drinking poor Mary's health on her birthday, tho' they never saw her, merely because she was a friend of Emma's, and the Vicar also sent me a brace of partridges" (III.220–21). When Charles met the family in Bury on the fraught occasion of Emma's first illness in the spring of 1830, he immediately charmed Mrs. Williams ("Grace Joanna") and the two daughters, Josepha Maria and Louisa Clare, by composing acrostics on their names, which Mrs. Williams reciprocated with an acrostic for him (III.259–62). When Emma returned to Bury after a month recuperating with the Lambs, Charles reported to Bernard Barton in late June that Emma "had been treated like a daughter by the good Parson and his whole family" (III.283).[34]

Emma's health, however, proved too precarious. In early spring 1831, she returned to the Lambs, ill yet again, with the understanding that her time in Bury had ended. Charles reported the final separation in late March to Emma's Dulwich friend Maria Fryer, who had visited during her first recovery:

---

33. Charles Lamb wrote to Fanny Kelly in March 1828: "Many thanks for your kind consideration about our young friend who is engaged to a clergyman's family near Bury, and it is settled that she goes there in April" (III.155).

34. The Moxon family holds a letter from the Reverend Williams to Emma at the time of her illness, expressing much sympathy; my thanks to John Moxon for access to this manuscript.

Found Children   183

> Emma came to us on Thursday last, having quite parted with Mrs. Williams, which has been a severe feeling, I believe, to both. . . . The mortification to her at being obliged to quit a family so kind to her has been very painful indeed. If anything could alleviate it, it would be the excessive kindness of the manner in which Mrs. Williams broke the necessity to her. . . . She appears to have combated against her disorder, and to have done every thing she could to give satisfaction at Fornham, but the indisposition would not let her. . . . She cried most bitterly, for she was deservedly attached to the Williams's, to the children, & the very household, who all did their best to make her situation agreeable to her. (Princeton 186–87)

Emma spent nearly three years, from spring 1828 to spring 1831, in Fornham, broken up by regular holiday visits with Charles and Mary in Enfield and by her first recovery visit in 1830. Mary was often ill and away from home under care, which made Emma's visits even more therapeutic for the solitary Charles. The only time he used the word "adopted" to refer to Emma is in a snapshot of the leave-taking cost of these holiday visits when Mary was also ill and away. From a letter to Bernard Barton in late July 1829: "I have had the loneliest time near 10 weeks, broken by a short apparition of Emma for her holydays, whose departure only deepend the returning solitude. . . . When I took leave of our adopted young friend at Charing Cross, 'twas heavy unfeeling rain, and I had no where to go. Home have I none—and not a sympathising house to turn to in the great city. Never did the waters of the heaven pour down on a forlorner head" (III.224).[35]

Emma Isola turned twenty-one in 1829, during her term as governess. Charles marked that milestone with a poem addressed "To a Young Friend, on her Twenty-First Birth-Day."[36] Once again, as in his request for album verses for Emma, Charles grounded Emma's identity in her immigrant Cambridge birth family. The poem imagines a day when friends of an aged Emma Isola will affirm that "This Dame for length of days, and virtues rare / With her respected Grandsire may compare." As an adoptee, Emma's lost past included not only the immigrant grandfather she never knew but, most painfully, the birth parents who were both dead by the time she was seven:

Grandchild of that respected Isola,
Thou shoulds't have had about thee on this day

---

35. For a Lamb-centric reading of the effect on Charles Lamb of Emma Isola's independence as a governess and her marriage, see Riehl, "Last Days," 2–12.

36. The poem was published in Lamb's *Album Verses* in 1830, which was the first book published by Edward Moxon in his new enterprise; Lamb, *Works,* 5.53–54 (text) and 310 (note).

Kind looks of Parents, to congratulate
Their Pride grown up to woman's grave estate.
But they have died, and left thee, to advance
Thy fortunes how thou may'st, and owe to chance
The friends which Nature grudg'd.

For the orphaned adoptee, the celebratory moment requires mourning the loss of biological kin. Emma's adoptive caregivers belong to a different kinship order of randomness and "chance," a subsequent set of "friends" who now substitute, haphazardly, for the lost originals whom "Nature grudg'd"—those first friends whose lives "Nature" cut short.

THE POLITICS OF ADOPTION

During the decade when the Lambs cared for Emma Isola, they moved northward from central London several times, into more open country. They first moved in 1823 from their Russell Street lodgings near Covent Garden to Islington three miles to the north; in 1827, the year Emma finished boarding school, they moved ten miles farther north to the village of Enfield; and in 1833, the year of Emma's marriage, they shifted five miles back toward town, to the village of Edmonton, where Charles and Mary are buried; during the Emma decade, Mary was ill for increasingly longer intervals, away from home under care. Even in their town days, Charles was a celebrated pedestrian, but the northward moves and his 1825 retirement installed walking at the vagabond center of daily life, as Charles reported in a letter to Robert Southey in August 1825: "Mary walks her twelve miles a day some days, and I my twenty on others" (III.23).[37] During her full year with the Lambs in 1827–28 and her subsequent holiday visits, Emma Isola regularly accompanied Charles on his rambles. In Thomas Noon Talfourd's 1837 account, "Lamb was fond of taking long walks in the country, and as Miss Lamb's strength was not always equal to these pedestrian excursions, [Emma] became his constant companion in

---

37. Mary wrote to Mrs. Vincent Novello in spring 1820, from Newington: "My brother walked seventeen miles yesterday before dinner. And notwithstanding his long walk to and from the office, we walk every evening; but I by no means perform in this way so well as I used to do. A twelve-mile walk one hot Sunday morning made my feet blister, and they are hardly well now" (II.273). Charles wrote to Bernard Barton in July 1829, after Emma had returned to Fornham and while Mary was still ill and away: "What I can do, and do overdo, is to walk, but deadly long are the days" (III.225). In the year of his death, Lamb wrote to his old friend Thomas Manning: "I walk 9 or 10 miles a day" (III.410).

Found Children

walks."[38] In May 1833, while Mary was again ill and away under care, Charles announced Emma's impending marriage in pedestrian terms, in a letter to William Wordsworth: "I am about to lose my old and only walk-companion, whose mirthful spirits were 'the youth of our house,' Emma Isola. . . . I am feeble, but cheerful in this my genial hot weather.—walk'd 16 miles yesterday" (III.371).

At least one of the walks shared by adoptive parent and adopted daughter took a pointedly political turn. One of Charles's favorite walks from Enfield aimed at the village of Waltham Cross, another five miles to the north.[39] The "Cross" that gave the village its name is, in Charles's words, "one of the Crosses which Edwd 1st caused to be built for his wife at every town where her corpse rested between Northhamptonshr and London." Reporting an excursion to see the monument in September 1827, when Emma was his regular "walk-companion," Charles included draft verses that drew a tight connection between Elinor's thirteenth-century royal fate and the life of Caroline of Brunswick, dead in 1821. From his letter to Bernard Barton (III.128):

> Strolling to Waltham Cross the other day, I hit off these lines:
>
>> A stately Cross each sad spot doth attest,
>> Whereat the corpse of Elinor did rest,
>> From Herdby fetch'd—her Spouse so honour'd her—
>> To sleep with royal dust at Westminster.
>> And, if less pompous obsequies were thine,
>> Duke Brunswick's daughter, princely Caroline,
>> Grudge not, great ghost, nor count thy funeral losses:
>> Thou in thy life-time had'st thy share of crosses.

Published in the *Englishman's Magazine* in September 1831, Lamb's lament for Queen Caroline, nearly a decade after her riotous end, underscores how the Lambs' adoption of Emma Isola—from its earliest moments in 1820 through her excursions with Charles—takes oppositional shape within the manifestly political context of adoption performed nationally by the life and times of Caroline of Brunswick and her adopted son William Austin, as set forth in chapter 2. A surrogate child is a disruptive, oppositional figure in national

---

38. Talfourd, *Letters*, 142.

39. Charles mentions at least one other walk to Waltham Cross in February 1828, when Emma was still there: "yesterday tramped to Waltham Cross" (III.152); in July 1829, when Maria Fryer was with the Lambs and Emma for Emma's holidays, Emma herself, in a rare surviving letter, records "a delightful walk to Waltham this morning" (III.223).

politics at precisely the moment when Charles Lamb, Mary Lamb, and Emma Isola met one another in Cambridge and launched their own untimely family experiment.

The published version of Charles's Waltham Cross poem rendered more explicit the "obsequies" and "funeral losses" attendant upon Caroline after her death in August 1821, a year after the Lambs had met Emma Isola in Cambridge and hosted her in London:

> Far different rites did thee to dust consign,
> Duke Brunswick's daughter, Princely Caroline.
> A hurrying funeral, and a banish'd grave,
> High-minded Wife! were all that thou could'st have.[40]

In the wake of her banishment from the coronation of her despised husband in July 1821, Queen Caroline died on August 7. On August 14, her funeral procession, featuring William Austin in one of the dedicated mourning coaches, churned a rowdy way through London, the crowds swelling near the Lambs' Russell Street lodgings. On that same hot London day of "riots, affray, and manslaughter," as Caroline's modern biographer puts it, Charles sent an invitation for cards "to-morrow evening at 8" to William Ayrton (the brother of his Cambridge host at Kenmare House the previous summer), alerting Ayrton that he would find as a mark of respect "closed windows on account of the demise of her Majesty" (II.318)"[41] The press reports of the queen's burial a few days later in her native Brunswick regularly logged her residuary legatee "Mr. William Austin" (no longer "young Austin") among her final band of mourners. When Charles wrote his will in 1830, after ensuring primary care for Mary, he named Emma Isola his own residuary legatee: the trustees "shall have power to pay the Residue of the said property to Emma Isola now residing at Fornham All Saints Bury Suffolk or in case that she may not be living to any child or children that she may have left born in lawful wedlock" (III.292). In its last phrases, the boilerplate legal language of the will repositioned the adopted legatee in a sanctioned line of biological descent.

---

40. Lamb, *Works*, 5.107 (text) and 338–39 (note).

41. Fraser, *Unruly Queen*, 462. A contemporary Queenite account noted the form of grudging tributes from establishment redoubts on the day of her death: "At the mansion of the Lord-Chancellor . . . the shutters in the lower part of the house were quite closed, and in the upper parts the blinds were drawn. At Carlton House, the shutters in front were all closed. Most of the houses in St. James's Square, including the late residence of her Majesty, were also in the same state, and similar marks of respect were observable . . . in the other fashionable squares and streets"; Nightingale, *Memoirs*, 299.

FOUND CHILDREN

During the uproar of Caroline's return to England and adultery trial in Lords from August to November 1820, Charles Lamb was a dedicated Queenite, like so many of the queen's champions largely motivated by his detestation of the former prince regent, now ruling as George IV. Throughout the late-Regency years of the run-up to the trial and its aftermath, Lamb published sharply pointed verses about political characters and topics in *The Champion,* John Thelwall's oppositional rag, his topics including the Spa Fields riots in 1816 and the Cato Street conspiracy in 1820.[42] Lamb clearly not only tracked the royal scandal, unfolding daily in great detail in the press, but was a lively participant. To take but one example, while populist London roiled on behalf of the queen, the new king threw regular fits with his counselors in which he threatened to withdraw to the family territory in Hanover and yield the throne to his brother, the Duke of York. Lamb in response to press gossip produced a quatrain titled "On a Projected Journey" that ran in *The Champion* on July 15 and 16, 1820:

> To gratify his people's wish
> See G[eorg]e at length prepare—
> He's setting out for Hanover—
> We've often wished him there.[43]

Writing to his friend Barron Field in Australia in August, Charles set an international poll: "Pray are you King's or Queen's men in Sidney? Or have thieves no politics?" (II.282). Precisely during this fraught extreme of royal family politics, Charles and Mary escaped the heat of London and the crowds agitating the scandal for vacation lodgings on the King's Parade in Cambridge. During evenings at Kenmore House on Trumpington Street, the stammering Charles and the intermittently mad Mary met the orphan Emma Isola, the embryonic moment of their own ectopic family performance.

It is telling that contemporary accounts of William Austin and later accounts of Emma Isola cannot resist inventing and policing transgressed sexual boundaries—Willy Austin is Caroline's incestuous partner and Emma Isola dwells with a pedophile. These false alarms measure the power of both adoptive figures to disturb and unsettle established order. During the 1820s, both surrogate families—one excessively public and one known chiefly in literary circles—posed primary narrative puzzles. While regularly experimenting with how to explain Emma's identity to friends and acquaintances, Charles

---

42. For an account of Lamb's contributions on these fronts, see especially Gardner, *Poetry and Popular Protest.*

43. Lamb, *Works,* 5.106 (text) and 337 (note).

188   CHAPTER 6

Lamb kept an interested eye on the various aftershocks of the Queen Caroline affair with residual Queenite sympathies, as in the Waltham Cross poem. After Caroline's death in 1821, William Austin stayed in the British news, even though he returned to live in Italy; popular press accounts continued to float rumors about his contested identity. Twice during the decade he returned to London to battle out in Chancery the terms of his inheritance as Caroline's residuary legatee. In the lives of both English adoptees, Italy supplied primary marks of alien status. William Austin's residence in Milan offered to the London press lurid reminders of the scandals of his adoptive mother's rowdy Italian period, capped by his commitment to a Milanese madhouse. A source of pride within her family, Emma Isola's Italian heritage was simultaneously racialized in the chromatic epithet that still follows her name, the "nut-brown maid."[44] When Charles introduced her in a letter to Bryan Waller Procter in January 1829, he offhandedly compounded the inflection of Emma as alien—she is "brown," "wild," and "Italian" (not to mention "silent" and "a girl"): "There is no mystery in my incognita. She has often seen you, though you may not have observed a silent brown girl, who for the last twelve years has run wild about our house in her Christmas holidays. She is Italian by name and extraction" (III.202). The untimely family stories of William Austin and Emma Isola by default disrupted biocentric and bionormative national narratives.

Standard accounts of Charles Lamb's career in literary history highlight a different signature event in the days when he and Mary met Emma: the publication of his first *Elia* essay, "The South Sea House," in the *London Magazine* in August 1820.[45] During the months of the royal trial, Charles's oppositional capital was itself performatively narrative, as he shaped his own identity as a surrogate outsider to establishment redoubts such as Oxbridge colleges. In the second *Elia* essay, "Oxford in the Vacation," written about his summer holidays in Cambridge in 1819 and 1820 and published in October 1820, Charles celebrated the freedom of the uncredentialed pedestrian who is, culturally, an impostor:

> I can here play the gentleman, enact the student. . . . Here I can take my
> walks unmolested, and fancy myself of what degree or standing I please. . . .
> The walks at these times are so much one's own. . . . The halls deserted, and
> with open doors, inviting one to slip in unperceived, and pay a devoir to
> some Founder, or noble or royal Benefactress (that should have been ours)

---

44. "Moxon has fal'n in love with Emma, our nut-brown maid"; Lamb, *Letters*, III.106. The phrase "nut-brown maid" refers to the title of a popular ballad ("The Nut-Brown Maiden"), on the topic of woman's fidelity.

45. Lamb, *Elia*, 1–8.

FOUND CHILDREN

whose portrait seems to smile upon their over-looked beadsman, and to adopt me for their own.[46]

In his Elia mask, Lamb fashioned his own surrogate identity at this 1820 moment under the sign of adoption, the mark of an outsider who for the next decade performed, oppositionally, as a surrogate parent to a surrogate child.

The history of that adoption left its record almost exclusively in letters and diaries. The *Elia* essays, Lamb's most well-known work, offer no direct references to Emma Isola, the historical child in this haphazard family. One of the most anthologized of those essays, "Dream Children: A Reverie" (1822), instead foregrounds childlessness, adoptive or otherwise. The narrator awakes from a dream of telling family tales to his phantom children, who bid him farewell: "We are nothing, less than nothing, and dreams. We are only what might have been."[47] Elsewhere the essays furnish evidence that Lamb circulated the figure of the Romantic child in especially masculinist and infantilized form. In "The Child Angel: A Dream" (1823), for example, Lamb constructed a figure whose "portion was, and is, to be a child for ever," to remain in "perpetual childhood."[48]

Instead of a focus on Lamb's peculiar inflection of the mythic Romantic child and its legacy of burdens, I close this final chapter with two moments in the *Elia* essays that point beyond those texts to the historical Emma Isola and her alliance with her adoptive father as a company of untimely outsiders, of glad misfits. In addition to Charles's stutter posing no impediment to their conversation, adoptive father and adopted daughter shared not only a fondness for vagabond ways but an outsider's relish for nonsense—nonsense as a performative refusal of the absurdities of prevailing, normalized behavior and establishment scripts. Two *Elia* essays, "The Old and the New School-Master" and "The Wedding," offer gateways to moments in the correspondence when Charles and Emma exhibit their shared adoptive perch outside what passes as the prescriptively proper and normal.

In the "School-Master" essay from 1825, which continued Charles's dispute with Anna Letitia Barbauld in the wake of their frosty meeting in 1824, the narrator suffers confinement in a coach with a stranger who quizzes him about every trivial matter that passes their view. When the insufferable seatmate at last exits the coach, "the truth now flashed upon me, that my companion was a schoolmaster" who, "expected to know a little of every thing,"

---

46. Lamb, 10; Lamb's habitual displacement of self generated the title focus (Oxford) of the essay, which is largely based on his holidays in Cambridge.

47. Lamb, 118.

48. Lamb, 278.

190 CHAPTER 6

is "superficially omniscient."[49] What Barbauld's modern pedagogy could not tolerate is nonsense. In her "Advertisement" to *Lessons for Children,* she wrote of her adopted nephew "Little Charles" that "a grave remark, or a connected story, however simple, is above his capacity; and *nonsense* is always below it; for Folly is worse than Ignorance." In May 1830, Emma and Charles traveled in a coach from Bury to Enfield, in the wake of Emma's first illness in Fornham. Charles's report of the journey in a letter to Sarah Hazlitt replayed the "School-Master" essay, but with this key difference: now he and Emma performed together an oppositional triumph of nonsense.

> We travelled with one of those troublesome fellow passengers in a stage coach that is call'd a well-informed man. For twenty miles we discoursed about the properties of steam, probabilities of carriages by ditto, till all my science, and more than all, was exhausted & I was thinking of escaping my torment by getting up on the outside, when getting into Bishop Stortford my gentleman spying some farming land put an unlucky question to me "what sort of crop of turnips I thought we should have this year." Emma's eyes turned to me, to know what in the world I could have to say, and she burst into a violent fit of laughter, maugre her pale serious cheeks, when with the greatest gravity I replied, that "it depended, I believed upon boiled legs of mutton." This clench'd our conversation, and my gentleman with a face half wise, half in scorn, troubled us with no more conversation scientific or philosophical for the remainder of the journey. (III.280)

Emma Isola here joins company with John Keats in Benjamin Robert Haydon's famous account of the "Immortal Dinner" in 1817, when Lamb in his cups repeatedly demands to inspect the phrenological organs of an unlucky tax official from the Stamp Office: "Keats and I hurried Lamb into the painting-room, shut the door and gave way to inextinguishable laughter."[50]

The *Elia* essay "The Wedding" (1825) supplies an uncanny anticipation of Emma's July 1833 London wedding at St. George's in Hanover Square. Invited to the wedding of a friend's daughter, the Elia narrator garbs himself in the language of adoption: "Being without a family, I am flattered with these temporary adoptions into a friend's family. . . . I am inducted into degrees of affinity." Filling in as a surrogate for the father in the ceremony, the dissident narrator risks disrupting the institutional script: "I do not know what business I have to be present in solemn places. I cannot divest me of unseason-

---

49. Lamb, 57–60.
50. Haydon, *Autobiography*; and Plumly, *Immortal Evening.*

FOUND CHILDREN

able disposition to levity upon the most awful occasions. I was never cut out for a public functionary."[51] In a letter to Louisa Badams, Charles's account of Emma's July 1833 wedding repeats the dissident script of the 1825 essay, but with a crucial difference. Performatively, adoptive father and adoptive daughter are now partners in outsider crime: "I was at church, as the grave Father, and behaved tolerably well, except at first entrance, when Emma in a whisper repressed a nascent giggle" (III.381).

I want to connect this nonsense-loving misbehavior of the adoptive pair in a London-bound coach and at Emma's wedding to the record of oppositional literary politics in the decades following Waterloo. Twenty years before Emma Isola's wedding, in 1814 Harriet Westbrook and Percy Bysshe Shelley pledged vows at the same altar at the same Hanover Square church, sanctioning with Church of England establishment ritual their 1811 Scottish elopement. In 1818 Basil Montagu senior, housing once again in London his hapless repatriated son Basil Caroline, supplied legal counsel for Shelley, now the partner of Mary Wollstonecraft Godwin, in Shelley's failed attempt to gain custody of his two children with Harriet, who had drowned herself in the Serpentine in Hyde Park a year earlier. The court cited Shelley's radical poem *Queen Mab* as evidence that he was unfit to be a parent. In 1840 Emma Isola Moxon, now the mother of young children, learned that her husband Edward, the publisher of a new one-volume *The Poetical Works of Percy Bysshe Shelley*, edited by his widow Mary Shelley, would be tried in the Queen's Bench Court for blasphemous libel; the smoking gun for the charge was an unexpurgated *Queen Mab*.[52] The presiding judge for Emma's husband's trial was Lord Denman, ironically one of the most eloquent advocates for the adoptive mother of William Austin in Queen Caroline's 1820 trial for royal adultery. Emma's husband's advocate at trial was Thomas Noon Talfourd, one of the executors of Charles Lamb's estate, who in 1837 had supplied the earliest published account of Emma's adopted life in *The Letters of Charles Lamb, with a Sketch of His Life*. In Talfourd's account, Charles and Mary at Cambridge "met with a little girl, who being in a manner alone in the world, engaged their sympathy, and soon riveted their affections. . . . Their regard for her increased; she regularly spent the holidays with them till she left school, and afterwards was adopted as a daughter, and lived generally with them until 1833, when she married Mr. Moxon" (II.141). At trial, Talfourd's eloquent speech for freedom of expression

---

51. Lamb, *Elia*, 271–74.

52. Moxon's 1839 four-volume edition of Shelley's poetry omitted sections of the poem that had been proved blasphemous in an 1821 trial, but Mary Shelley decided to restore the passages for the one-volume 1840 edition. Her "Postscript" to the "Editor's Preface," dated November 6, 1839, states, "At my request the publisher has restored the omitted passages of Queen Mab" (xi).

CHAPTER 6

won the day but lost the verdict.[53] Lord Denman, sympathetic, ruled that the law was nevertheless the law, and Emma's husband was convicted of publishing blasphemous libel but sentenced only to pay court costs.[54] The law was the law: like a proscribed poem or unsanctioned speech, or even the passing madness of a nascent giggle, adoption remained outside the laws and norms of the nation for another century.

Emma Isola's publisher husband Edward Moxon died in 1858, when Emma was fifty; Emma lived another thirty-three years until her death in Brighton in 1891. There were seven Moxon children who survived into adulthood, but Emma maintained a life not bounded by domesticity; a Moxon family letter indicates that in the summer of 1849, for example, she took a summer holiday in the Malvern Hills with her old Dulwich schoolmate Maria Fryer, without husband and without children, and with conversations that surely often turned on their memories of Emma's adoptive family. In the aftermath of Edward's death, the Moxon publishing firm eventually fell on financial hard times, but the Moxon name was so valued in civic culture that several public efforts were made to ensure Emma's support, including a grant from the Queen's Civil List in 1874. But I close at the death of Emma's husband, forty years after the deaths of her biological parents in 1814 and 1815 and a quarter century after the death of her adoptive father in 1834. At this latest moment of too many griefs, including the death of her first son Edward in 1841, Emma suffered being posed for a portrait in a new medium, a photograph in widow's garb (figure 5).

It is not entirely fanciful to read in that formal visage of grief the trace of the impulse to share with her adoptive father their instinct to upstage, however fleetingly, the nonsensical absurdities of normative culture, which mapped them both, adopted daughter and adoptive father, as outsiders, suffering the outrages of diminishment.

---

53. Talfourd, *Speech for the Defendant.* In his opening remarks to the jury, Talfourd invoked the name of Charles Lamb, "to whom the wife of the defendant was as an adopted daughter" (note the qualifier "as," from a lawyer).

54. Thomas, "Prosecution," 329–34.

FIGURE 5. Emma Isola Moxon, 1858. Used with permission of John Moxon.

CONCLUSION

Untimely Adoption

And the tally? Severely diminished, William Austin died unremarked in a London asylum in 1857, six years after the state of Massachusetts passed the first de jure adoption legislation in the Anglophone world. In Thomas Carlyle's 1881 recollection, Basil Caroline Montagu "ended by a bad road" in 1830 in Cambridge, his death unnoticed in any records of his adoptive caregivers. Alone among the three historical children of Romantic-period adoption featured in these chapters, Emma Isola Moxon's death in Brighton in 1891 captured national view, headlined as Charles Lamb's adopted daughter, even though the phrase had no legal import. Among the supporting cast of adoptees registered in passing in these pages, Thomas Day's purloined foundling Sabrina Sidney, later the widowed Mrs. Bicknell, died in Greenwich in 1843, where she had briefly managed schoolboy life for William Austin. Charles Barbauld, who behaved as "Little Charles" on nearly every page of his adopted mother's *Lessons for Children,* died in London in 1847, after a career in medicine. Jane Austen's adopted older brother Edward, after 1812 Edward Austen Knight, died at Godmersham in Kent in 1852, survived by nine of his eleven children. In *Emma,* the adoptee Frank Churchill paired off in marriage with the adoptee Jane Fairfax, their subsequent lives as unavailable as the fates of the half dozen illegitimate offspring Emma Woodhouse imagines of Churchill agency. Bessie Florence Gibson Shelley, the adopted daughter and only child of Percy Florence Shelley, who was the sole surviving biological child of Mary

• 194 •

Wollstonecraft Godwin and Percy Bysshe Shelley, died as the widowed Lady Scarlett in 1934, eight years after Parliament passed the nation's first de jure adoption legislation in 1926.

In final sections of the Adoption of Children Act, 1926, the bureaucratic state both acknowledged and folded into law the prehistory of de facto adoption in England and Wales. The twelve sections of the act included a cleanup section 10, "Provisions as to existing de facto adoptions." Here is the entirety of section 10 (in which the act signifies by the term "infants" "a person under the age of twenty-one"):

> Where at the date of the commencement of this Act any infant is in the custody of, and being brought up, maintained and educated by any person or two spouses jointly as his, her or their own child under any de facto adoption, and has for a period of not less than two years before such commencement been in such custody, and been so brought up, maintained and educated, the Court may, upon the application of such person or spouses, and notwithstanding that the applicant is a male and the infant a female, make an adoption order authorizing him, her or them to adopt the infant without requiring the consent of any parent or guardian of the infant to be obtained, upon being satisfied that in all the circumstances of the case it is just and equitable and for the welfare of the infant that no such consent should be required and that an adoption order should be made.[1]

Having long supplied the culture with vehicles of ad hoc utility, de facto adoption, clearly familiar, was now legitimized. With backdoor blessings, section 10 exempted preexisting de facto adoptive care from two new restrictions on de jure adoption elsewhere in the act. The first, a requirement for parental consent, remains, with many disputed variations, a familiar feature of adoptive law. The second, the act's anxious prohibition of the adoption of a female child by a single male, has shifted in the subsequent history of adoption law into battles on different fronts, such as the rights of same-sex couples to adopt. But in 1926, any de facto adoption with legs longer than two years was exempt from either of these two new statutory guardrails. In the eyes of the state in 1926, de facto adoption, long absent from common law, at last entered the legal realm legislatively. Simultaneously, basic principles of modern de jure adoption first became law in England and Wales, including permanently "extinguishing" parental rights of birth parents and defining the status of the

---

1. Adoption of Children Act, 1926 [16 & 17 Geo.5. Ch.29.]; https://www.legislation.gov.uk/.

adoptee "as though the adopted child was a child born to the adopter in lawful wedlock."

In light of this pivot in the legal history of Anglophone adoption, the temptation to spin adoption history as a tale of progress might fasten on other language in section 10, such as the shift from informal Romantic-period phrases about "charge" and "care" to the new lockdown legal formula "brought up, maintained and educated" and the guiding standard of "the welfare of the infant." But other features of the 1926 act argue that it achieved at best a great leap sideways in the history of British adoption law.[2] Most tellingly, the biogenealogical property system remained untouched by the new law. Any new adoption order "shall not deprive the adopted child of any right to or interest in property to which the child would have been entitled," and such an order "shall not confer on the adopted child any right to or interest in property as a child of the adopter." Real and personal property rights, old or new, were walled off from any effect in the 1926 act, which also preserved a residual trace of the common law aversion to adoption as an outsider threat: the new law prohibited any adoption order "in respect of any infant who is not a British subject and so resident."

In tallied effect, the de facto adoptions in this book also lobby against a progressive reading. These adoptions resist being lumped together as the baseline of an adoption narrative that aims itself Whiggishly toward perfected forms of contemporary de jure adoption.[3] The leap forward of two hundred years from Romantic-period adoption instead stares down failure on too many global fronts, from the craven kidnapping of adoption to help criminalize abortion by the US Supreme Court in 2022 to the spectacle of purloined children from war-torn Ukraine being shopped adoptively in Russia as tools of national image-making.[4] In the context of this book's focus on British history, in July 2022 the UK government issued a parliamentary report on the abuses of adoption in the "Baby Scoop" period of the mid-twentieth century: "The Violation of Family Life: Adoption of Children of Unmarried Women 1949–1976."[5] The report called for "an apology by the Government and an official recognition that what happened to these mothers was dreadful and wrong."[6] Because the wreckage of the broken politics and practices of too

---

2. For a reading of the 1926 act as a "desire to maintain the status quo," see McCauliff, "First English Adoption Law," 675.

3. Jenny Keating's account of the national debates leading to the 1926 Adoption Act underscores how, instead of new middling-class family formations, these debates foregrounded the hot mess of childcare (or its absence) in urban working-class culture from the middle of the nineteenth century through the first World War.

4. See Hipchen, "Dobbs Issue"; and Kristof, "Russia Traffics."

5. For "Baby Scoop" history, see Fessler, *Girls Who Went Away*; and Solinger, *Wake Up.*

6. House of Commons, "Violation."

much modern de jure adoption urges detours from the primary tasks of this book, I return to adoptee subjectivity to restate my primary claim: the history of Romantic-period adoption supplies a new window into adoptee person-hood, then and now. Divorced from the illusion of seamless progress, conti-nuity between old and new instead takes this repeated shape: in the wake of Romantic-period childhood, doubly differentiated adoptees wrestle with seg-regated exceptionalism entangled with the diminishments of familial remove, yielding a fraught heritage of nonpersonhood from which emerge, unaccount-ably, both victims and survivors, who are not infrequently one and the same. Under the banner of the untimely, adoptees gather with the excluded.

The politics of these imbricated forms of Romantic-period adoption mani-fest in untimeliness. Adoptions in this period behave untimely in that, extra-legally, they confound temporal sequences, the quotidian sites of which are generational family structures, enshrined in common law bionormatively. When the London press attacked the adoptee William Austin in the wake of Queen Caroline's death as "that non-descript Billy Austin," the primary refer-ent in "non-descript" was the derailment of biological sequence, signifying an interruption caused by a newly discovered biological specimen "that has not been previously described or identified," discommodiously. When west-country locals were puzzled by "an unexplained child" under the adoptive care of the Wordsworth siblings, the explanatory power of normative family sequence failed to come to their aid. When the lawyer Basil Montagu's third wife distinguished between "my Sons, real, and adopted," she invoked biologi-cal origins to launch two inopportune narrative sequences defining identity in the family. When Charles Lamb's friends registered Emma Isola as "a kind of adopted daughter," the hesitation in the modifier "kind of" underscored a temporal glitch in bionormative family narrative, a glitch already at work in the very phrase "adopted daughter." My argument, in short, is that the title of this chapter, "Untimely Adoption," is redundant. Adoption is always already untimely.

The narrative spin-offs of untimeliness are mystery, an open form, and its cousin secrecy, a closed form. Who was the mysterious adopted Child in Caroline of Brunswick's household? The state investigated off the record, in failed secrecy. The unexplained child in the west country and his strange adoptive caregivers warranted secret investigation by a hapless field detective from the Home Office, the butt of later "Spy Nozy" jokes.[7] At some later point, some hand cut away pages from the father Basil Montagu's adoption memoir.

---

7. For a brief history of the Home Office surveillance of the west-country radicals, see Gill, *Wordsworth*, 127–28. Coleridge later dined out on an embellished anecdote about over-heard conversations about Spinoza, which were allegedly reported as suspicious remarks about "Spy Nozy."

Charles Lamb's apothecary mistook Emma Isola for a Miss Lamb, to her distress, and her adoptive father could never settle on a single phrase to explain her to his circle. Emma's obituary in 1891 muddled its headline claim that she was "Charles Lamb's adopted daughter" when its own text narrated their meeting in 1820: Emma "was afterwards domiciled in their house almost as a daughter." Both mystery and secrecy generate multiple narratives. Whereas the multiplicity of the unknown can transfigure narrative telos by its very open-endedness, secrecy collapses into closed silence. Because secrecy plagues so much of the history of adoption, a progressive adoption narrative fails to register how dystopian practices repeat instead of reform. As evidence, I add to the adopted children of history the children of one last Romantic-period writer, children who were born and survived, diminished, off the record, in secrecy.

SPURIOUS CHILDREN:
L.E.L.'S ABANDONED PROGENY

To bookend these antecedent histories of Romantic-period adoption, which launched with the abandoned children of Thérèse Levasseur, I turn at close to the abandoned children of Letitia Elizabeth Landon, who publishing as L.E.L. dominated the British poetry market in the 1820s and 1830s until her mysterious death in 1838. From the vantage of late Romanticism, Landon's secret history as an unwed relinquishing birth mother previews from the culture of de facto adoption the de jure regime of secrecy and shame that dominated postwar adoption in the mid-twentieth century in the "Baby Scoop" era. In contrast to a tale of progress, the history of adoption suggests that such systemically fraught scenes of distress and abuse end in diminishment and non-personhood again and again.

On November 15, 1802, the Deptford laundress Sophia Austin handed over her four-month-old second child, William Austin, to caregivers at the Princess of Wales's rebellious household on Blackheath, above Greenwich. One month earlier, on October 14, Letitia Elizabeth Landon was born in the West London neighborhood of Brompton, the daughter of John Landon, a partner in an army-goods agency, and his wife Catherine. Landon's mother Catherine was the illegitimate daughter born in France of an unknown gentleman and Letitia Bishop, the maternal grandmother who took in her namesake and granddaughter when Landon's mother, abandoned by her husband in the postwar financial crash, later turned her unmarried pregnant daughter out of the house.

In 1820, while London convulsed during the homecoming of Queen Caroline, in whose rowdy train bobbled the disruptive figure of an adopted child, a handful of poems signed only by the initial "L." began appearing in the London weekly the *Literary Gazette*. By the time Mary Shelley returned to London in the late summer of 1823, determined not to abandon her sole surviving child, the poems of "L." had upscaled into a verse industry branded as "L.E.L.," the literary rage of the decade turbocharged by the wildly successful publication of Landon's volume *The Improvisatrice* in 1824. Landon's meteoric career as L.E.L., cannily managed by the editor of the *Literary Gazette*, William Jerdan, tantalized gossipy London for the better part of two decades, ending in scandal-mongering headlines about her sudden marriage and unexplained death in 1838 on the Gold Coast of Africa—suicide? or murder?

Landon's dauntingly prolific career as a writer persists as one of the puzzles of late Romanticism, her subsequent demotion in the canon into footnotes about her death as much of a riddle as her two decades of success and fame. In 2000 the revelation of facts well-hidden in her lifetime rearranged the puzzle board. During the peak of her fame in the 1820s, Landon gave secret birth to and abandoned to foster and adoptive care three children fathered by her editor William Jerdan, none of whom she ever saw again. This belated tale emerged when a descendent of one of the children living in Japan, Michael Gorman, corresponded with an American researcher, Cynthia Lawford, who had tracked baptismal records of two of the children and published her discoveries in September 2000 in a "Diary" piece in the *London Review of Books*. Details building on Lawford's discoveries have since been fleshed out in substantial new biographies of both Jerdan and Landon.[8]

At the front end of Romanticism, we know nothing of Thérèse Levasseur's five abandoned children, apart from the father's very public confession of their fates. But Landon's three abandoned children have now emerged into focus. The first child was a girl, Ella, born probably in September 1823 near Ramsgate, where her pregnant unwed mother, turned out of her own mother's home, sheltered out of view; the baby was christened in London in April 1824. After foster care, Ella probably worked as a governess until she emigrated to Australia in 1852; marrying the ship's captain, she raised five children in Melbourne. The second child is the least known of the three, a boy, Fred, born probably in 1826 and who likely wound up in the West Indies, in Trinidad. The third child was another girl, Laura, born June 20, 1829, in Tunbridge Wells. Not christened until her majority in 1850, the 1851 census lists her living with foster parents Theophilus and Mary Ann Goodwin in Islington; Landon's

---

8. Lawford, "Diary"; and Matoff, *Conflicted Life*; Miller, *L.E.L.*

biographer, Lucasta Miller, proposes that the childless Goodwins "adopted Laura," who later married after the death of her adoptive Goodwin mother.[9]

William Jerdan was the Svengali who engineered the secretive and diminished lives of these children, a dubious skill he honed with at least two dozen acknowledged children, legitimate and illegitimate; his children with Landon were christened with the surname Stuart, Jerdan's mother's maiden name. The children knew the identity of their mother; "Letitia" and "Landon," for example, appear as family names in the extensive branches of Ella Stuart Gregson's Australian family. Jerdan's biographer, Susan Matoff, reports that, according to family lore, Ella "had no time for her sister Laura, disliked Jerdan intensely—and was very bitter always about her Mother."[10] The traces of her birth mother's relinquishing affect now signify across L.E.L.'s vast published and unpublished archive, sometimes hiding in plain sight, as in this untitled epigraph to a chapter in the first volume of her 1837 novel *Ethel Churchill*:

> Life has dark secrets; and the hearts are few
> That treasure not some sorrow from the world—
> A sorrow silent, gloomy, and unknown,
> Yet colouring the future from the past.
> We see the eye subdued, the practised smile,
> The word well weighed before it pass the lip,
> And know not of the misery within:
> Yet there it works incessantly, and fears
> The time to come; for time is terrible,
> Avenging, and betraying.[11]

Finer-grained measurements now await readers introduced to the language and structures of de facto adoption in the Romantic century.

The jurist William Blackstone's prescriptive 1765 *Commentaries on the Laws of England* opens the chapter "Of Parent and Child" with this sentence: "Children are of two sorts; legitimate, and spurious, or bastards."[12] The capacious modern category of the spurious collects a host of falsehoods, hoaxes, and bogus claims: a false pregnancy, yet another undiscovered poem by Shakespeare, a dubious conclusion in statistics, a rare bird no one else has ever seen. All these modern counterfeit items bear the lingering semantic mark of the original spurious object: a bastard, a child located on the wrong side of what

---

9. Miller, *L.E.L.*, 143.
10. Matoff, *Conflicted Life*, 578.
11. Landon, *Ethel Churchill*, I.136.
12. Blackstone, *Commentaries*, I.434.

passes judicial muster as normal. The old human drive to divide is sharp and stark: a child born within the norm is true; a child born or placed outside the norm is false, a spurious being. Inheriting Blackstone's affirmation of a deep-seated human instinct to sort humans into the true and the false, untimely adoptees under modern de jure regimes still too often dwell, diminished, on the spurious side of the border, bearing a doubly differentiated burden inherited from Romantic childhood.

APPENDIX

Austen Family Accounts of the Edward Austen Adoption

As the chapters in this book demonstrate, even though adoption did not exist in common law, British culture regularly employed forms of the word "adopt" to name de facto surrogate childcare prior to the legislation of de jure adoption in 1926. In press headlines, for example, William Austin is the "adopted son" of Queen Caroline and Emma Isola is the "adopted daughter" of Charles Lamb. To track forms of such a pragmatic and instrumental lexicon in a single archive, the Austen family narrative of the Edward Austen kinship adoption offers a rich record, from correspondence in 1797 to the most recent family memoir published in 2017. Awareness of these materials encourages scholarship to tap the brakes when it is tempted to misread such de facto adoptions through a modern lens as "official," "formal," or even "legal."

It is abundantly clear that Austen family accounts from the beginning regularly used the word "adoption" to narrate the story of Edward Austen. In 1869 the first-published family biography, *A Memoir of Jane Austen,* put the matter in these terms: "Her second brother, Edward, had been a good deal separated from the rest of the family, as he was early adopted by his cousin, Mr. Knight, of Godmersham Park in Kent and Chawton House in Hampshire; and finally came into possession both of the property and the name."[1] The phrase "early adopted by his cousin Mr. Knight" has two effects worth marking. First, this

---

1. Austen-Leigh, *Memoir,* 12.

204 APPENDIX

event in Edward Austen's history belongs to his childhood rather than his adulthood (when other related events "finally" happened), but exactly what period "early" signifies is left open; second, the adoption is also a transaction exclusively among males. In 1884 the first family edition of Austen letters settled for "adopted" rather than "early adopted," again marking the adoption as a property transaction among males alone: "Having no children, Mr. Knight adopted Edward Austen, George Austen's second son, and, dying in 1794, left him all his property."[2] The fountainhead family biography published in 1913, *Jane Austen: Her Life and Letters, a Family Record,* tilts the adoption chronology toward "finally" rather than "early" and now includes Mrs. Knight among the company: the Knight couple "took a fancy to young Edward, had him often to their house, and eventually adopted him. . . . There was no issue of the marriage of Mr. and Mrs. Knight, and by degrees they made up their minds to adopt Edward Austen as their heir."[3] The 1913 modifiers "eventually" and "by degrees" register early twentieth-century caution (or uncertainty) about what the term "adoption" signified a century earlier, just as "officially" and "formal" mark modern confusion about these Romantic-period events.

The most significant family document dwelling behind these published family sources is an 1848 account of the adoption by Edward's and Jane's brother Henry Austen, recorded by his niece Fanny Lefroy two years before his 1850 death, with his mark of provenance: "I tell the tale as it was told to me." Although subsequent biographies had access to this account in manuscript, Henry Austen's full account was not published until 1989, in Deirdre Le Faye's rewriting of the 1913 *Family Record.*[4] Henry's memories open with the 1779 meeting of the recently married Knights and the young Edward Austen:

> Mr. and Mrs. Knight from Godmersham came to Steventon Parsonage in their way to some place where they were intending for a time to remain. They took the child with them by way of amusement, returning him to his home after a few weeks absence. . . . No particular consequences at that time ensued, or seem to have been expected from this mark of preference for one little boy. Some time afterwards, probably more than a year, further advances were made (though not understood as such) in the way of adoption.

---

2. Austen, *Letters,* ed. Brabourne, I.10. Edward was the third son; the second son, George, was mentally impaired and was boarded out for his lifetime.

3. Austen-Leigh and Austen-Leigh, *Jane Austen: Her Life and Letters,* 47–48.

4. Austen-Leigh, Austen-Leigh, and Le Faye, *Jane Austen: A Family Record,* 40–41. Portions of Henry Austen's account are paraphrased in *Chawton Manor and Its Owners* in 1911 (see note 9) and quoted in Tucker, *Jane Austen: A Goodly Heritage,* in 1983.

Rather than a high-stakes adoption introduction framed by ceremony as in the Wellings silhouette (see chapter 3), this is a gradually unfolding arrangement that nearly escapes being understood as something called "in the way of adoption." Henry then offered an anecdote that attributes relinquishing adoptive agency to Mrs. Austen. The Knights proposed that Edward spend a school holiday in Godmersham; Mr. Austen, anxious that Edward would forget his Latin, was reluctant to agree, "but whilst he hesitated a few simple words from his Wife gently turned the scale—'I think, my Dear, you had better oblige your cousins, and let the Child go.'" But whereas Isabella Knightley in *Emma* would be primed at this point to sound alarms about child abandonment ("To give up one's child! I really never could think well of any body who proposed such a thing to any body else"), Henry Austen provided an unalarming sequel, opening with a tautological sentence worthy of his sister:

> Edward Austen returned from Godmersham ostensibly as much Edward Austen as ever, & remained for some years as such under the care of his natural Parents.—By degrees, however, it came to be understood in the family that Edward was selected from amongst themselves as the adopted son & Heir of Mr. Knight; and in further course of time he was taken more entire possession of.

In Henry Austen's account, the adoptive process happens gradually and, in language, passively: "By degrees it came to be understood." Instead of an active account ("the Knights adopted Edward"), "adopt" takes subordinate, participial form, which locates Edward in a male property narrative: he is "the adopted son & Heir of Mr. Knight." Even that fact is not tethered to an exact event, as it spins out "in further course of time." The final phrase "taken more entire possession of" inflects other phrases used by the culture for surrogate care ("taking the charge of," "undertaking the care of," or "under the protection of") in terms of property and ownership.

None of these Austen family accounts registers the 1783 Wellings silhouette, the icon now widely used to introduce and frame the story. A family heirloom, as a piece of evidence it came late to the adoption story in scholarship, in accounts by George Holbert Tucker in 1983 and again by Deirdre Le Faye in 1989 in her revision of the 1913 *Family Record*: "It seems that 1783 was the year in which adoption was *finally* agreed upon, as a silhouette bearing that date was painted by William Wellings to commemorate *the event*. It depicts Mr. Austen *formally* presenting his son to Mrs. Knight, while Mr. Knight, leaning on the back of his sister Jane's chair, looks on

206   APPENDIX

approvingly."[5] Le Faye, the authoritative modern curator of the Austen biographical archive, in her encyclopedic *Chronology* also tags the 1812 name change as "*officially* confirmed."[6] The prevailing effect of this influential scholarship is that Edward Austen's adoption is now regularly pegged as a discrete "event" tied to a specific year, 1783, and often described, anachronistically, as an "official" or "formal" adoption; the fact that the 1812 name change required a royal charter shades the event toward the modern status of "legal." My claim is that such representations of the Edward Austen history risk distorting this Romantic-period adoption through a lens polished by modern de jure adoption, with misshaping effects on the way we read de facto adoption in Jane Austen's fiction.

Before turning to remark several curious features in the adoption history that disrupt the modern picture, there is one last instance of the term "adoption" in the family archive to register, which is also the earliest and most contemporary instance of the term. In late 1797, Catherine Knight, since 1794 the widow of Thomas Knight II residing at Godmersham, decided to retire to nearby Canterbury on annuity, which required her to persuade Edward and Elizabeth Austen and their rapidly growing family of four children to relocate from their Bridges family home, Rowling, to Godmersham. Edward Austen took some persuading, which survives in a set of letters first published by a Chawton neighbor of the Knight family, W. H. Pollock, in 1899.[7] In response to the proposal, Edward Austen addressed his adoptive mother Mrs. Knight, formally, as "My Dearest Madam" and resisted the offer: "Believe me, therefore, my dear Madam, equally sincere when I say it is impossible for us in this Instance to accede to your Plan. I am confident we should never be happy at Godmersham whilst you were living at a smaller and less comfortable House" (86). Catherine Knight was not to be dissuaded, however, and she pressed her case in the voice of an adoptive mother: "From the time that my partiality for you induced Mr. Knight *to treat you as our adopted child* I have felt for you the tenderness of a Mother, and never have you appeared more deserving of affection than at this time" (87; emphasis added). Several gendered features of Romantic-period adoption bear remark in this sentence. Unlike the published family accounts, both the sentence and the adoption launch with female

---

5. Austen-Leigh, Austen-Leigh, and Le Faye, *Jane Austen: A Family Record*, 41 (emphasis added); and Tucker, *Jane Austen: A Goodly Heritage*, 119. Tucker is cautious about using the 1783 date of the artifact to date the adoption: "That he was adopted is true, but it was definitely not during his early childhood. . . . Although the adoption did eventually take place, it was the outcome of a gradual deeper acquaintance" (119). The silhouette was first reproduced in a Janeite collection of images in 1901; see chapter 3, note 5.

6. Le Faye, *Chronology*, 432; emphasis added.

7. Pollock, *Jane Austen, Her Contemporaries*, 85–89.

APPENDIX 207

agency: "my partiality for you." Catherine Knight the widow then proved herself a canny business agent as she seamlessly shifted gears from female agency to the demands of property and the language of a patriarch:

> I am desirous of making the Deed irrevocable, during your life; for your being kept in a state of dependence on my wish, or perhaps caprice, would not be less painful to you, than disagreeable to myself. [But if] a promise under my own hand, as binding as words can make it [will suffice to the trustees] I shall not object to such a Mode; but this and many other points we can discuss when I see you. *You will observe, my dear Edward, that I depend upon your obedience to my wish.* (88; emphasis added)

The cool temperature of this last sentence sounds not unlike Sir Thomas Bertram laying down the law to his adoptive niece Fanny Price in *Mansfield Park*. The letter is then signed "Yr most sincere friend, C.K."—not "Yr cousin" or even, impossibly, "Yr mother." Edward Austen was a blood relative of Thomas Knight but not of Catherine Knight, except in the prevailing legal sense— especially problematic for a widow—that the two Knights in marriage had become one (male) person. It helps to recall that in abundant (and abundantly controversial) forms of modern de jure adoption, courts issue new birth certificates in which the name of the adoptive mother replaces and erases the name of the birth mother, but there is no such fungibility of maternal names in Romantic-period adoption. In such a fraught landscape of kinship, Catherine Knight chooses friendship as a leveling category to close her letter, after her brief assumption of the voice of an adoptive mother and her return to the voice of propertied patriarchal authority.

To recover the Edward Austen history as an unfolding Romantic-period de facto adoption accomplished "by degrees" instead of a foreshortened modern picture of an "official" or "formal" event, it helps to flag several curious features in the way that history has taken modern shape. First is the oddness of the assumption that a young newlywed couple of the landed gentry in 1779, Thomas Knight II and Catherine Knatchbull, were already engaged in the preparatory groundwork of adoption on their wedding journey. Catherine Knatchbull was twenty-seven at the time of the marriage and her husband was forty-five. Did they begin marriage anticipating that their reproductive lives would be "without issue"? Perhaps, but thirteen years later in Thomas Knight's 1792 will, when Catherine was forty and he was fifty-eight, boilerplate legal language in the document still made legal room for biological offspring, before the will turned to the status of Edward Austen several pages later:

To the use of the first son of the body of me the said Thomas Knight on the body of the said Catherine my wife lawfully to be begotten and the Heirs Male of the body of such first son lawfully issuing and for default of such issue to the use of the second son of the body of the said Thomas Knight on the body of the said Catherine lawfully to be begotten and the heirs male of the body of such second son lawfully issuing [and on through third and] fourth fifth and sixth and all and every other Son and Sons of the body of me the said Thomas Knight on the body of the said Catherine lawfully to be begotten.[8]

Thomas Knight II died two years later "without issue." My point is that lawful male issue was always the default template for the transfer of property, regardless of adoptive backup plans. In the 1792 will, such a baked-in surplus of potential legitimate blood heirs supplies an ironic gloss on Emma Woodhouse's fanciful speculations in the wake of the death of Mrs. Churchill in *Emma,* the aunt (by marriage) and adoptive mother of Frank Churchill: "Half a dozen natural children, perhaps—and poor Frank cut off!"

A 1911 family biography, *Chawton Manor and Its Owners,* offered more cautious reproductive claims about the Knights and Edward Austen: "But his adoption by his patrons must have been a gradual affair. They can only have been married a very short time when he first attracted their notice, and the idea of adopting a distant cousin as their heir would not arise until some time afterwards," a caution endorsed by the modern biographer George Holbert Tucker in 1983.[9] That "some time afterwards" is now almost always locked in as an "event" in 1783, on the basis of the Wellings image. But in the immediate wake of the 1783 silhouette occasion (of whatever sort), how did the new adoptive family bond together as a new unit, as the modern way would prescribe? In September 1784, Thomas and Catherine Knight spun off to the continent for ten months, "accompanied by Mrs. K's brothers Wyndham and Charles Knatchbull, her friend Miss Harriet Townshend and Mr Lewis Cage their Kentish neighbor, plus four servants and a dog"—but no Edward Austen.[10] One year after their return in July 1785, in July 1786 Edward Austen launched four solo Grand Tour years on the continent, returning in July 1790. The math runs like this: for five of the seven years after the 1783 image, Edward Austen and his adoptive parents traveled their separate ways, which simply measures

---

8. The National Archives, PROB 11/1252/42.

9. Austen-Leigh and Knight, *Chawton Manor,* 157; and Tucker, *Jane Austen: A Goodly Heritage,* 118–20.

10. Le Faye, *Chronology,* 96–97.

APPENDIX   209

the difference between bonding imperatives of modern adoption and adoptive habits of the landed gentry in the middle of the Romantic century.

The 1783 Wellings image also locks in the association of the adoption with a particular place, Godmersham in Kent, the crown jewel of the Knight estate. The distortion submerged in this association is that the other primary fact regularly cited in the history of the adoption, the change of surname from Austen to Knight, is tethered not to Godmersham but to the other main property in the Knight estate, Chawton in Hampshire. The 1913 family biography is very clear about the link between the 1812 name change and Chawton: "On the death of Mrs. Knight—his kind and generous patron and friend—in October of that year, Edward and all his family took the name of Knight: a name which had been borne by every successive owner of the Chawton Estate since the sixteenth century."[11] The legal restriction requiring the name change in order to inherit Chawton travels back through the 1792 will of the adoptive father Thomas Knight II and the 1779 will of his father Thomas Knight I to the 1737 will of his mother Elizabeth Knight, which cites the "strict obligations" created by her seventeenth-century ancestor Sir Richard Knight "to do all that in me lies to preserve and establish the sirname of Knight that the same and no other sirname should be of use by the owner of the Estate heretofore of Sir Richard Knight now deceased."[12] For modern adoptees who navigate the multiplicity and arbitrariness of birth and adoptive names, the fungibility of male family names in this Knight family history will verge on a mad species of the comic. The first two of Elizabeth Knight's husbands, William Woodward and Bulstrode Peachey, dutifully changed their surnames to Knight upon marriage to Elizabeth. Her third husband and surviving heir Thomas Knight I was by that name working on his third surname: born Thomas Brodnax, he first changed his name to Thomas May to inherit other property and then changed from Thomas May to Thomas Knight in order to meet the "strict obligation" attached to the Chawton property, which he passed along to his son Thomas Knight II, who passed it along to his adopted heir Edward Austen. Because these were matters of landed property and inheritance, such changes of name required either a Private Act of Parliament or a Royal License; a grumpy member of Parliament complained about the frequency of dealing with Thomas Brodnax (a.k.a. Thomas May a.k.a. Thomas Knight): "This gentleman gives us so much trouble, that the best way would be to pass an Act for him to use whatever name he pleases").[13] Thirty years after the Wellings silhouette, when Catherine Knight died in 1812 and Edward Austen's lawyers set to work on

---

11. Austen-Leigh and Austen-Leigh, *Jane Austen: Her Life and Letters*, 256.

12. The National Archives, PROB 11/688/170.

13. Tucker, *Jane Austen: A Goodly Heritage*, 19.

the change of name required to inherit Chawton, the vehicle that prompted Jane Austen to practice "making a better K" was a Royal License instead of a Private Act of Parliament, a copy of which now hangs on the curated walls of Chawton Cottage, the outbuilding on the Chawton Estate that from 1809, courtesy of the adopted Edward Austen, provided a home for his widowed birth mother and his sisters Cassandra and Jane.[14]

More accurately than troops of researchers from both academic and Janeite divisions, a blood relation comes closest among modern writers to getting the Edward Austen adoption right. Caroline Jane Knight, the "fifth great-niece of Jane Austen," wrote this in her 2017 memoir about her Austen and Knight ancestors: "It was about 1783 when Thomas and Catherine informally adopted fifteen-year-old Edward, and he became heir to the Knight fortune—there was no legal adoption process at that time."[15] But her chronology still pegs the event to the 1783 icon, even as the sentence frames the adoption as "informal," walled off from access to de jure adoption.

---

14. A copy of the Royal License issued in "Whitehall Nov. 10, 1812" was published on the first page of the official record ("Published by Authority") in the *London Gazette*, no. 16671 (from Saturday, November 21, to Tuesday, November 24, 1812).

15. Knight, *Jane & Me*, 83.

BIBLIOGRAPHY

Abramowicz, Sarah. "Childhood and the Limits of Contract." *Yale Journal of Law & the Humanities* 21, no. 1 (Winter 2009): 37–100.

Alryyes, Ala. *Original Subjects: The Child, the Novel, and the Nation.* Cambridge, MA: Harvard University Press, 2001.

Anthony, Katharine. *The Lambs: A Story of Pre-Victorian England.* New York: Knopf, 1945.

Ariès, Philippe. *Centuries of Childhood: A Social History of Family Life.* New York: Random House, 1962.

Ashe, Thomas. *The Spirit of "The Book"; or, Memoirs of Caroline Princess of Hasburgh, a Political and Amatory Romance.* 3 vols. London: Allen, 1812.

Aspinall, A., ed. *The Letters of King George IV, 1812–1830.* 3 vols. Cambridge, UK: Cambridge University Press, 1938.

Austen, Jane. *Emma.* Edited by Richard Cronin and Dorothy McMillan. Cambridge, UK: Cambridge University Press, 2005.

———. *Jane Austen's Letters.* Edited by Deirdre Le Faye. 3rd ed. Oxford, UK: Oxford University Press, 1995.

———. *Later Manuscripts.* Edited by Janet Todd and Linda Bree. Cambridge, UK: Cambridge University Press, 2008.

———. *Letters of Jane Austen.* Edited by Edward, Lord Brabourne. 2 vols. London: Bentley, 1884.

———. *Mansfield Park.* Edited by John Wiltshire. Cambridge, UK: Cambridge University Press, 2005.

———. *Northanger Abbey.* Edited by Barbara Benedict with Deirdre Le Faye. Cambridge, UK: Cambridge University Press, 2006.

———. *Persuasion.* Edited by Janet Todd and Antje Blank. Cambridge, UK: Cambridge University Press, 2006.

BIBLIOGRAPHY

———. *Pride and Prejudice.* Edited by Pat Rogers. Cambridge, UK: Cambridge University Press, 2006.

———. *Sense and Sensibility.* Edited by Edward Copeland. Cambridge, UK: Cambridge University Press, 2006.

Austen-Leigh, J. E. *A Memoir of Jane Austen, by Her Nephew J. E. Austen Leigh.* 3rd ed. London: Bentley, 1872.

Austen-Leigh, William, and Richard Arthur Austen-Leigh. *Jane Austen: A Family Record.* Rev. Deirdre Le Faye, London: Hall/Macmillan 1989

———. *Jane Austen: Her Life and Letters, a Family Record.* London: Smith, Elder, 1913.

Austen-Leigh, William, and Montagu George Knight. *Chawton Manor and Its Owners: A Family History.* London: Smith, Elder, 1911.

Bailey, Joanne. *Parenting in England 1760–1830: Emotion, Identity, and Generation.* Oxford, UK: Oxford University Press, 2012.

Barbauld, Anna Letitia. *Lessons for Children.* London: n.d.; first printed 1778–79 in 2 vols.; expanded to 4 vols.; frequently reprinted.

———. *The Works of Anna Letitia Barbauld, with a Memoir, by Lucy Aikin.* London: Longman, 1825.

Barker, Juliet. *Wordsworth: A Life.* New York: Viking, 2000.

Behlmer, George. *Friends of the Family: The English Home and Its Guardians, 1850–1940.* Stanford, CA: Stanford University Press, 1998.

Behrendt, Stephen C. *Royal Mourning and Regency Culture: Elegies and Memorials of Princess Charlotte.* New York: St. Martin's, 1997.

Bell, Neil. *So Perish the Roses.* New York: Macmillan, 1940.

Belle. Directed by Amma Asante, written by Misan Sagay, Fox Searchlight Pictures, 2013.

Berlant, Lauren. "The Theory of Infantile Citizenship." *Public Culture* 5, no. 3 (Spring 1993): 395–410.

Blackstone, William. *Commentaries on the Laws of England.* 4 vols. Oxford, UK: Clarendon, 1770.

Blum, Carol. *Rousseau and the Republic of Virtue: The Language of Politics in the French Revolution.* Ithaca, NY: Cornell University Press, 1986.

The Book. London, 1813.

Boswell, John. *The Kindness of Strangers: Child Abandonment in Europe from Late Antiquity to the Renaissance.* New York: Pegasus, 1988.

Bowlby, Rachel. *A Child of One's Own: Parental Stories.* Oxford, UK: Oxford University Press, 2013.

Brewer, Holly. *By Birth or Consent: Children, Law, and the Anglo-American Revolution in Authority.* Chapel Hill: University of North Carolina Press, 2005.

Burke, Edmund. *A Letter from Mr. Burke, to a Member of the National Assembly.* London: Dodsley, 1791.

Bury, Lady Charlotte. *The Diary of a Lady-in-Waiting.* Edited by A. Francis Steuart. 2 vols. London: John Lane, 1908.

Butler, Marilyn. "Introduction." In *Frankenstein, or The Modern Prometheus: The 1818 Text,* ix–li. Oxford, UK: Oxford University Press, 1993.

Byrne, Paula. *The Real Jane Austen: A Life in Small Things.* New York: HarperCollins, 2012.

Camp, Anthony J. *Royal Mistresses and Bastards: Facts and Fiction, 1714–1936.* London: privately printed, 2007. Subsequent addenda on the author's website: http://anthonyjcamp.com/.

Carlyle, Thomas. *The Carlyle Letters Online.* Durham, NC: Duke University Press. https// carlyleletters.dukeupress.edu.

———. *Reminiscences*. Edited by James Anthony Froude. 2 vols. London: Longmans, 1881.

Cavell, Stanley. *The Claim of Reason: Wittgenstein, Skepticism, Morality, and Tragedy*. Oxford, UK: Oxford University Press, 1979.

———. *In Quest of the Ordinary: Lines of Skepticism and Romanticism*. Chicago: University of Chicago Press, 1988.

Christensen, Jerome. *Romanticism at the End of History*. Baltimore: Johns Hopkins University Press, 2000.

Clark, Anna. "Queen Caroline and the Sexual Politics of Popular Culture in London, 1820." *Representations* 31 (Spring 1990): 47–68.

———. *Scandal: The Sexual Politics of the British Constitution*. Princeton, NJ: Princeton University Press, 2006.

Coleridge, Samuel Taylor. *Biographia Literaria*. Edited by James Engell and W. Jackson Bate. 2 vols. Princeton, NJ: Princeton University Press, 1983.

Coleridge, Sara Fricker. *Minnow among Tritons: Mrs. S. T. Coleridge's Letters to Thomas Poole, 1799–1834*. Edited by Stephen Potter. London: Nonesuch, 1934.

Cornwall, Barry. *Charles Lamb: A Memoir*. London: Moxon, 1866.

Courtney, Winifred F. *Young Charles Lamb 1775–1802*. New York: New York University Press, 1983.

Cranston, Maurice. *Jean-Jacques: The Early Life and Work of Jean-Jacques Rousseau, 1712–1754*. New York: Norton, 1983.

Cunningham, Hugh. *Children and Childhood in Western Society since 1500*. 3rd ed. London: Routledge, 2021.

———. *The Children of the Poor: Representations of Childhood since the Seventeenth Century*. Oxford, UK: Blackwell, 1991.

———. *The Invention of Childhood*. London: BBC, 2006.

Damrosch, Leo. *Jean-Jacques Rousseau: Restless Genius*. New York: Houghton Mifflin, 2005.

Dart, Gregory. *Rousseau, Robespierre and English Romanticism*. Cambridge, UK: Cambridge University Press, 1999.

Davidoff, Leonore, and Katherine Hall. *Family Fortunes: Men and Women of the English Middle Class, 1780–1850*. Chicago: University of Chicago Press, 1987.

Day, Thomas. *The History of Sandford and Merton*. 3 vols. London: Debrett, 1783.

Diver, Alice. "'Monstrous Othering': The Gothic Nature of Origin-Tracing in Law and Literature." *Adoption & Culture* 9, no. 2 (2021): 247–75.

Edgeworth, Maria. *Belinda*. Edited by Kathryn J. Kirkpatrick. New York: Oxford University Press, 1994.

Emma. Directed by Autumn de Wilde, screenplay by Eleanor Catton, Universal Pictures, 2020.

Emma. Directed by Jim O'Hanlon, screenplay by Sandy Welch, BBC, 2009.

Evans, Tanya. *"Unfortunate Objects": Lone Mothers in Eighteenth-Century London*. London: Palgrave, 2005.

Farington, Joseph. *The Diary of Joseph Farington*. Edited by Kenneth Garlick, Angus Macintyre, and Kathryn Cave. 17 vols. New Haven, CT: Yale University Press, 1978–98.

Ferguson, Frances. "The Afterlife of the Romantic Child: Rousseau and Kant Meet Deleuze and Guattari." *South Atlantic Quarterly* 102, no. 1 (Winter 2003): 215–34.

———. "The Novel Comes of Age: When Literature Started Talking with Children." *differences: A Journal of Feminist Cultural Studies* 28, no. 1 (May 2017): 37–63.

214 BIBLIOGRAPHY

———. "Rousseau, *Emile*, and Britain." In *Jean-Jacques Rousseau and British Romanticism*, edited by Russell Goulbourne and David Higgins, 187–207. London: Bloomsbury, 2017.

Fessler, Ann. *The Girls Who Went Away: The Hidden History of Women Who Surrendered Children for Adoption in the Decades before Roe v. Wade.* New York: Penguin, 2006.

Finch, Jeremiah Stanton. "Charles Lamb's 'Companionship in Almost Solitude.'" *Princeton University Library Chronicle* 6, no. 4 (1935): 179–99.

Fraiman, Susan. *Unbecoming Women: British Women Writers and the Novel of Development.* New York: Columbia University Press, 1993.

Fraser, Flora. *The Unruly Queen: The Life of Queen Caroline.* New York: Knopf, 1996.

Freud, Sigmund. "Family Romances." In *The Standard Edition of the Complete Psychological Works of Sigmund Freud,* vol. 9, 235–42. London: Hogarth, 1959.

Frost, Ginger. *Illegitimacy in English Law and Society 1860–1930.* Manchester, UK: Manchester University Press, 2016.

Fulcher, Jonathan. "The Loyalist Response to the Queen Caroline Agitations." *Journal of British Studies* 34, no. 4 (October 1995): 481–502.

Fulford, Roger. *George the Fourth.* London: Duckworth, 1935.

Galperin, William. *The Historical Austen.* Philadelphia: University of Pennsylvania Press, 2003.

———. *The History of Missed Opportunities: British Romanticism and the Emergence of the Everyday.* Stanford, CA: Stanford University Press, 2017.

Gardner, Jane F. *Family and Familia in Roman Law and Life.* Oxford, UK: Oxford University Press, 1998.

Gardner, John. *Poetry and Popular Protest: Peterloo, Cato Street, and the Queen Caroline Controversy.* New York: Palgrave, 2011.

Garside, Peter, and Rainer Schöwerling. *The English Novel 1770–1829.* Oxford, UK: Oxford University Press, 2000.

George, M. Dorothy. *Catalogue of Political and Personal Satires Preserved in the Department of Prints and Drawings in the British Museum.* London: British Museum, 1978.

Gigante, Denise. *Book Madness: A Story of Book Collectors in America.* New Haven, CT: Yale University Press, 2022.

Gill, Stephen, ed. *The Cambridge Companion to William Wordsworth.* Cambridge, UK: Cambridge University Press, 2003.

———. *William Wordsworth: A Life.* Oxford, UK: Clarendon, 1989.

Godwin, William. *The Diary of William Godwin.* Edited by Victoria Myers, David O'Shaughnessy, and Mark Philp. Oxford, UK: Oxford Digital Library, 2010. http://godwindiary.bodleian.ox.ac.uk.

———. *An Enquiry Concerning Political Justice.* 2 vols. London: Robinson, 1793.

———. *Transfusion; or the Orphans of Uberwalden, by the Late William Godwin Jun with a Memoir of His Life and Writings by His Father.* 3 vols. London: Macrone, 1835.

Goody, Jack. *The Development of the Family and Marriage in Europe.* Cambridge, UK: Cambridge University Press, 1983.

Graham, David, and John Tribe. "Basil Montagu QC (1770–1851): A Portrait of an Early 19th Century Life in Literature and the Law." Rochester, NY: Social Science Research Network (SSRN), January 2009, online. DOI: 10.2139/ssrn.1328460.

Gray, Dennis. *Spencer Perceval: The Evangelical Prime Minister, 1762–1812.* Manchester, UK: Manchester University Press, 1963.

BIBLIOGRAPHY

Hansard, T. C. *The Parliamentary Debates,* New Series, vol. 10, March 16, 1824, col. 1103.

Hansard, House of Lords Debate, July 16, 1889, vol. 338 cc502–14.

Haydon, Benjamin Robert. *Autobiography of Benjamin Robert Haydon.* Oxford, UK: Oxford University Press, 1927.

Heidegger, Martin. *Being and Time.* Translated by Joan Stambaugh. Albany: State University of New York Press, 1996.

Heller-Roazen, Daniel. *Absentees: On Variously Missing Persons.* New York: Zone Books, 2021.

Hibbert, Christopher. *George IV: Prince of Wales, 1762–1811.* London: Longman, 1972.

———. *George IV: Regent and King, 1811–1830.* London: Allen Lane, 1973.

Hill, Constance. *Jane Austen: Her Homes & Her Friends.* London: John Lane, 1901.

Hipchen, Emily, ed. "The Dobbs Issue." Special issue, *Adoption & Culture* 10, no. 2 (2022): 163–378.

Hitchcock, Susan Tyler. *Mad Mary Lamb: Lunacy and Murder in Literary London.* New York: Norton, 2005.

Homans, Margaret. "Adoption and Essentialism." *Tulsa Studies in Women's Literature* 35, no. 2 (2002): 257–74.

———. *Bearing the Word: Language and Female Experience in Nineteenth-Century Women's Writing.* Chicago: University of Chicago Press, 1986.

———. *The Imprint of Another Life: Adoption Narratives and Human Possibility.* Ann Arbor: University of Michigan Press, 2013.

House of Commons and House of Lords Joint Committee on Human Rights. "The Violation of Family Life: Adoption of Children of Unmarried Women 1949–1976." July 15, 2022. https:// publications.parliament.uk/pa/jt5803/jtselect/jtrights/270/summary.html.

Huish, Robert. *Memoirs of Her Late Majesty Caroline.* 2 vols. London: T. Kelly, 1821.

Hunt, Lynn. *The Family Romance of the French Revolution.* Berkeley: University of California Press, 1992.

Hunt, Tamara L. "Morality and Monarchy in the Queen Caroline Affair." *Albion* 23, no. 4 (Winter 1991): 697–722.

Jackson, Mark. *New-Born Child Murder: Women, Illegitimacy and the Courts in Eighteenth-Century England.* Manchester, UK: Manchester University Press, 1997.

Johnson, Claudia. *Equivocal Beings: Politics, Gender, and Sentimentality in the 1790s: Wollstonecraft, Radcliffe, Burney, Austen.* Chicago: University of Chicago Press, 1995.

———. *Jane Austen: Women, Politics, and the Novel.* Chicago: University of Chicago Press, 1988.

Johnson, Samuel. *A Dictionary of the English Language.* London, 1755.

———. *Johnson's Dictionary.* Rev. H. J. Todd. London, 1818.

Jones, Christine Kenyon. "Ambiguous Cousinship: *Mansfield Park* and the Mansfield Family." *Persuasions On-Line,* 31, no. 1 (Winter 2010).

Jones, Wendy. *Jane on the Brain: Exploring the Science of Social Intelligence with Jane Austen.* New York: Pegasus, 2017.

Joshua, Essaka. *Physical Disability in British Romantic Literature.* Cambridge, UK: Cambridge University Press, 2020.

Kaplan, Laurie. "*Emma* and 'the children in Brunswick Square.'" *Persuasions,* 31 (2009): 236–47.

Keating, Jenny. *A Child for Keeps: The History of Adoption in England, 1918–45.* New York: Palgrave Macmillan, 2009.

Keats, John. *Keats's Poetry and Prose.* Edited by Jeffrey N. Cox. New York: Norton, 2009.

Kertzer, David I., and Marzio Barbagli. *Family Life in the Long Nineteenth Century, 1789–1913*. Vol. 2 of *The History of the European Family*. New Haven, CT: Yale University Press, 2001.

Knight, Caroline Jane. *Jane & Me: My Austen Heritage*. Victoria, Australia: Greyfriar, 2017.

Kristof, Nicholas. "Russia Traffics in Ukrainian Children." *New York Times,* November 25, 2022, section A, 25.

Lamb, Charles. *Elia and the Last Essays of Elia*. Edited by Jonathan Bate. New York: Oxford University Press, 1987.

Lamb, Charles, and Mary Lamb. *The Letters of Charles and Mary Lamb*. Edited by E. V. Lucas. 3 vols. London: Methuen, 1935.

———. *The Works of Charles and Mary Lamb*. Edited by E. V. Lucas. Vol. 5: *Poems and Plays*. London: Methuen, 1903.

Landon, Letitia Elizabeth (L.E.L.). *Ethel Churchill: or, The Two Brides*. 3 vols. London: Colburn, 1837.

Laqueur, Thomas W. "The Queen Caroline Affair: Politics as Art in the Reign of George IV." *Journal of Modern History* 54, no. 3 (September 1982): 417–66.

Latchford, Frances. *Steeped in Blood: Adoption, Identity, and the Meaning of Family*. Montreal: McGill-Queen's University Press, 2019.

Lawford, Cynthia. "Diary." *London Review of Books,* September 21, 2000, 36–37.

Le Faye, Deirdre. *A Chronology of Jane Austen and Her Family, 1600–2000*. 2nd ed. Cambridge, UK: Cambridge University Press, 2013.

Leighton, Kimberly. "Addressing the Harms of Not Knowing One's Heredity: Lessons from Genealogical Bewilderment." *Adoption & Culture* 3 (2012): 63–107.

Lifton, Betty. *Twice Born: Memoirs of an Adopted Daughter*. New York: McGraw Hill, 1975.

Lloyd, H. Evans. *George IV, Memoirs of His Life and Reign*. London: Treuttel & Würtz, 1830.

Londoño, Ernesto. "Stolen at Birth: Chilean Adoptees Uncover Their Past." *New York Times,* December 18, 2021, section A, 4.

Lucas, E. V. *The Life of Charles Lamb*. 2 vols. London: Methuen, 1905.

Mackintosh, James. *Memoirs of the Life of the Right Honorable Sir James Mackintosh*. Edited by Robert James Mackintosh. 2 vols. London: Moxon, 1835.

Marshall, John. *Royal Naval Biography*. Vol. 1, Pt. 1. London: Longman, 1823.

Matoff, Susan. *Conflicted Life: William Jerdan, 1782–1869*. Brighton, UK: Sussex Academic Press, 2011.

McCalman, Iain. *Radical Underworld: Prophets, Revolutionaries, and Pornographers in London, 1795–1840*. Oxford, UK: Oxford University Press, 1993.

McCarthy, William. *Anna Letitia Barbauld: Voice of the Enlightenment*. Baltimore: Johns Hopkins University Press, 2008.

McCauliff, C. M. A. "The First English Adoption Law and Its American Precursors." *Seton Hall Law Review* 16, no. 3 (1986): 656–77.

McClure, Ruth K. *Coram's Children: The London Foundling Hospital in the Eighteenth Century*. New Haven, CT: Yale University Press, 1981.

McLeod, John. *Life Lines: Writing Transcultural Adoption*. London: Bloomsbury, 2015.

Mellor, Anne K. *Mary Shelley: Her Life, Her Fiction, Her Monsters*. New York: Routledge, 1989.

Meyers, Mitzi. "De-Romanticizing the Subject: Maria Edgeworth's 'The Bracelets,' Mythologies of Origin, and the Daughter's Coming to Writing." In *Romantic Women Writers: Voices and*

BIBLIOGRAPHY

Countervoices, edited by Paula R. Feldman and Theresa M. Kelley, 88–110. Hanover, NH: University Press of New England, 1995.

Mignot, Jean-François. "Full Adoption in England and Wales and France: A Comparative History of Law and Practice, 1926–2015." *Adoption & Fostering* 41, no. 2 (2017): 142–58.

Miller, Lucasta. *L.E.L.: The Lost Life and Scandalous Death of Letitia Elizabeth Landon, the Celebrated "Female Byron."* New York: Knopf, 2019.

Mills, Charles. *The Racial Contract.* Ithaca, NY: Cornell University Press, 1997.

Mitchell, David T., and Sharon L. Snyder. *Narrative Prosthesis: Disability and the Dependencies of Discourse.* Ann Arbor: University of Michigan Press, 2000.

Molloy, J. Fitzgerald. *Court Life below Stairs, or London under the Last Georges 1760–1830.* London: Downey, 1897.

Moore, Doris Langley. *The Late Lord Byron: Posthumous Dramas.* Philadelphia: Lippincott, 1961.

Moore, Lorrie. "Attention Working Writers: Lorrie Moore Admires What You Do." *New York Times Sunday Book Review,* March 26, 2020, p. 8.

Moore, Wendy. *How to Create the Perfect Wife.* New York: Basic Books, 2013.

Moxon, Emma Isola. *Emma Isola Moxon Autograph Album.* Special Collections, Houghton Library, Harvard University MS Eng 601.66, fol. 10.

Murray, Douglas. "Jane Austen's 'passion for taking likenesses': Portraits of the Prince Regent in *Emma.*" *Persuasions* 29 (2007): 132–44.

Nelson, Claudia. *Family Ties in Victorian England.* Bloomington: Indiana University Press, 2007.

———. *Little Strangers: Adoption and Foster Care in America 1850–1929.* Bloomington: Indiana University Press, 2003.

———. "Review of Carolyn Steedman, *Strange Dislocations.*" *The Lion and the Unicorn* 22, no. 1 (1998): 122–25.

Nelson, Claudia, and Emily Hipchen, "Victorian Childhood and Children: A Conversation with Claudia Nelson." *Adoption & Culture* 9, no. 1 (2021): 12–23.

Nelson, Claudia, Julie-Marie Strange, and Susan B. Egenolf, eds. *British Family Life, 1780–1914.* 5 vols. London: Pickering & Chatto, 2013.

Nightingale, Joseph. *Memoirs of the Public and Private Life of Queen Caroline* (1821). Edited by Christopher Hibbert. London: Folio Society, 1978.

———. *Memoirs of Queen Caroline.* London: Robinson, 1820.

Nixon, Cheryl. *The Orphan in Eighteenth-Century Law and Literature.* Burlington, VT: Ashgate, 2011.

Novy, Marianne. "Memoirs and the Future of Adoption." *Adoption & Culture* 9, no. 2 (2021): 308–24.

———. *Reading Adoption: Family and Difference in Fiction and Drama.* Ann Arbor: University of Michigan Press, 2005.

O'Rourke, James. "The 1831 Introduction and Revisions to *Frankenstein*: Mary Shelley Dictates Her Legacy." *Studies in Romanticism* 38, no. 3 (Fall 1999): 365–85.

———. "'Nothing More Unnatural': Mary Shelley's Revision of Rousseau." *ELH* 56, no. 3 (Fall 1989): 543–69.

Parr, Joy. *Labouring Children: British Immigrant Apprentices to Canada, 1869–1924.* Toronto: University of Toronto Press, 1980.

Patterson, Orlando. *Slavery and Social Death: A Comparative Study.* Cambridge, MA: Harvard University Press, 1982.

Peel, Ellen. "Adoption, Tragedy, and the Failed Search for Origins in *Frankenstein*." *Adoption & Culture* 7, no. 2 (2019): 244–53.

Pinsky, Robert. *At the Foundling Hospital*. New York: Farrar, Straus & Giroux, 2016.

Plotz, Judith. *Romanticism and the Vocation of Childhood*. New York: Palgrave, 2001.

Plumly, Stanley. *The Immortal Evening*. New York: Norton, 2014.

Pollock, Walter Herries. *Jane Austen, Her Contemporaries and Herself: An Essay in Criticism*. London: Longmans, 1899.

Poovey, Mary. *The Proper Lady and the Woman Writer: Ideology as Style in the Works of Mary Wollstonecraft, Mary Shelley, and Jane Austen*. Chicago: University of Chicago Press, 1985.

Reed, Mark L. *Wordsworth: The Chronology of the Middle Years, 1800–1815*. Cambridge, MA: Harvard University Press, 1975.

Reynolds, Frederick. *Fortune's Fool; A Comedy, in Five Acts*. London: Longman, 1796.

Richardson, Alan. *Literature, Education, and Romanticism*. Cambridge, UK: Cambridge University Press, 1994.

———. "Romanticism and the End of Childhood." *Nineteenth-Century Contexts* 21, no. 2 (1999): 169–89.

Richman, Jared. "The Other King's Speech: Elocution and the Politics of Disability in Georgian Britain." *The Eighteenth Century* 59, no. 3 (Fall 2018): 279–304.

Riehl, Joseph R. "The Last Days of Charles Lamb: Emma Isola." *Charles Lamb Bulletin* n.s., 85 (January 1994): 2–12.

Robinson, Henry Crabb. *Diary, Reminiscences, and Correspondence of Henry Crabb Robinson*. Edited by Thomas Sadler. London: Macmillan, 1872.

———. *Henry Crabb Robinson on Books and Their Writers*. Edited by Edith J. Morley. 3 vols. London: Dent, 1938.

Rose, Lionel. *The Massacre of the Innocents: Infanticide in Britain 1800–1939*. London: Routledge, 1986.

Ross, Ernest Carson. *Charles Lamb and Emma Isola: A Survey of the Evidence Relevant to Their Personal Relationship*. London: Charles Lamb Society 1950; rep. 1991.

Rousseau, Jean-Jacques. *Confessions*. Translated by Angela Scholar. Oxford, UK: Oxford University Press, 2000.

———. *Emile, or On Education*. Edited by Allan Bloom. New York: Basic Books, 1979.

———. *Julie, or the New Heloise*. Translated by Philip Stewart and Jean Vaché. Hanover, NH: University Press of New England, 1997.

Rowland, Ann Wierda. *Romanticism and Childhood: The Infantilization of British Literary Culture*. Cambridge, UK: Cambridge University Press, 2012.

Rudy, Sayres. "The Anxious Kinship of the Vanishing Adoptee." *Adoption & Culture* 7, no. 2 (2019): 206–30.

Sahlins, Marshall. *What Kinship Is—And Is Not*. Chicago: University of Chicago Press, 2013.

Said, Edward. *Culture and Imperialism*. New York: Knopf, 1993.

Salazar, Rothman. *Randy Nelson: Sex, Sailors, and Napoleonic War*. Bologna: University of Bologna Press, 1969.

Salih, Sara. "The Silence of Miss Lambe: *Sanditon* and Fictions of 'Race' in the Abolition Era." *Eighteenth-Century Fiction* 18, no. 3 (2006): 329–53.

Sampson, Fiona. *In Search of Mary Shelley*. New York: Pegasus, 2018.

Sandford, Margaret E. *Thomas Poole and His Friends*. 2 vols. London: Macmillan, 1888.

BIBLIOGRAPHY

Sants, H. J. "Genealogical Bewilderment in Children with Substitute Parents." *British Journal of Medical Psychology* 37, no. 2 (1964): 133–40.

Schor, Esther. *Bearing the Dead: The British Culture of Mourning from the Enlightenment to Victoria*. Princeton, NJ: Princeton University Press, 1994.

Secrets & Lies. Written and directed by Mike Leigh, October Films, 1996.

Selman, Peter. "Global Trends in Intercountry Adoption: 2001–2010." *Adoption Advocate* 44 (2012), National Council for Adoption.

Shakespeare, William. *The Norton Shakespeare*. Edited by Stephen Greenblatt et al. 3rd ed. New York: Norton, 2015.

Shell, Marc. *Children of the Earth: Literature, Politics, and Nationhood*. Oxford, UK: Oxford University Press, 1993.

Shelley, Mary. *Frankenstein; or, The Modern Prometheus*. Edited by Susan J. Wolfson. New York: Longman, 2003.

———. *The Journals of Mary Shelley, 1814–1844*. Edited by Paula Feldman and Diana Scott-Kilvert. Oxford, UK: Oxford University Press, 1987.

———. *The Letters of Mary Wollstonecraft Shelley*. Edited by Betty Bennett. 3 vols. Baltimore: Johns Hopkins University Press, 1980.

———. *Mary Shelley's "Literary Lives" and Other Writings*. Vol. 3, *French Lives*. Edited by Clarissa Campbell Orr. London: Pickering & Chatto, 2002.

———. "Rousseau. 1712–1778." In *Lives of the Most Eminent Literary and Scientific Men of France*. 2 vols. In Dionysius Lardner, ed., *Cabinet Cyclopedia*. London: Longman, 1839.

Simpson, David. *Romanticism and the Question of the Stranger*. Chicago: University of Chicago Press, 2013.

Sisman, Adam. *The Friendship: William Wordsworth and Samuel Taylor Coleridge*. New York: Viking, 2007.

Smeeton, George. *The Important and Eventful Trial of Queen Caroline, Consort of George IV, for "Adulterous Intercourse," with Bartolomeo Bergami*. London: Smeeton, 1820.

Solinger, Rickie. *Wake Up Little Susie: Single Pregnancy and Race before Roe v. Wade*. New York: Routledge, 1992.

Southey, Robert. Online edition of Southey's correspondence at *Romantic Circles*. Edited by Ian Parker and Lynda Pratt. https://romantic-circles.org/editions/southey_letters/l.

Stampone, Christopher. "'Obliged to yield': The Language of Patriarchy and the System of Mental Slavery in *Mansfield Park*." *Studies in the Novel* 50, no. 2 (Summer 2018): 197–212.

Stanback, Emily. *The Wordsworth-Coleridge Circle and the Aesthetics of Disability*. New York: Palgrave, 2017.

Stanhope, Lady Hester. *Memoirs of the Lady Hester Stanhope*. 3 vols. London: Colburn, 1845.

St Clair, William. *The Godwins and the Shelleys: A Biography of a Family*. Baltimore: Johns Hopkins University Press, 1989.

———. *The Reading Nation in the Romantic Period*. Cambridge, UK: Cambridge University Press, 2004.

Steedman, Carolyn. *Strange Dislocations: Childhood and the Idea of Human Interiority*. Cambridge, MA: Harvard University Press, 1989.

Stevens, Jacqueline. *Reproducing the State*. Princeton, NJ: Princeton University Press, 1999.

Sunstein, Emily W. *Mary Shelley: Romance and Reality*. Baltimore: Johns Hopkins University Press, 1989.

Swift, Jonathan. *The Writings of Jonathan Swift*. Edited by Robert A. Greenberg and William B. Piper. New York: Norton, 1973.

Szalai, Jennifer. "Where Have All the Liberals Gone?" *New York Times,* May 12, 2022, section C, 1.

Talfourd, Thomas Noon. *The Letters of Charles Lamb, with a Sketch of His Life*. 2 vols. London: Moxon, 1837.

Talfourd, T. N. *Speech for the Defendant, in the Prosecution of The Queen v. Moxon, for the Publication of Shelley's Works*. London: Moxon, 1841.

Thomas, Donald. "The Prosecution of Moxon's Shelley." *The Library* 33, no. 4 (December 1978): 329–34.

Thompson, E. P. *The Making of the English Working Class*. New York: Vintage, 1966.

Tomalin, Claire. *Jane Austen: A Life*. New York: Knopf, 1998.

Tucker, George Holbert. *Jane Austen: A Goodly Heritage*. Manchester, UK: Carcanet, 1983.

Tuite, Clara. *Romantic Austen: Sexual Politics and the Literary Canon*. Cambridge, UK: Cambridge University Press, 2002.

Turner, Beatrice. *Romantic Childhood, Romantic Heirs*. Cham, Switzerland: Palmer Macmillan, 2017.

Uglow, Jenny. *The Lunar Men: Five Friends Whose Curiosity Changed the World*. New York: Farrar, Straus & Giroux, 2002.

Waddams, S. M. *Law, Politics, and the Church of England: The Career of Stephen Lushington 1782– 1873*. Cambridge, UK: Cambridge University Press, 1992.

Wade, Laura. *The Watsons, Adapted from the Unfinished Novel by Jane Austen*. London: Oberon Books, 2018.

Wagner, Gillian. *Barnardo*. London: Weidenfeld & Nicholson, 1979.

———. *Children of the Empire*. London: Weidenfeld & Nicholson, 1982.

Wahrman, Dror. "Middle-Class Domesticity Goes Public." *Journal of British Studies* 32, no. 4 (October 1993): 396–432.

Walker, Eric C. "Adoption, Abortion, and Nonpersons," *Adoption & Culture* 10, no. 2 (2022): 192–96.

———. *Marriage, Writing, and Romanticism: Wordsworth and Austen after War*. Stanford, CA: Stanford University Press, 2009.

———. "Rewriting Romantic Revision: A New Byron Letter." *Keats-Shelley Journal* 53 (2004): 20–24.

Wardle, Ralph M. "Basil and Anna Montagu: Touchstones for the Romantics." *Keats-Shelley Journal* 34 (1985): 131–71.

Whitaker, F. R., and H. P. Stokes. "The Isola Papers," reprinted from the *Cambridge Review* (November 1915 and January 1916); Henry Paine Stokes Papers collection, MS Add. 8699/1/5, Cambridge University Library.

White, Terence de Vere. "A Lost Correspondence: Letters from Italy from 2nd Marquess of Sligo to Rt Hon. Lord Lowther." *The Twentieth Century* 163 (March 1958): 233.

Wilson, Eric G. *Dream-Child: A Life of Charles Lamb*. New Haven, CT: Yale University Press, 2022.

Wollstonecraft, Mary. *Thoughts on the Education of Daughters*. London, 1787.

———. *Vindication of the Rights of Woman*. Edited by Deidre Lynch. New York: Norton, 2009.

Wordsworth, Dorothy. *Journals of Dorothy Wordsworth*. Edited by E. de Selincourt. 2 vols. Oxford, UK: Oxford University Press, 1941.

Wordsworth, Mary. *The Letters of Mary Wordsworth, 1800–1855*. Edited by Mary E. Burton. Oxford, UK: Oxford University Press, 1958.

Wordsworth, William. *The Fenwick Notes of William Wordsworth*. Edited by Jared Curtis. Bristol: Bristol Classical Press, 1993.

———. *"Lyrical Ballads," and Other Poems, 1797–1800*. Edited by James Butler and Karen Green. Ithaca, NY: Cornell University Press, 1992.

———. *Poems, in Two Volumes, and Other Poems, 1800–1807*. Edited by Jared Curtis. Ithaca, NY: Cornell University Press, 1983.

Wordsworth, William, and Dorothy Wordsworth. *The Letters of William and Dorothy Wordsworth*. Vol. 1, *The Early Years 1787–1805*. Edited by Ernest de Selincourt, rev. Chester L. Shaver. Oxford, UK: Oxford University Press, 1967.

———. *The Letters of William and Dorothy Wordsworth*. Vol. 2, *The Middle Years, Part I: 1806–1811*. Edited by Ernest de Selincourt, 2nd ed., rev. Mary Moorman. Oxford, UK: Oxford University Press, 1969.

———. *The Letters of William and Dorothy Wordsworth*. Vol. 3, *The Middle Years, Part II: 1812–1820*. Edited by Ernest de Selincourt, 2nd ed., rev. Mary Moorman and Alan G. Hill. Oxford, UK: Oxford University Press, 1970.

Wordsworth, William, and Mary Wordsworth. *The Love Letters of William and Mary Wordsworth*. Edited by Beth Darlington. Ithaca, NY: Cornell University Press, 1981.

Young-Bruehl, Elisabeth. *Childism: Confronting Prejudice against Children*. New Haven, CT: Yale University Press, 2012.

Zelizer, Viviana. *Pricing the Priceless Child: The Changing Social Value of Children*. New York: Basic Books, 1985.

Zunshine, Lisa. *Bastards and Foundlings: Illegitimacy in Eighteenth-Century England*. Columbus: The Ohio State University Press, 2005.

INDEX

abandonment, child: and adoption narratives, 31n80; in *Emma,* 107, 205; in *Frankenstein,* 111–17; by Letitia Landon, 198–200; in *Mansfield Park,* 76–77; and Rousseau, 2–3, 7; and Mary Shelley, 28, 106, 111, 113, 117, 121, 127, 199; Mary Shelley on Rousseau's, 106, 118–21

adoption, de facto, viii, 4–10, 14–18, 27, 32, 50, 112, 134, 195–98, 200–207; and Jane Austen, 80, 89, 91, 93, 96; of Emma Isola, 163–70, 173, 175, 180

adoption, de jure, viii, 4, 9–10, 15–18, 27, 33, 50, 76, 175, 194–98, 201, 203, 206–7, 210

adoption, kinship, 6, 7, 11, 15, 32, 126, 132, 175, 180, 203–10; and Austen's fiction, 71–80, 85–86, 88, 91, 98; in *Frankenstein,* 112–14

adoption, untimely, viii, ix, 4–9, 20, 22, 27–28, 68, 71, 75, 88, 106, 122, 164, 186, 188–89, 194–98, 201

Adoption Act of 1926, 9, 17, 18n19, 19, 68, 195–96

adoption and law: and age-of-consent law and exceptionalism, 23; and civil code tradition in Europe, 4, 13, 18; and contracts, child custody, and equity courts, 18; in English common law, 4, 9, 13–19, 81, 195–97, 203; in France, viii, 3–6, 17–19,

37, 39; and Roman law and practice, 4, 18, 40. *See also* Adoption Act of 1926

adoption and repatriation: in *Emma,* 95–96; of Emma Isola, 171–72; in *Mansfield Park,* 82–87; of Basil Caroline Montagu, 155; in *The Watsons,* 85–87

adoption lexicon in the Romantic century: and Austen's fiction, 15–16; in Samuel Johnson's 1755 *Dictionary,* ix, 14–16, 82n20, 93n36; in the *OED,* 15

adoption narratives, 13, 29–32; and national narratives, 30

Aiken family members: Anna Letitia Aiken (later Barbauld; adoptive mother of Charles Aiken), (*see* Barbauld, Anna Letitia); Charles Aiken (adopted son of Anna Letitia Barbauld), 11–13; John Aiken (birth father of Charles Aiken and brother of Anna Letitia Barbauld), 11–13; Lucy Aiken (birth sibling of Charles Aiken), 11–13; Martha Aiken (birth mother of Charles Aiken), 12–13

Alryyes, Ala, and childhood and the novel, 5, 39–40

Anthony, Katharine. *See* Lamb, Charles, biographical accounts

Index

Ariès, Philippe, and history of childhood, 19

Ashe, Thomas, and *The Spirit of "The Book,"* 46–47

Austen, Jane: brother Edward's adoption, 73–76, 203–10; Chawton home, 76

Austen, Jane, biographical accounts: Paula Byrne, 73–74; Deirdre Le Faye, 205–6; Claire Tomalin, 74n7; George Holbert Tucker, 204n4, 205, 206n5

Austen, Jane, novels of: *Emma*, 6, 15, 17, 28, 47, 71, 177–78, 208; *Mansfield Park*, 6, 15, 16, 27n60, 71, 207; *Northanger Abbey*, 16, 79n14, 100; *Persuasion*, 16, 102, 161–62; *Pride and Prejudice*, 70, 79n14, 125; *Sanditon*, 86; *Sense and Sensibility*, 15n11, 16, 79n14, 89n32; *The Watsons*, 6, 85–87

Austen family members: Cassandra Austen (sister of Jane Austen), 210; Cassandra Leigh Austen (mother of Jane Austen), 73, 210; Edward Austen, later Knight (older brother of Jane Austen), 6, 73–76, 203–10; Elizabeth Bridges Austen (later Knight; wife of Edward Austen), 75; Fanny Austen, (niece of Jane Austen), 75; George Austen (father of Jane Austen), 73, 204; George Austen (impaired older brother of Jane Austen), 73n5; Henry Austen (brother of Jane Austen), 204–5

Austin, William, 5–6, 14, 28; birth and relinquishment, 40–41; in caricature, 47–49, 52–55; with Caroline in Europe, 50–54; death and burial, 68; and death of Caroline, 57–59; identity in Delicate Investigation, 43–47; letters to birth mother, 50, 51, 53, 57; in London during queen's divorce trial, 54–57; in queen's will as residuary legatee, 58–59; return to Italy, 59–64; return to UK and lunacy hearing, 64–66; at school in Greenwich, 35–36

Austin, William, biographical accounts: Anthony J. Camp, 42n11; Flora Fraser, 42n11; Roger Fulford, 68n73; Christopher Hibbert, 42n11

Austin family members: Caroline Austin (younger sister of William Austin), 50n32; Job Austin (older brother of William Austin), 50n32; Samuel Austin (birth father of William Austin), 38, 41, 50n32, 63; Samuel Austin (younger brother of William Austin), 50n32, 61–62, 64; Sophia Austin (birth mother of William Austin), 38, 41, 46, 50n32, 63–64

Barbauld, Anna Letitia: as adoptive mother of Charles Aiken, 11–13; quarrels with Charles Lamb, 180–81, 189–90. *See also* Aiken family members

Barker, Mary, and illness of Basil Caroline Montagu, 156–58

Barnardo, Thomas, 33, 68

bastards and bastardy, 7, 14n6, 15, 17, 31, 200–201; and William Austin, 42n11, 48–49, 52, 59, 66; William Blackstone, 17, 92, 200; in *Emma*, 91–93, 102–3; Letitia Landon, 198–200; William Wordsworth's French daughter, 132. *See also* illegitimacy; spuriousness and adoptee personhood

Behlmer, George, and adoption and common law, 18

Behrendt, Stephen, and death of Princess Charlotte, 39n3

Belinda (Edgeworth): and Thomas Day, 35; and *Emma*, 35, 71, 100, 103–4; and *Northanger Abbey*, 104n56

Bell, Neil. *See* Lamb, Charles, biographical accounts

Belle (film), 81n18

Belle, Dido Elizabeth, and *Mansfield Park*, 81

Bennett, Betty. *See* Shelley, Mary, biographical accounts

Bentley, Richard, and 1831 *Frankenstein*, 113n13

Bergami, Bartolomeo. *See* Pergami, Bartolomeo

Berlant, Lauren, 40n7

Betham, Matilda, and Emma Isola's autograph album, 168

Bicknell, Sabrina. *See* Sidney, Sabrina

Bishop, Letitia, grandmother of Letitia Landon, 198

Blackstone, William: and adoption in common law, 17; Austen reference to, in *Emma*, 92; on children in common law, 200–201; on guardians and wards in common law, 17; and US Supreme Court *Dobbs* abortion decision, 17n16

Index

Book, The, and record of Delicate Investigation, 45–46, 48

Boswell, John, and adoption narrative, 31

Bowlby, Rachel, and prehistory of adoptive parenthood, 4n8

Brewer, Holly, and Enlightenment exceptionalism of childhood, 23n44

Brougham, Henry: in caricature, 48–49, 55; and death of William Austin, 68–70; as ghost writer for Princess Caroline, 69–70

Brougham, James (brother of Henry Brougham), and rumor of William Austin's identity, 60

Brown, Louise, and in vitro fertilization history, 16

Burdett, Francis: in 1813 caricature, 48–49, 48 fig. 1; in 1820 caricature, 55

Burke, Edmund, and Rousseau, 3

Burney, Charles (brother of Frances Burney), and school at Greenwich, 35–36

Bury, Lady Charlotte, and Princess Caroline, 49–50

Butler, Marilyn: on 1831 alterations to *Frankenstein*, 113n12; on failed parenthood in *Frankenstein*, 111

Byrne, Paula. *See* Austen, Jane, biographical accounts

Byron, George Gordon, Lord, and correspondence with Mary Shelley, 107–8, 110

Camp, Anthony J. *See* Austin, William, biographical accounts

Canning, George, and *Frankenstein*, 110–11; and Princess Caroline, 111

Car, Dorcas, and purloined adoptees of Thomas Day, 35. *See also* Sidney, Sabrina

Carlyle, Thomas, 122; and Basil Caroline Montagu, 153, 159–60, 162

Caroline, Princess of Wales, 5–6, 14, 35; and Jane Austen, 69, 89–90; and William Austin, 38–39, 41–46, 49n27, 50–51, 58, 60–61; Charles Lamb, 185–86; and Mary Shelley, 107, 111. *See also* Caroline, Queen

Caroline, Queen, 6, 9, 14, 199, 203; and Edward Austen, 80n15; and William Austin, 37–38, 55, 57n51, 58n53, 62–66, 80n15; and Mary Shelley, 105–7, 111, 121–22, 126; and Charles Lamb, 165, 178n25,

185–86. *See also* Caroline, Princess of Wales

Castlereagh, and Queen Caroline trial melodrama in Paris, 67

Cavell, Stanley, and Romantic abandonment, 27

Charlotte, Princess (daughter of the Prince and Princess of Wales), 39, 43, 52, 70

Charlotte, Queen (wife of George III), 38

child custody and contract law, 23

childhood and Romantic-period adoption, vii, 3–10, 197, 201; and adoption narratives, 29–33; and Jane Austen, 91; and William Austin, 39, 51; and figure of Romantic child, 19–28; and Charles Lamb, 189; and Basil Caroline Montagu, 129, 131, 139–40, 142, 144, 162; and Mary Shelley, 106, 112, 115–17. *See also* exceptionalism, liberal; liberalism and adoption history

Christensen, Jerome, and untimely Romanticism, viii, 5, 9, 27

chromatism. *See* race and Romantic-period adoption

Clark, Anna: and sexual scandal, 40; and trial of Queen Caroline, 55n41

class and Romantic-period adoption, 13–14, 23–24, 33, 196n3; and Jane Austen, 72, 86; and William Austin, 37–38, 49, 54, 67; and Mary Shelley, 114, 118

Cobbett, William, 46n22; in 1820 caricature, 55

Coleridge, Hartley (son of Samuel Taylor Coleridge), and "Intimations Ode," 144

Coleridge, Samuel Taylor: and divorce trial of Queen Caroline, 56n44; falling-out with Wordsworth, 152; "Foster-Mother's Tale," 140–41; and "Intimations Ode" (Wordsworth), 21; *Lyrical Ballads*, 129, 141; trip to Germany, 146; Spy Nozy anecdote, 197n7

Coleridge, Sara Fricker (estranged wife of Samuel Taylor Coleridge), and illness of Basil Caroline Montagu, 156–57

Commentaries on the Laws of England (Blackstone), 17, 200

common law, English. *See* adoption and law

contingency and Romantic-period adoption. *See* haphazard family, the

Coram, Thomas, and London Foundling hospital, 32, 33n86

Cornwall, Barry, and Emma Isola identity, 166

Courtney, Winifred F. *See* Lamb, Charles, biographical accounts

Cranston, Maurice, and Rousseau biography, 2n2

Cruikshank, George, and William Austin caricature, 53–54

Cunningham, Hugh: and history of childhood, 34, 39; and "sanctification of children," 5, 20

Damrosch, Leo, and Rousseau biography, 2n2

Darwin, Charles, and adoptive identity, 22n41

Davidoff, Leonore, and history of middling classes, 13

Day, Thomas: and Rousseau, 35; adopting Sabrina Sidney, 34–35, 100

Deleuze, Gilles, and age of consent law, 24n46

Delicate Investigation, the, 35, 38, 41, 43–45

Denman, Lord: and William Austin, 66n69; and Moxon trial, 191

Descartes, Rene, and adoptive subjectivity, 22n41

Dickens, Charles, and adoption history, 32n32

differentiation and adoption, 5; doubled differentiation and adoptee subjectivity, 6, 13, 20, 23, 24, 26, 27, 197

diminishment and adoptee personhood, viii, ix, 5–9, 26–28, 49, 59, 66, 71, 144, 162, 192, 194, 198, 200–201. *See also* Heller-Roazen, Daniel

disability: and adoption and narrative in *Emma*, 72, 103; of Charles Lamb and Frederick Isola, 169–70

Diver, Alice, and *Frankenstein*, 111n10

Douglas, Lord and Lady, and Delicate Investigation, 43–44

Edgeworth, Maria: *Belinda*, 35, 71, 100, 103–4; *Patronage*, 79

Edward I, King, and Charles Lamb poem about Queen Elinor, 185–86

Eldon, Lord, and William Austin, 60, 66n69

Elia, Essays of (Charles Lamb): "The Child Angel: A Dream," 189; "Dream Children: A Reverie," 189; "Mackery end, in Hertfordshire," 122, 164; "The Old and the New School-Master," 189–90; "Oxford in the Vacation," 188–89; "The South Sea House," 188; "The Wedding," 190–91

Eliot, George, and adoption, 32n32

Emma (film, de Wilde), 93n37

Emma (film, O'Hanlon), 88, 90–91

Emma. See Austen, Jane, novels of: *Emma*

Enquiry Concerning Political Justice, An (Godwin), 4, 132–33

exceptionalism, liberal: and adoption, 4–5, 13, 22–24, 26, 197. *See also* childhood and Romantic-period adoption

Ferdinand, Prince Louis, and reputed parentage of William Austin, 60

Ferguson, Adam, and Romantic historiography of childhood, 29

Ferguson, Frances, 19–20, 24–25, 87n29, 143

Fessler, Ann, and "Baby Scoop" adoption era, 196n5

Finch-Hatton, Lady Elizabeth, and *Mansfield Park*, 81

Fitzgerald, Lord, and 1889 adoption legislation, 17

Fortune's Fool (Reynolds), ix

Foucault, Michel, 23n42

Foundling Hospital, London, 1, 32–34, 106; 1816 print of, 109 fig. 3

Frankenstein (Shelley), vii, 7, 106, 110, 111–18

Fraser, Flora. *See* Austin, William, biographical accounts

Frederick, Prince William, and Emma Isola, 178n25

Freud, Sigmund: and adoption genealogy, 22n41; and fantasy of adoptee status elevation, 51; and interiority, 27

Fryer, Maria, and Emma Isola, 174n20, 179, 192

Fulford, Roger. *See* Austin, William, biographical accounts

Galperin, William, and probabilistic fiction, 111n9

INDEX

227

Gardner, Jane F., and Roman adoption, 18n23

Gardner, John, and Charles Lamb's politics, 187n42

gender and Romantic-period adoption, 1, 9, 23–24, 74, 87, 93–94, 165, 181, 206

George, Prince of Wales (later George IV). *See* Wales, Prince of, and later Prince Regent

George III, King, 38, 54, 66

George IV, King, 38, 59, 187. *See also* Wales, Prince of, and later Prince Regent

Gigante, Denise. *See* Lamb, Charles, biographical accounts

Godwin, William, 4, 106–7, 132–34

Godwin, William, Jr., 106, 107n2

Goodwin, Mary Ann, and Theophilus Godwin, adoptive parents of Laura Stuart (Landon), 199–200

Goody, Jack, and history of childhood, 18n22

Gorman, Michael, descendent of Ella Stuart Gregson and Letitia Landon, 199

Guattari, Félix, and age-of-consent case law, 24n46

Hall, Catherine, and history of middling classes, 13

Hamilton, Lady, and death of Queen Caroline, 57, 58n54

haphazard family, the, viii, ix, 5–9, 34–40, 70, 77, 106, 128, 144, 151, 160, 178, 189; and adoptee contingency, viii, ix, 5, 16, 25, 39, 40, 45, 49, 67–68, 71–72, 99–103, 143–44, 154, 174; and the aleatory, ix; chance, 2, 58, 184; and the random, ix, 142, 184

Haydon, Benjamin Robert, and the Immortal Dinner, 190

Heidegger, Martin, and human abandonment, 27

Heller-Roazen, Daniel: and personhood theory, vii, viii, 5, 26–27. *See also* diminishment and adoptee personhood; lessening and adoptee personhood; nonpersonhood and adoptee identity; nonpersons and adoptee identity; personhood, adoptee

Hibbert, Christopher. *See* Austin, William, biographical accounts

Hipchen, Emily, and *Frankenstein,* 111n10

Hitchcock, Susan Tyler. *See* Lamb, Charles, biographical accounts

Homans, Margaret: on adoption and nation, 39–40; on *Frankenstein,* 111n10; and origin searches, 29n69, 29–31; on *Silas Marner,* 32n85

Hood, Lord and Lady, and death of Queen Caroline, 57, 58n53

Hôpital des Enfants Trouvé, Paris, 1, 109

Hunt, Lynn, and nation and family, 39–40

Hunt brothers (John and Leigh), and plans to publish P. B. Shelley's poetry, 124–25

identity and Romantic-period adoption, viii, 4, 6, 8, 13–14, 20, 197, 200; and Jane Austen, 70–71, 76, 88, 91–94, 97–98; and William Austin, 37, 41–49, 53–62, 66–68; and Emma Isola, 165–67, 183, 187–89. *See also* nonpersonhood and adoptee identity; personhood, adoptee; subjectivity and Romantic-period adoption

illegitimacy: and adoptive personhood, 200–201; in Blackstone's *Commentaries,* 17, 200–201; in *Emma,* 91–93, 102–3; and Letitia Landon, 198–200; of Basil Montagu, 128–29; and Rousseau, 1–4; and William Wordsworth, 132. *See also* bastards and bastardy

indigeneity and repatriation adoption narrative and politics, 33

"Intimations Ode" (Wordsworth), 20–21, 31, 116, 144–45

Isola, Emma (later Moxon): birth, 165; at boarding school, 178–79; children and death, 163, 192; deaths of birth parents of, 165; in 1858 photograph, 192–93, 193 fig. 5; governess career, 172–73, 177–83; Italian heritage, 167–68; marriage to Edward Moxon, 173–74, 190–91; meeting Lambs, 165

Isola biography. *See* Lamb, Charles, biographical accounts

Isola family: Elizabeth Humphreys (sister of Mary Humphreys and aunt of Emma Isola), 165, 169–77; Agostino Isola (grandfather of Emma Isola), 165, 183–84; Charles Isola (birth father of Emma Isola), 165, 183–84; Frederick Isola (brother of Emma Isola), 169–70; Harriet Isola (sister of Emma Isola), 165, 169;

228 INDEX

Mary Humphreys Isola (birth mother of Emma Isola), 165, 183–84

Jerdan, William, biological father of children of Letitia Landon, 199–200

Johnson, Claudia: on *Emma,* 100; on *Frankenstein,* 116–17

Johnson, Samuel. *See* adoption lexicon in the Romantic century

Jones, Wendy, on cognitive neuroscience in *Emma,* 76

Joshua, Essaka, and Romantic-period disability, 169n16

Kant, Immanuel, and adoptee subjectivity, 22n41

Keating, Jenny, and British adoption history, 33n88, 196n3

Keats, John, 55; and *Emma* and "negative capability," 102n54; and *Emma* and "Ode on a Grecian Urn," 101n49; with Emma Isola at the Immortal Dinner, 190

Kent, Edwardina, and Princess Caroline, 42n12

Kertzer, David I., and adoption in revolutionary France, 18n24

Kingsolver, Barbara, and repatriation narrative and indigeneity, 83n22

Knight family: Caroline Jane Knight, fifth-great niece of Jane Austen, 210; Catherine Knatchbull Knight, adoptive mother of Edward Austen, 73, 75, 204, 206; Edward Austen Knight, 73–76, 203–10; Thomas Knight II, adoptive father of Edward Austen, 73–75, 203–10; Wellings silhouette, 73 fig. 2

Kristof, Nicholas, and adoptive child trafficking in Ukraine and Russia, 196n4

Lamb, Charles, adoptive parent of Emma Isola, 8–9, 14, 55; death in 1834, 166; *Elia* essays, 188–91; and Emma's governess preparation, 178–82; and Emma's illness while governess, 182–83; and Emma's wedding, 173–74; encouraging Cambridge and Italy connections for Emma, 167–68; meeting Emma in 1820, 164–65, 170–71; negotiating adoption boundaries with Emma's Cambridge family, 168–77;

pedestrian politics, 184–85; Queenite and oppositional politics, 185–88; quarrel with Anna Letitia Barbauld, 180–81; and Mary Shelley, 106, 110, 122–23; as sibling pair with older sister Mary, 164–65; stutter and Emma's brother Frederick, 169–70; terms for Emma, 166–67

Lamb, Charles, biographical accounts: Katharine Anthony, 164n5; Neil Bell, 164n5; Winifred Courtney, 169; Denise Gigante, 166nn8–9; Susan Hitchcock, 166n2; E. V. Lucas, 166; Joseph Riehl, 183n35; Ernest Carson Ross, 164; Eric G. Wilson, 164n5, 166n7, 166n9

Lamb, Mary, adoptive parent of Emma Isola, 8, 14; death in 1847, 166; and Emma's governess preparation, 178–82; and Emma's wedding, 173–74; and language prep for Emma, 122, 168, 181; matricide, 164, 177n22; meeting Emma Isola in 1820, 164–65, 170–71; pedestrian politics, 184–85; and Mary Shelley, 106, 122; as sibling pair with younger brother Charles, 164–65

Landon, Catherine, and John Landon, birth parents of Letitia Elizabeth Landon, 198

Landon, Letitia Elizabeth (L.E.L.), 9; and child abandonment and illegitimacy, 198–200

Landor, Walter Savage, and Emma Isola, 168

Lane, John, and Basil Montagu family, 131, 147–48

Laqueur, Thomas W., and divorce trial of Queen Caroline, 55n41

Lardner, Dionysius, and Mary Shelley's biography of Rousseau, 106, 118

Latchford, Frances, and intellectual history of adoption, 21–22, 22n41, 23n42

Lawford, Cynthia, and Letitia Landon's illegitimate children, 199

Lawrence, Thomas, and Princess Caroline, 43

Le Faye, Deirdre. *See* Austen, Jane, biographical accounts

Leigh, Mike, *Secrets and Lies* (film), 67, 99

Leighton, Kimberly, and genealogical bewilderment, 25n53

lessening and adoptee personhood, 5, 26. *See also* Heller-Roazen, Daniel

Lessons for Children (Barbauld), 12–13, 189–90

INDEX

Levasseur, Thérèse, and abandoned children with Rousseau, 1–3, 9, 198

liberalism and adoption history, 4, 22–26, 28, 114, 143, 158. *See also* exceptionalism, liberal; universalism, liberal

Lifton, Betty, and adoptee identity, 50n31

Lindsay, Sir John, father of Dido Belle, 81. *See also* Mansfield, Lord

Liverpool, Lord, and William Austin, 60

Locke, John, and childhood, 133, 139

Londoño, Ernesto, and adoption in Chile, 30n75

Lucas, E. V. *See* Lamb, Charles, biographical accounts

Lushington, Stephen, and William Austin, 58, 60, 61, 64, 68

Lyrical Ballads (Wordsworth and Coleridge), 129–44; "Anecdote for Fathers" (Wordsworth), 142–44; "The Foster Mother's Tale" (Coleridge), 140–41; "The Idiot Boy" (Wordsworth), 20, 144; "The Thorn" (Wordsworth), 145; "To My Sister" (Wordsworth), 141–42; "We Are Seven" (Wordsworth), 20, 142, 144

Manby, Thomas, and Princess Caroline, 43, 60

Mansfield, Lord: and slavery and adoption in *Mansfield Park*, 80–81

Mansfield Park. See Austen, Jane, novels of: *Mansfield Park*

Marsh, Peggy, Wordsworth family servant in Dorset and Somerset, 137, 141, 147

Matoff, Susan, and William Jerdan biography, 199–200

McCarthy, William, and Barbauld biography, 11n2

McCauliff, C. M. A., and 1926 Adoption Act, 196n2

McClure, Ruth K., and London Foundling Hospital, 2n2

McLeod, John: on adoption geography, 32; on adoption narratives, 31–32; and adoptive identity, 31; on *Secrets & Lies*, 99n44

Meath, Earl of, and proposed UK adoption legislation in 1889, 17

Mellor, Anne K. *See* Shelley, Mary, biographical accounts

Meyers, Mitzi, and Romantic childhood, 22

Mignot, Jean-François, and modern adoption demography, 19n26

Miller, Lucasta, and Letitia Landon biography, 199–200

Mills, Charles, and liberalism and race, 23n42

Mitchell, David T., and *Emma* and disability theory, 72, 103

Montagu, Basil, birth father of Basil Caroline Montagu: and Basil Caroline's illness, 156–58; and Basil Caroline's navy service, 149–52; biographical sources, 130n4; birth, 128; and birth of Basil Caroline and death of wife Caroline, 130; and death of Mary Wollstonecraft, 138–39; education at Charterhouse and Cambridge, 131; and falling-out between Coleridge and Wordsworth, 152; falling-out with Wordsworth, 158–59; and Godwinian radicalism, 132–33; later life and death, 161; in London, 131–35; marriage, 129; marriage to Laura Rush and death of Laura Rush, 146–48; meeting William Wordsworth, 132; relinquishment of Basil Caroline to adoptive care of Wordsworth siblings, 134–35; P. B. Shelley's custody trial, 159; visit to Cumbria with Basil Caroline, 153–55; visit to Dorset, 138; writing adoption memoir, 129–30, 158

Montagu, Basil Caroline: anonymity in London and Cambridgeshire, 159–61; birth and Brampton kin, 130–31; death and burial, 161; in Cambridgeshire with father and John Lane, 146–50; in navy, 150–52; in Cumbria with the Wordsworth circle, 152–59; in Dorset and Somerset with Wordsworth siblings, 134–46; in London with father Basil, 131–34

Montagu family: Alfred Montagu (son of Basil Montagu and Laura Rush), 147; Algernon Montagu (son of Basil Montagu and Laura Rush), 147, 152, 155; Anna Skepper Montagu (third wife of Basil Montagu), 128, 151–52; Anne Skepper Montagu (daughter of Anna Skepper), 151, 160–61; Basil Montagu (bastard son of the Earl of Sandwich and Martha Ray; *see* Montagu, Basil, birth father of Basil Caroline Montagu); Basil Caroline Montagu (son of Basil Montagu and Caroline Want; *see* Montagu, Basil Caroline); Caroline Want Montagu (first wife of

Basil Montagu), 129–30; Charles Montagu (son of Basil Montagu and Anna Skepper), 151; Emily Montagu (daughter of Basil Montagu and Anna Skepper), 151; Laura Rush Montagu (second wife of Basil Montagu), 146–48; Robert Montagu (bastard son of the Earl of Sandwich), 149–51; William Montagu (son of Basil Montagu and Laura Rush), 147, 149

Moore, Lorrie, and the Edward Austen adoption, 74

Moore, Wendy, and history of Sabrina Sidney, 34–35

Moxon, Edward (husband of Emma Isola), publisher, 166, 171, 173, 175–76; death, 192

Moxon, Emma Isola. *See* Isola, Emma

Moxon, John (great-great-grandson of Emma Isola Moxon and Edward Moxon), 168n13, 170n17, 179n27, 182n34, 193 fig. 5

Murray, Douglas, and representations of the Prince Regent in *Emma,* 101n50

Myers, Mitzi, and romantic childhood, 22

Myers, Tom, and Wordsworth adoption scheme, 136

nation and adoption, viii, 5–10, 14, 18–19, 28–30, 32, 35, 194, 196; and Jane Austen, 69–70; and William Austin, 37–41, 44, 47, 50, 59, 65–68; in biocentric Britain, 5, 38–40, 59, 67–68, 72, 96–97, 122, 169, 188; and the Lambs and Emma Isola, 164–65, 186, 188; and modern adoption narratives of Korea, China, Guatemala, Germany, Ireland, US, Ukraine, Russia, and Chile, 30, 196; and Basil Caroline Montagu, 132n6; in revolutionary France, viii, 4–6, 13, 17–19, 37–39; and Mary Shelley, 121, 123

Nelson, Claudia, and history of childhood, viiin2, 19

Nightingale, Joseph, and honorific account of William Austin, 57

Nixon, Cheryl, and orphans in Romantic century, 16

nonpersonhood and adoptee identity, 13, 197–98. *See also* Heller-Roazen, Daniel

nonpersons and adoptee identity, vii–viii, 5, 26–28, 88. *See also* Heller-Roazen, Daniel

Northanger Abbey. See Austen, Jane, novels of: *Northanger Abbey*

Novy, Marianne: on adoption memoirs, 129n1; on adoption narratives, 31; on *Mansfield Park,* 83n23

O'Hanlon, Jim, and film of *Emma,* 88, 90–91

O'Rourke, James: on *Frankenstein,* 114; on Mary Shelley's Rousseau biography, 118n21

Oxford, Lady: and 1813 William Austin cartoon, 48–49, 48 fig. 2; in 1813 Jane Austen letter, 69

Patterson, Orlando, and "natal alienation" in slavery, 27n60

Peel, Ellen, and *Frankenstein,* 111n10

Pergami, Bartolomeo (also Bergami), 39, 50; in caricature, 54–55

personhood, adoptee, viii, 14, 20, 26–27, 197. *See also* Heller-Roazen, Daniel

Persuasion. See Austen, Jane, novels of: *Persuasion*

Phillips, Adam, and Romantic childhood, 4

Pinney, Azariah, and John Pinney (brothers), and Racedown home in Dorset, 135, 141

Pinochet, Augusto, and adoption in Chile, 30n75

Pinsky, Robert, and the London Foundling Hospital, 2n1

Plotz, Judith, and romantic childhood, 21–22

Poovey, Mary. *See* Shelley, Mary, biographical accounts

Pride and Prejudice. See Austen, Jane, novels of: *Pride and Prejudice*

Procter, Bryan Waller, and Mary Shelley, 110, 124–26

race and Romantic-period adoption: in *Fortune's Fool,* ix; and Charles Lamb and Emma Isola, 188; in *Mansfield Park,* 77, 80; in *The Watsons,* 86–87. *See also* liberalism and adoption history; slavery and Romantic-period adoption

Ray, Martha, birth mother of Basil Montagu, 128; name in Wordsworth's "The Thorn," 145

repatriation. *See* adoption and repatriation

Reynolds, Frederick, *Fortune's Fool,* ix

INDEX

Richardson, Alan, and romantic childhood, 19, 22, 28

Richman, Jared, and speech impairment in the Romantic century, 169n16

Riehl, Joseph R. *See* Lamb, Charles, biographical accounts

Robinson, Henry Crabb: on divorce trial of Queen Caroline, 56n44; and Wordsworth-Coleridge quarrel, 152; on Wordsworth-Basil Montagu quarrel, 159; on Emma Isola, 166, 168

Roe, Nicholas, and Basil Caroline Montagu, 134n12

Rogers, Samuel, and Emma Isola, 174

Romantic child, the. *See* childhood and Romantic-period adoption

Romanticism, untimely. *See* adoption, untimely

Romilly, Sir Samuel, and Basil Caroline Montagu, 158

Ross, Ernest Carson. *See* Lamb, Charles, biographical accounts

Rousseau, Jean-Jacques: *Confessions*, 2–3; Thomas Day's conjugal experiment, 34–35; *Emile*, 3; *Emma*, 6, 71, 88; Godwin's *Enquiry*, 133–34; *Julie*, 3; and national child, 5, 37; as subject of Shelley biography, 106, 118–21

Rowland, Ann Weirda, and Romantic childhood, 20–21, 29, 30

Rudy, Sayres: on adoptee anxiety, 25–26; on adoption genealogy and history, 22n41, 32; on intersectional theory, 27n60

Sahlins, Marshall, and kinship theory, 71n3

Said, Edward, and *Mansfield Park*, 80

Salih, Sara, and race in Austen, 86

Sampson, Fiona. *See* Shelley, Mary, biographical accounts

Sanditon. *See* Austen, Jane, novels of: *Sanditon*

Sandwich, Earl of, father of Basil Montagu, 7, 14, 128. *See also* Montagu family

Sants, H. J., and genealogical bewilderment, 25n53

schizoanalysis, 24n46

Schor, Esther, and death of Princess Charlotte, 39n3

Secrets and Lies (film), 67, 99

Selman, Peter, and modern adoption demographics, 19n26

Sense and Sensibility. *See* Austen, Jane, novels of: *Sense and Sensibility*

Shakespeare, William, and "propinquity of blood" in *Lear*, 17n17

Shell, Marc: on adoption in revolutionary France, 18n24; on adoption in Rome, 18n23

Shelley, Mary: abandonment and 1831 introduction to *Frankenstein*, 117–18; adoption and 1831 revisions to *Frankenstein*, 111–17; child abandonment and biography of Rousseau, 7, 118–21; custody battle with Sir Timothy Shelley, 105–8; falling-out with Montagu family, 123–26; friendship with Lamb family, 122–23; residence near Foundling Hospital, 106–10; return to England in 1823, 7, 28, 106–7; survived by adopted granddaughter Flossie Gibson Shelley, 126–27

Shelley, Mary, biographical accounts: Betty Bennett, 126; Anne Mellor, 117; Mary Poovey, 122n23; Fiona Sampson, 118; William St Clair, 126; Emily W. Sunstein, 118, 126–27

Shelley family: William Godwin (father of Mary Shelley; *see* Godwin, William); Bessie Florence Gibson Shelley (adopted daughter of Percy Florence Shelley), 126–27; Mary Shelley (*see* Shelley, Mary); Percy Bysshe Shelley (husband of Mary Shelley), 190–91; Percy Florence Shelley (son of Mary Shelley), 106, 126–27; Sir Timothy Shelley (father of Percy Bysshe Shelley), 7, 105, 107–8; Mary Wollstonecraft (mother of Mary Shelley; *see* Wollstonecraft, Mary)

Sidney, Sabrina (later Bicknell), 34–36, 71, 100

Skepper, Anna Benson (third wife of Basil Montagu). *See* Montagu family

Skepper, Anne (daughter of Anna Benson Skepper). *See* Montagu family

slavery and Romantic-period adoption, 26–27, 34, 110, 135; and Jane Austen's fiction, 71, 77–82, 87, 94, 177–78. *See also* race and Romantic-period adoption

Sligo, Lord, and William Austin abroad, 52

Smith, Sir Sidney, and Princess Caroline, 43

Snyder, Sharon, and disability theory and *Emma,* 72, 103

Solinger, Rickie, and Baby Scoop adoption, 196n5

Southey, Robert, and Basil Caroline Montagu's Keswick illness, 152, 156–57

Spirit of The Book, The (Ashe), 46–47

spuriousness and adoptee personhood, 200–201. *See also* bastards and bastardy; illegitimacy

Stampone, Christopher, and race in *Mansfield Park,* 81

Stanback, Emily, and Charles Lamb's disability, 169

Stanhope, Lady Hester, and William Austin, 43

St Clair, William. *See* Shelley, Mary, biographical accounts

Steedman, Carolyn, and Romantic childhood, 27

Steeped in Blood (Latchford), 22–23, 113n12

Stevens, Jacqueline: on adoption and nation, 39–40; on Roman adoption, 18n23

Stewart, Dugald, and Romantic historiography of childhood, 29

Stikeman, Thomas, page of Princess Caroline, 35, 50n32

Stone, John Hurford, and adoption in revolutionary France, 19

Stone, Lawrence, and history of childhood, 19n27

Stuart, Ella, illegitimate daughter of Letitia Landon, 9, 199–200

Stuart, Fred, illegitimate son of Letitia Landon, 9, 199–200

Stuart, Laura, illegitimate daughter of Letitia Landon, 9, 199–200

subjectivity and Romantic-period adoption, vii, viii, 13, 20, 27–28, 197. *See also* identity and Romantic-period adoption; nonpersonhood and adoptee identity; nonpersons and adoptee identity; personhood, adoptee

Sunstein, Emily W. *See* Shelley, Mary, biographical accounts

Sutherland, Dr. A. R., and William Austin's madness, 64

Swift, Jonathan, and Houyhnhnms, 143

Szalai, Jennifer, and history of liberalism, 23n43

Talfourd, Thomas Noon: and Moxon trial, 191; and Lamb biography, 191

Thelwall, John: and proposed monument to Queen Caroline, 63; as publisher for Lamb, 187

Thompson, E. P., and laboring class childhood, 33–34

Todd, H. J., and Johnsonian lexicography, ix

Tomalin, Claire. *See* Austen, Jane, biographical accounts

Tucker, George Holbert. *See* Austen, Jane, biographical accounts

Tuite, Clara, and adoption in Austen, 71

Turner, Beatrice, and genetic determinism in the fiction of William Godwin Jr., 107n2

Uglow, Jenny, and Sabrina Sidney, 100n45

UN Convention on the Rights of the Child, 140

universalism, liberal, 4, 23

Vallon, Annette, mother of Caroline Wordsworth, 132

Victoria, Queen, 38

Wade, Laura, and Jane Austen's *The Watsons,* 85n24

Wales, Prince of, and later Prince Regent, 5–6, 35, 38–39, 43–45, 47, 51–52, 54, 69, 101, 178n25, 187. *See also* George IV, King

Wales, Princess of. *See* Caroline, Princess of Wales; Caroline, Queen

Want family: Arabella Want (sister of Caroline Want), 131; Caroline Want Montagu (birth mother of Basil Caroline Montagu), 128, 130; Charlotte Want (sister of Caroline Want), 128; Henrietta Want (sister of Caroline Want), 161; Robert Want (father of Caroline Want), 130

Watsons, The. See Austen, Jane, novels of: *The Watsons*

Wedgwood, Sarah, and marriage prospects of Basil Montagu, 138

Welch, Sandy, and O'Hanlon *Emma* film, 88, 90–91

Wellings, William, and Edward Austen adoption silhouette, 73–74, 73 fig. 2, 205–6, 209

Whitbread, Samuel, and William Austin, 49

Wilde, Sir Thomas, and William Austin's madness, 64

Williams, Grace, and Emma Isola's term as governess, 182–83

Williams, Helen Maria, and adoption in revolutionary France, 19

Williams, Jane, and Mary Shelley, 110

Wilson, Eric G. *See* Lamb, Charles, biographical accounts

Wiltshire, John, and slavery in *Mansfield Park,* 81

Wolfson, Susan, and text of *Frankenstein,* 112n11

Wollstonecraft, Mary: on adoption, 111; death, 138–39; and Rousseau, 3–4

Wordsworth, Dorothy: abroad in Germany, 146; adoptive care of Basil Caroline Montagu in Dorset and Somerset, 137–46; with Basil Caroline Montagu in Cumbria, 155–56; death, 161; and illness of Basil Caroline Montagu, 156–58; and illness of Laura Rush Montagu, 148–49; plans for adoptive care of Basil Caroline Montagu, 135–37; return to Cumbria, 147

Wordsworth, William: abroad in Germany, 146; adoptive care of Basil Caroline Montagu in Dorset and Somerset, 139–46; death, 161; falling-out with Basil Montagu, 158–59; friendship with Basil Montagu, 132; illegitimate child in France, 132; "Intimations Ode," 20–21, 31, 144–45; Charles Lamb letter to, about Emma Isola, 167; Basil Montagu and Laura Rush marriage and death, 146–48; quarrel with Coleridge, 152; with Basil Caroline Montagu in Cumbria, 155–59; poems in *Lyrical Ballads* (see *Lyrical Ballads*)

Wordsworth family: Caroline Wordsworth (illegitimate daughter of William Wordsworth), 132; Christopher Wordsworth (brother of Dorothy Wordsworth), 137; Dorothy Wordsworth (adoptive parent of Basil Caroline Montagu; *see* Wordsworth, Dorothy); John Wordsworth (brother of Dorothy Wordsworth), 147; Johnny Wordsworth (son of Mary and William Wordsworth), 152; Mary Wordsworth (wife of William Wordsworth), 138, 152, 155, 158; William Wordsworth (brother of Dorothy Wordsworth and adoptive parent of Basil Caroline Montagu; *see* Wordsworth, William)

Wrangham, Francis, 131, 137, 143

York, Duke of (brother of George IV), 187

Young-Bruehl, Elisabeth, and modern childism, 24n48

Zelizer, Vivienne, and "sacralization" of children, 5, 20, 30

Zunshine, Lisa: on adoption narratives, 31; on eighteenth-century bastards and foundlings, 14n6, 15n11; on mysterious natural children in *Emma,* 103

FORMATIONS: ADOPTION, KINSHIP, AND CULTURE
Emily Hipchen and John McLeod, Series Editors

This interdisciplinary series encourages critical engagement with all aspects of non-normative kinship—such as adoption, foster care, IVF, surrogacy, and gamete transfers—especially as they intersect with race, identity, heritage, nationality, sexuality, and gender. Books in the series explore how these constructions affect not only those personally involved but also public understandings of identity, personhood, migration, kinship, and the politics of family.

Haphazard Families: Romanticism, Nation, and the Prehistory of Modern Adoption
    ERIC C. WALKER

Adoption Fantasies: The Fetishization of Asian Adoptees from Girlhood to Womanhood
    KIMBERLY D. MCKEE

Adoption across Race and Nation: US Histories and Legacies
    EDITED BY SILKE HACKENESCH

The Politics of Reproduction: Adoption, Abortion, and Surrogacy in the Age of Neoliberalism
    EDITED BY MODHUMITA ROY AND MARY THOMPSON